CONFUCIAN FEMINIST

Memoirs of Zeng Baosun
(1893–1978)

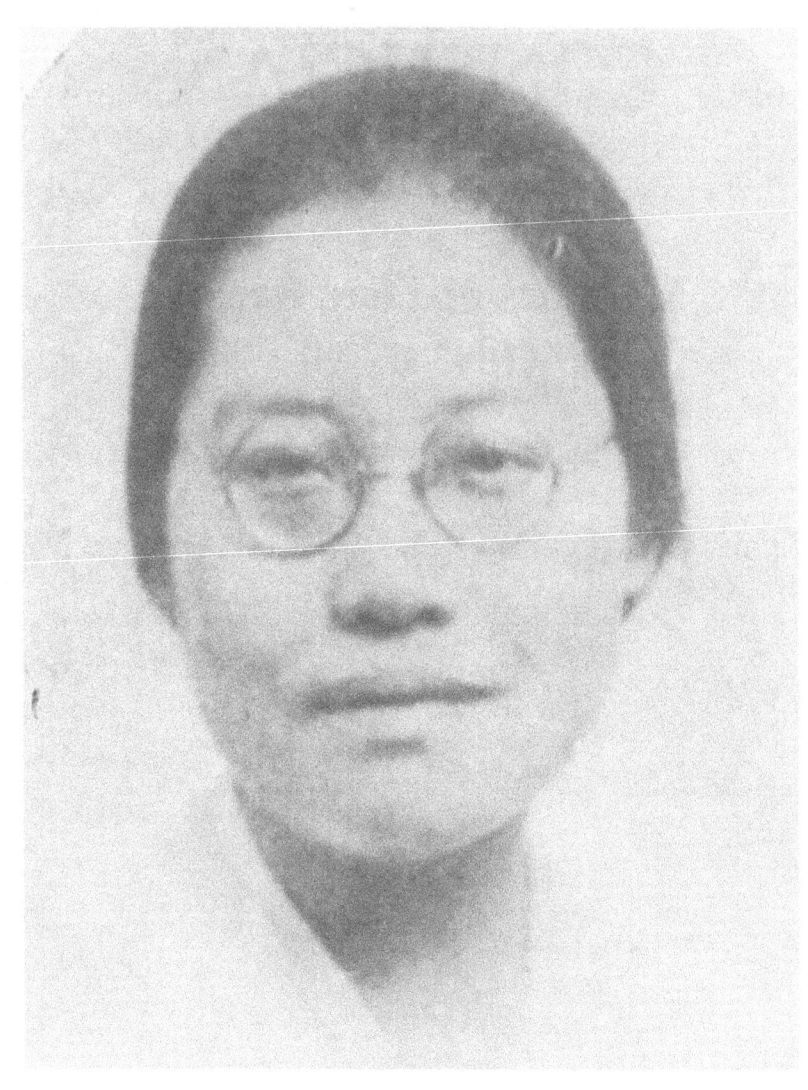

Zeng Baosun

TRANSACTIONS
of the
AMERICAN PHILOSOPHICAL SOCIETY
Held at Philadelphia
For Promoting Useful Knowledge
Volume 92, Part 1

CONFUCIAN FEMINIST

Memoirs of Zeng Baosun (1893–1978)

Translated and Adapted by
Thomas L. Kennedy

American Philosophical Society
Philadelphia • 2002

Copyright © 2002 by the American Philosophical Society for its *Transactions* series. All rights reserved.

ISBN: 0-87169-921-4
US ISSN: 0065-9746

Library of Congress Cataloging-in-Publication Data

Zeng, Baosun, 1893-
  [Zeng Baosun hui yi lu. English]
  Confucian feminist : memoirs of Zeng Baosun (1893-1978)/translated and adapted by Thomas L. Kennedy.
    p. cm.—(Transactions of the American Philosophical Society, ISSN 0065-9746; vol. 92, pt. 1)
  Includes bibliographical references and index.
  ISBN 0-87169-921-4 (pbk.)
  1. Zeng, Baosun, 1893- 2. Educators—China—Biography. 3. Feminists—China—Biography. 4. Feminism—China. 5. Confucianism. I. Kennedy, Thomas L. II. Title. III. Series.

LA2383.C52 Z459 2002
370'.92—dc21
[B]
                                                                                    2001045786

Design and Composition
Maryland Publishing Services

Contents

Translator's Foreword ix
Translator's Introduction: Who Is Zeng Baosun? xi
Principal Events in the Life of Zeng Baosun and Related World Events xvi
Locations from the Memoirs of Zeng Baosun xxi
Partial Family Tree of Forebears and Relatives of Zeng Baosun xxii

PART I: Family and Early Education

Chapter 1   My Family 3

Chapter 2   Prosperity Hall 8

Chapter 3   My Early Education 14

Chapter 4   Life in the Mission Schools 23

Chapter 5   Finding Christ in China 27

PART II: To School in England

Chapter 6   On the Way to Study in England 35

Chapter 7   Middle School in England 39

Chapter 8   New Friends 43

Chapter 9   A Difficult Decision 46

Chapter 10   Westfield College 49

Chapter 11   Student Life at Westfield College 52

Chapter 12	A Modern Girls' School for China	56
Chapter 13	World War I	59
Chapter 14	Oxford and Cambridge	63

PART III: The Yifang School for Girls

Chapter 15	Going Home	69
Chapter 16	The Yifang Girls' Middle School	74
Chapter 17	The Campus at Yifang	77
Chapter 18	An Experiment with Democracy	80
Chapter 19	The May Fourth Movement	84
Chapter 20	April 8, 1927: One Day in the Chinese Revolution	89
Chapter 21	Revolution Comes to Yifang	92

PART IV: War with Japan

Chapter 22	The World Christian Council	99
Chapter 23	The Institute of Pacific Relations	101
Chapter 24	Yifang's Second Rebirth	105
Chapter 25	War Comes to Hunan	108
Chapter 26	Escape to Hong Kong	112
Chapter 27	Japanese Occupied Hong Kong	115
Chapter 28	With the Guerillas in Hunan	121

PART V: Exile in Taiwan

Chapter 29	The Third Rebirth of Yifang	131
Chapter 30	The Fall of Changsha	134
Chapter 31	The Pavilion of Everlasting Farewell	139
Chapter 32	Joys and Sorrows in Taiwan	143
Chapter 33	The United Nations Commission on the Status of Women	147
Chapter 34	Nixon Resigns from Office	150

Afterword 157
Some Thoughts after Reading the Memoirs of Zeng Baosun 158
A Note on Materials 161
Index 163

Translator's Foreword

Ms. Zeng Baosun's Memoirs are not, in my judgment, suited to a close translation. There are several reasons for this, all of which stem from the purpose of the translation: to make accessible to Western readers the life experiences and reflections of an exceptional Chinese woman. With this purpose in mind, I attempted to make the text accurate with respect to the central themes of Ms. Zeng's life and, at the same time, readily readable for persons with an interest in, but little familiarity with, life in early twentieth-century China. To accomplish this, I have removed some passages, principally those that describe in detail geographical, architectural, or medical conditions or objects that do not have a direct bearing on the central themes of Ms. Zeng's life and career. These as well as the many names of Chinese friends, colleagues, and relatives that I have removed from the text have great meaning for some Chinese readers. For Western readers, they can obscure the important messages conveyed by her life experiences with information that is of little interest or does little to further understanding. I beg the forgiveness of Ms. Zeng and her many surviving friends, colleagues, and relatives.

I have added some material and inserted some transitional and interpretive passages. The added materials are, for the most part, identifications of persons, books, places, or Chinese terms essential to an understanding of Ms. Zeng's life and career. I have done this through the use of appositional clauses or by otherwise incorporating explanatory material directly into the text, thus sparing the reader frequent reference to endnotes. I hope readers will find the resulting rendition both informative and readable. I have introduced transitional and interpretive passages in places where the Chinese narrative moves abruptly from one topic to the next, a style not uncommon among Chinese writers who assume their intended readers have the necessary background knowledge to follow such moves. These passages have been added often at the beginning or at the end of chapters or within chapters when there are such unannounced changes of subject. Sometimes, my purpose is to call the readers' attention to the new topic and, at other times, I supply an interpretation of some topic in the original text that is self evident to many Chinese readers but may be perplexing to Western readers.

Finally, I have rearranged some parts of the text, divided chapters in some cases, and incorporated parts of several chapters into others in an effort to bring coherence to the presentation of materials for the Western reader. The incorporated materials are drawn, in most cases, from the nine topical chapters of reminiscences that follow the final chapter of the memoir. The lengthy poem that appears in Chapter 34 is the only instance in which I have introduced substantive content not in the original Chinese edition. I found this poem among Ms. Zeng's papers at the Institute of Modern History of the Academia Sinica in Taiwan, Republic of China.

In translating Chinese names, I have made clarity for the Western reader my principal concern. I have retained the Chinese order of family name first followed by the given names but in some cases I have departed from the names used in the text for the sake of simplicity. For example, I have used the popular name for well known historical figures such as Zeng Guofan or Zeng Jize. In naming close family members, I have avoided using expressions such as "fifth brother" or "seventh uncle." Instead I have used the given name that is used in the text with a term indicating the relationship, e.g. uncle, cousin etc. When more than one given name for one person is used in the text, I have used the one that is used first or most frequently. In all cases, I have used only one name for each person throughout the translation.

I wish to thank colleagues and friends of long standing at the Institute of Modern History for making the facilities and the personnel of the Institute available to me twice while this work was in preparation. The Chinese Christian Literature Council of Hong Kong, the original publisher of the Chinese edition, has kindly facilitated the publication of this English rendition. Professor Yang Tianhong of the Department of History of Sichuan Normal University has extended invaluable assistance as has Mr. Yang Tianqing of the Foreign Affairs Section. Mrs. Elizabeth Siler, my daughter, provided essential editorial and other specialized assistance. Responsibility for errors or imperfections in the final rendition are the sole responsibility of the translator.

I also wish to express my gratitude to the American Philosophical Society in Philadelphia and the Washington State China Relations Council for support for travel and research associated with the preparation of this rendition. Washington State University also has granted me professional leave and the Department of History has provided various forms of needed secretarial and logistical support.

Thomas L. Kennedy

Translator's Introduction

Who Is Zeng Baosun?

In 1893, in the remote countryside of south China, in Hunan Province, two children were born: a boy and a girl. The boy, on December 26, in the village of Shaoshan in the western drainage of the Xiang River; the girl, earlier in the year, just as spring was coming on, in the small village of Xiangxiang, a few miles to the south. Both of these young lives were caught up in the waves of foreign influence that spread across China in the years following the disastrous defeat by Japan in 1895.

The boy drew deeply from the reservoir of strength and purpose that had enabled his prosperous peasant family to survive for generations. As a young man, he mobilized peasant resentment at government neglect and landlord abuse, fusing Marxist political dogma and domestic rebellion into a revolution that sought to transform Chinese society and recapture its sovereignty. Though he borrowed freely from foreign ideology, he never set foot outside of China until the midpoint of the twentieth century.

The girl was nurtured in the bosom of a great landholding family. An older generation of firm Confucian conviction launched her on a course of intellectual and social development that sought to renew Chinese civilization, in the twentieth century, on the foundation of its Confucian past. She experienced a new world of foreign education, discovered the common ground shared by Christian and Confucian beliefs, pioneered modern education for Chinese women, fought for the independence of her homeland, and spoke out for Christian values and women's equality in national and international forums.

The boy was Mao Zedong (1893–1976), his name synonymous with peasant-based communist revolution. The girl, Zeng Baosun (1893–1978), was not nearly so well known. But her life, specifically the lessons it holds for those struggling to come to terms with the past as they move toward an uncertain future, has attracted the attention of the Chinese reading public world wide.

The rural society of Hunan and the extended Confucian family in which Zeng Baosun was reared had a formative influence on her character. The values that motivated her throughout life— an enduring belief in the power of education to improve the human condition, dedication to the betterment of the condition of women, and commitment to moderate political and social change— had their origins in her early education. From the second decade of the twentieth century until her death in

1978, the values formed during her early years were tested frequently in the international environment in which she moved. Missionary schools in China and university life in England brought conversion to Christianity and deep conviction to its spiritual tenets. China's struggle with communist revolution and Japanese aggression ignited in Ms. Zeng a fierce commitment to conservative nationalism that built upon, rather than rejected, the inherited values of her youth.

Hunan Province lies deep in the heartland of China, far from the coastal cities that, at the turn of the century, were home to foreign traders, missionaries, and diplomats. The rich rice lands of Hunan were linked to the national market by the Xiang River flowing northward through eastern Hunan into Dongting Lake and the Yangzi. On the banks of the Xiang was the provincial capital, Changsha. The small village of Xiangxiang lay about forty miles to the southwest of Changsha, far from the river, deep in the hills. This was the home of the great Hunanese general and statesman, Zeng Guofan (1811–1872), Zeng Baosun's great grandfather, who had rescued the faltering Qing Dynasty (1644–1912) from the Taiping Rebellion (1851–1865). It was where Zeng Baosun spent most of her girlhood years.

Remarkably, the tiny village of Xiangxiang was home to another young woman who defied the social mores of her day: Cai Chang (1900–1990), a radical student returned from study in post WWI France, a survivor of the Chinese Communists epic Long March, and one of the first women to serve on the Party's Central Committee. Sometime in the early twentieth century, these two young women came to a fork in the road that led them away from the traditional society of their youth. Zeng Baosun took the road "less traveled."

Hunan was a bastion of the old society where the great families clung tenaciously to traditional ways. Hunanese were a breed apart, known for their singleness of purpose and disdain for outsiders. Chinese of other provinces called Hunanese "mules" and foreign missionaries referred to Hunan as the "city with iron gates." In Hunan, as elsewhere in early twentieth-century China, individual behavior and social activity were strictly regulated by traditional norms and ritual practice. Nowhere was this more evident than in the social controls extended to women. The subordination of women in the traditional family, the restrictions on women's social activities, the limitations on educational opportunity, and the egregious practice of footbinding were well known features of Chinese society which, in conservative Hunan, were observed rigorously, though not without exception. Zeng Baosun's home and family life led her to test these norms imposed by traditional society.

The family into which Zeng Baosun was born was a stronghold of Confucian values, and there is none stronger than family solidarity. The descendants of the sainted Zeng Guofan, the paragon of nineteenth-century Confucianism, held strictly to a frugal life style and valued the human development of family members and service to society above the acquisition of material wealth. Both male and female members of this family were beneficiaries of this enlightened Confucian outlook, each valued as an inheritor of the Great Tradition of Confucianism with vast potential for moral development and service to others. Widely known as the doyenne of Confucianism in her day was Zeng's youngest daughter, Mrs. Nie Zeng Jifen (1852–1942). This is not to say that the women of the Zeng family were not constrained by the dictates of the traditional social order. Nevertheless, prosperity tempered by a sense of social responsibility enabled this family to exemplify the Confucian emphasis on human development—even to the point that it tested the limits of traditional gender roles.

This may help to explain one very puzzling aspect of Zeng Baosun's personal development. Though she esteemed family relationships beyond all others and revered the distinguished heritage of the Zeng family, she never married. This is all the more baffling because, in the society in which she grew up, it was virtually unheard of for women to remain single. In her memoirs, Ms. Zeng is quite open with her emotions toward siblings and other family members but she is silent about her personal feelings regarding marriage, except to thank her father for not arranging a marriage for her. She also thanked him for not standing in the way of her conversion to Christianity or blocking her study in England. These three aspects of her life are clearly related. Christianity and overseas study would never have been compatible with an arranged marriage. One can only speculate that, as she grew to maturity, her life became so dedicated to religious activities and reaching professional goals that the time for marriage passed her by unnoticed. The emotional need for companionship was no doubt supplied by her long and warm relationship with her cousin, Zeng Yuenung, whom she regarded as a brother. Not only was he her lifelong companion, he too had been educated in England and shared with her a keen interest in Christianity.

Zeng Baosun first ventured beyond the boundaries of rural Hunan and the nurturing influences of her family to enter the genteel world of mission schools for women in the coastal city of Shanghai. Following the suppression of the anti-Christian, anti-foreign Boxer Uprising of 1900, the Christian mission movement in China flourished during the first two decades of the twentieth century. Missionary efforts to win converts, establish schools, and provide medical facilities complemented the wave of government-sponsored reformism that swept through the provinces during these years. It was in the cities of East China, however, where the Protestant missions mounted their greatest efforts. In cities such as Shanghai, Christian schools were numerous. This was the heyday of Christian education. It would end abruptly in the 1920s as a wave of nationalism moved across China railing against the scourge of imperialism and the missions that it had spawned.

During these years, Zeng Baosun tasted the spirit of rebellion afoot among Chinese youth, but, the conservative values of her family prevailed, buttressed by the moral tenets of Christianity in the institutional setting of mission schools. There, education, not rebellion, was valued as the proper vehicle for bringing about social and political change. Ms. Zeng's conversion to Christianity directed her away from the rebellious youth of her day and led to a lasting friendship with missionary educator Louise Barnes, a relationship that brought her to Westfield College of the University of London during WWI.

Zeng Baosun's conversion took root in the first two decades of the twentieth century. In the 1920s she struggled mightily to reconcile her foreign faith with the powerful new nationalism. On her return to China, she encountered almost immediately the tumult of the May Fourth Movement of 1919—Chinese youth demonstrating against Japan's imperialist demands on China's sovereignty and the corrupt warlord government that had yielded to them. The violent nationalism that moved through Chinese society in the wake of the May Fourth Movement, much of it directed by the infant Chinese Communist Party, posed formidable obstacles to Zeng Baosun's efforts to establish a modern, non-political middle school for Chinese women. Confronted by such obstacles and by Japan's naked aggression in the 1930s, she drew deeply from the spiritual values of her Christian faith and took comfort and encouragement from her family and friends. A resolute spirit of nationalism born of the struggle against communist rebels and Japanese invaders inspired her to hold to the dream of unlimited educational opportunity for Chinese women in a strong, independent China. This vision guided her through turmoil and personal deprivation during WWII and the heartbreak that came with the communist victory in 1949.

After 1950, while on Taiwan, she parlayed her role as an international spokesperson for Christianity and China's Nationalist government and her tireless advocacy of educational opportunity for women into a new role as grande dame of women's interests. In her most important of several international assignments, she represented the Chinese Nationalist government in the United Nations Commission on the Status of Women. Ill health marred her declining years but did little to dampen her spirit. Though she gradually withdrew from life in the public eye and more and more enjoyed her relationships with family and former students, President Nixon's reversal of U.S. China policy and his historic trip to the communist controlled mainland caused her no end of consternation. Her lengthy poem written after Nixon's resignation excoriating his perfidy toward the Nationalist Chinese on Taiwan left no doubt that ill health and advancing age could not silence a voice that for decades had cried out in support of honesty, fairness, and democracy.

I have not attempted to fit this exceptional life into the theoretical constructs that explicate the emergence of Chinese women. As a document of personal disclosure, Ms. Zeng's memoir provides an understanding of feminism that stands apart from the familiar depiction of women's emancipation accompanied by sweeping social change. The Confucian feminism of Zeng Baosun emphasized the feminist commitments to leadership, service to the community, and improvement in the condition of women, but always within an established social and economic order that changed only gradually within guidelines imposed by traditional culture. These guidelines represent the conservative nationalist ideology that intersected with and reinforced her Confucian feminism. In Europe of the 1930s, a similar nationalist ideology devolved into crude fascism. In China, this devolution was tempered by the emergence of a feminist movement that was at once humanistic and democratic and, at the same time, traditional. The genius of Ms. Zeng's memoir is the insight it provides into the subtleties of this feminism—driven, as it was, by religious humanism and directed by conservative culturalism.

Ms. Zeng's insights are not always stated plainly; more often they are masked in the rhetoric of traditional autobiography. Though she abandoned the conventional form of the chronological autobiography (*ziding nianpu*), she retained its characteristic reserve. For the most part, she chooses not to speak directly to such issues as feminism or state ideology. In the style of the traditional autobiography, she lets her experiences speak for themselves and her readers take from them what they will. I will do the same.

Principal Events in the Life of Zeng Baosun and Related World Events

1893   Zeng Baosun born

        (1893 Mao Zedong born)

        (1894–95 Japan defeats China in Sino–Japanese War)

1897   Zeng Baosun begins family school in Beijing

        (1898 Empress Dowager suppresses "100 Days Reform")

        (1899–1900 Boxer Uprising)

1900   Zeng Baosun returns to family home in Xiangxiang, Hunan Province

1902   Zeng Baosun moves with family to Nanjing

1903   Zeng Baosun returns to Xiangxiang with grandmother

1904   Zeng Baosun accompanies grandmother to Changsha, capital of Hunan
Zeng Baosun enrolls in missionary school in Shanghai

        (1904–05 Russia defeats Japan in Russo–Japanese War)

1905   Zeng Baosun transfers to Wuben School

1906–07   Zeng Baosun enrolled in Hangzhou Provincial Normal School

1908   Zeng Baosun at uncle's residence in Hubei

1909   Zeng Baosun enrolls in Mary Vaughan High School for Girls in Hangzhou

1911   Zeng Baosun baptized in the Church of England
Uncle Zeng Jirong baptized a Christian

        (1911–12 Republican Revolution overthrows Manchu Qing Dynasty)

        (1912–16 Presidency of Yuan Shikai)

Principal Events in the Life of Zeng Baosun

1912	Zeng Baosun accompanies Ms. Louise Barnes to England to attend school, enrolls in Worthing Church House School, and transfers to Blackheath Upper Middle School
1913	Ms. Barnes resigns from Church of England Mission to remain in England with Zeng Baosun Zeng Baosun enrolls in Westfield College, University of London

(1914–18 World War I)

1915	Zeng Baosun resolves to establish a modern school for girls in China

(1916 Yuan Shikai dies)

1916	Zeng Baosun awarded Bachelor of Science Degree from University of London
1916–17	Zeng Baosun pursues graduate study at Oxford, Cambridge, and the University of London
1916	Zeng Baosun's grandmother, Ms. Guo Yun, dies

(1917–28 Warlord rule in China)

1917	Zeng Baosun returns to China via the United States and Canada

(1917–23 New Culture Movement in China)

1918	Zeng Baosun establishes Yifang Girls' Middle School in Changsha and serves as principal

(1919 May Fourth Movement; John Dewey and Bertrand Russell visit China)

1919–21	Zeng Baosun serves concurrently as principal of First Women's Normal School, Changsha

(1921 Chinese Communist Party established)

1921	Yifang vandalized by radicals and communist sympathizers

(1925 Anti–imperialist May Thirtieth Movement in China; Dr. Sun Yatsen, leader of United Front, dies; Chiang Kaishek succeeds to leadership)

(1926–28 Chiang Kaishek leads Northern Expedition against warlords and imperialists)

1927	Yifang taken over by Peasants Association; Zeng Baosun and some staff escape to Shanghai; Ms. Barnes dies in Shanghai

(1927 Chiang Kaishek expels Communists from United Front)

1928	Yifang reopened; Zeng Baosun attends meeting of World Christian Council in Jerusalem
	(1928 Nominal unification of China by Nationalists; Chiang Kaishek, president)
1929	Zeng Baosun's father dies while she is attending meeting of Institute of Pacific Relations in Kyoto, Japan
	(1930 Communists temporarily seize Changsha forcing closing of Yifang)
1931	Zeng Baosun recuperating at Yantai, Shandong Province
	(1931 Japanese occupy Manchuria; Communists establish Soviets in Jiangxi Province)
1932	Yifang reopens
	(1932 Japanese establish puppet state of Manchukuo in Manchuria)
	(1934–35 Nationalist forces overrun Jiangxi Soviets; Communists escape on Long March to Yan'an in Northwest)
1936	YMCA sponsors Zeng Baosun in twelve city lecture tour
	(1937 Japanese and Chinese forces clash south of Beijing; World War II in Asia; Second United Front of Nationalists and Communists to resist Japan; Japanese forces massacre Chinese civilians at Nanjing)
1937	Zeng Baosun's mother, Ms. Chen, dies at Changsha
	(1938 Japanese bomb Chansha; Yifang damaged, closes; Zeng Baosun and family members flee to brother's home in Nanning, Guangxi Province)
1938–39	Zeng Baosun represents China at meeting of World Christian Council in Madras, India; lecture tour of the British Isles
1939	Zeng Baosun returns to China; resides in Hong Kong
	(1940 Japan joins the Axis powers)
	(1941 Dec. 7, Japan bombs Pearl Harbor; United States declares war on Axis powers; China joins Allies; Communist–Nationalist United Front unravels)
	(1941 December, Japanese occupy Hong Kong)
1942	Zeng Baosun returns from Hong Kong to Xiangxiang via French territory of Guangzhouwan

Principal Events in the Life of Zeng Baosun   xix

1942–45   Zeng Baosun cooperating with anti–Japanese guerillas in Hunan

        (1945 Aug 15, Japan surrenders)

        (1945–49 Communist-Nationalist civil war)

1946   Yifang reopens with Zeng Baosun as principal

1948   Zeng Baosun elected to National Assembly from Xiangxiang District

        (1948 National Assembly elects Chiang Kaishek and Li Zongren as President and Vice President of the Republic of China)

        (1949 Changsha taken by communist forces; Zeng Baosun leaves to attend World Peace Conference in India)

        (1949 Communists victorious in civil war; Nationalists flee to Taiwan)

1950   Zeng Baosun returns from India to Hong Kong

        (1950 Korean War; China enters on North Korean side)

1951   Zeng Baosun accepts Nationalist Government's invitation to reside on Taiwan; Brother Zeng Zhaohua killed in airplane accident

1952   Zeng Baosun represents Republic of China at the United Nations Commission on the Status of Women in Geneva

1953   Donghai University established at Taizhong, Taiwan; Zeng Baosun meets Vice President Richard Nixon at groundbreaking

        (1953 Korean War armistice)

1954   Zeng Baosun participates in National Assembly reelection of Chiang Kaishek as President of Republic of China on Taiwan; named Vice Chairman of Planning Commission for Recovery of the Mainland

        (1954 Chinese prisoners of war from Korea choose repatriation in Taiwan)

1956   Zeng Baosun represents Republic of China at meeting of Asian Anti–Communist League in Manila

1959   Zeng Baosun contracts cancer in left breast

1961   Recurrence of cancer

1964   Cataract removed from right eye

        (1965–75 Vietnam War)

1968 Celebration of fiftieth anniversary of establishment of Yifang

1969 Ms. Xiao Xiaohui, cousin and close companion of Zeng Baosun, succumbs to Parkinson's

(1971 Republic of China withdraws from United Nations)

(1972 President Richard Nixon visits Peoples Republic of China)

Locations From the Memoirs of Zeng Baosun

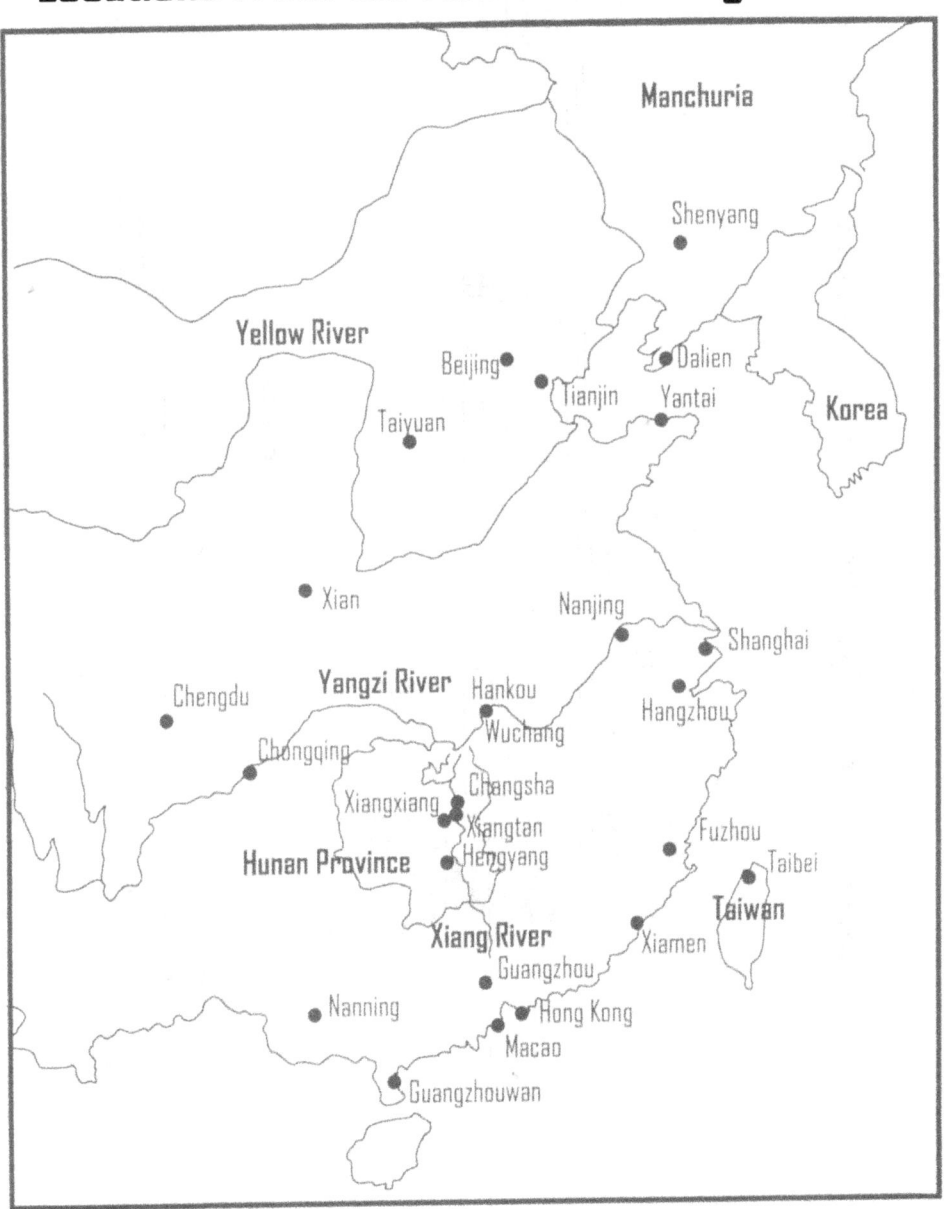

Partial Family Tree of Forebears and Relatives of Zeng Baosun

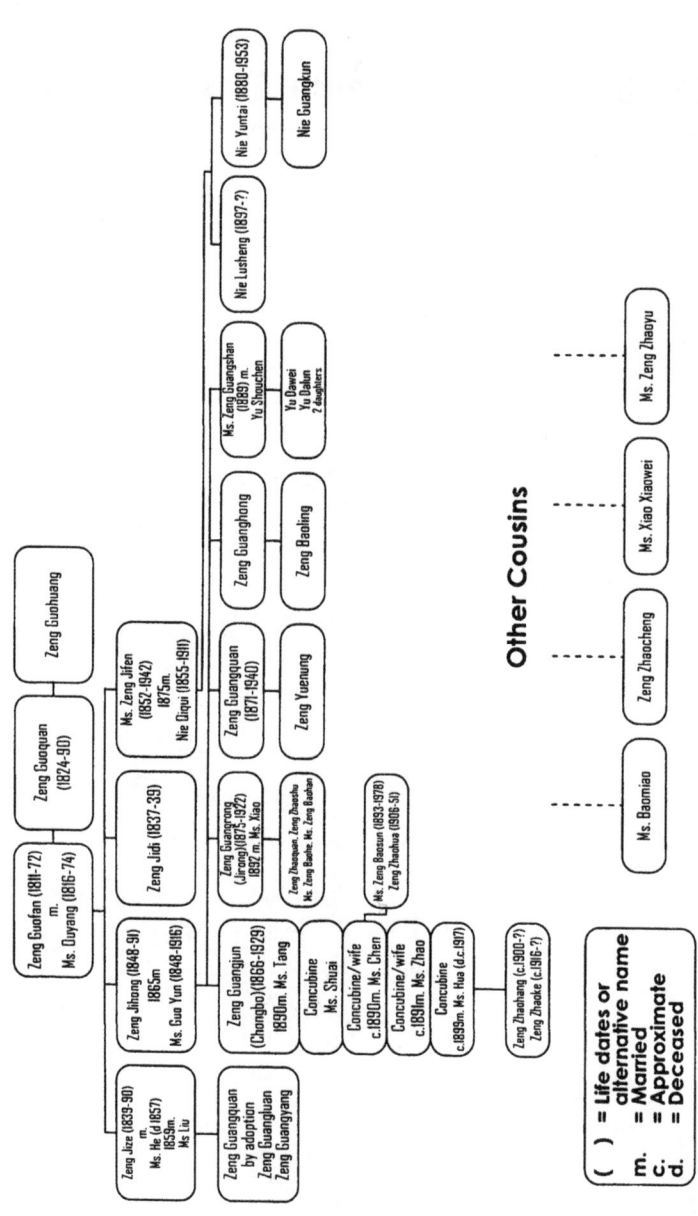

Part I

Family and Early Education

Chapter 1

My Family

I was born during the Qing Dynasty in the nineteenth year of the reign of Emperor Guangxu (1893) during the first month of the lunar calendar, on the same date, tradition has it, as the birth date of Qu Yuan (c.340–278 B.C.), who was China's earliest and perhaps its greatest poet. Our home province, Hunan, in the middle Yangzi valley is the area in which Qu Yuan had lived. My father gave me the name Baosun (precious iris) and the alternate name Pingfang (peaceful and pleasant). He selected this alternate name because the character for "Ping" was used in Qu Yuan's alternate name.

My great-grandfather was Marquis Zeng Guofan, known also by the honorary name Wenzheng (cultured and sincere)—posthumously conferred by the emperor. The accomplishments that led to this honor are recorded in the histories and countless other volumes; there is no need for me to recount them here. His talents, both literary and military, his essays on morality, and his administrative accomplishments are legendary.

My great-grandmother, Madam Ouyang, was a refined woman, the youngest daughter, of a great family. Her father, Mr. Ouyang Ningzhi, had been great-grandfather's tutor. Mr. Ouyang admired great-grandfather's talent and recognized his superior character; he knew that great honor and good fortune lay ahead for Zeng Guofan so he arranged the betrothal.

Madam Ouyang and Zeng Guofan had three sons. The first, Jidi, died in infancy. The second son, Jize, inherited the rank of Marquis from Zeng Guofan; later he served as imperial ambassador to England, France, Germany, and Russia. In that capacity, in 1881, he concluded the "Ili Treaty" recovering for China territories earlier lost to Russia. In recognition of his service to the Empire, the emperor posthumously conferred on him the honorary name Huimin (kind and clever).

The third son, Jihong, was my grandfather. As a youth he devoted himself tirelessly to study and was very skilled in mathematics. He also studied English so that he might read foreign books. Unfortunately, he drove himself beyond his endurance and contracted tuberculosis; he lingered on for three or four years. Despondent over his failure in the highest level civil-service examinations, he died in 1882 in Beijing. Only thirty-three, he left a widow and five children.

Though widowed while she was still young, my grandmother, Madam Guo, did not remarry. She was in poor health and had five children to raise, four boys and a girl. The oldest was my father. His given name was Guangjun; he was also known as Chongbo. He was only fifteen when grandfather died. At that time, grandfather's only brother, Zeng Jize, was in England, so the family turned to great-grandfather's younger brother, Uncle Zeng Guoquan, also known by his posthumous honorary name Zhongxiang (loyal and helpful), for its principal support. Grandmother escorted grandfather's body back to his family home in Hunan and laid him peacefully to rest. From then on, she devoted herself wholeheartedly to the education of her children, living sometimes in the family home in Xiangxiang in Hunan and sometimes in Changsha at Hongjiajing, a residence purchased by Zeng Jize.

Grandmother's dedication to learning and Confucian principles had been developed both in her family and in the family into which she married. She was the third daughter of Guo Peilin of Qishui in Hubei Province. While her father was serving as intendant of the Huaiyanghai Circuit, the pseudo-Christian rebellion of the Taipings (1851–1865) swept through the province. Guo Peilin sent his family to safety before the Taipings arrived but died a hero's death himself defending his city, amply demonstrating his Confucian humanity and determination to do what was right, as well as his loyalty to the throne and love of China. Inspired by her father's life and his death, grandmother dedicated herself to the Confucian Way and the education of her grandchildren. She had quite a high level of Chinese education in her home, however, she used to say, "It was not until I married into the Zeng family when I was nineteen that I studied the great books, such as the annotated thirteen classics and the imperially approved outlines of the general history of China, under the guidance of Zeng Guofan."

Because my grandfather had not passed the highest level civil-service examinations, grandmother was determined that my father should study for the examinations without distraction. Her determination bore fruit in 1889 when, at age twenty-three, he passed the examinations and was admitted to the Hanlin Academy, the highest academic institution in the Empire. He was the youngest civil-service graduate ever inducted into this body. In part, this was the result of grandmother's supervision of his studies and, in part, it was father's natural talent. Father's accomplishment erased the regret family members felt about grandfather's failure to pass the examinations.

Grandmother accomplished all this despite the fact that she suffered from a type of paralysis contracted in her youth that restricted her movement. She spent most of her time in the outer rooms of her home reading, writing letters, practicing calligraphy, or composing poetry. She authored the *Yifangguan Shichao* [collected poems from the hall of culture and virtue]. In her leisure time she liked to cultivate orchids and make condiments.

Although she didn't get about much she knew everything great or small that went on in her home and served as the arbiter of right and wrong. She was very reasonable in administering discipline and instruction, never reprimanding a wrongdoer in front of others. Instead, she would call whoever was at fault into her room and quietly explain what they had done wrong, comparing it to incidents from the past. Her aim was to show the wrongdoers the error of their ways, to urge them to repent and to change their behavior.

As an older person, she also loved to read magazines and newspapers and talk about politics and current events. She used to say, "General Yuan Shikai (1859–1916) will probably be *bolixitiande* someday." At the time, we didn't understand what she meant. Later when General Yuan became first president of the Republic of China, we realized it meant "president" and admired her vision.

She frequently showed others, including her grandchildren, how to do things; then she would step aside and observe. When my older cousin, Baoling, and I were learning to embroider, grandmother would take a few stitches to show us how and then tell us to continue. Baoling's mother died when she was only ten years old. After that, grandmother cared for her. When Uncle Jirong moved his family to Zhejiang Province, he left his son Zhaoquan with grandmother. So the two of them were reared, for the most part, by grandmother. Baoling later studied to be a teacher in Hangzhou, the capital city of Zhejiang, but before graduation she left to marry Yao Yuanyu of Changsha. Zhaoquan was among the first group of students from Qinghua University to attend a university in the United States and the first from our generation to study abroad.

Yuenung also was the son of one of father's younger brothers and the fifth male born in my generation of our family. The children of my father's brothers were like siblings to me. We referred to the males in this generation as brothers and assigned them a numerical designation corresponding to the order of their birth. It was from among these, that I found my dearest and closest companion, my "fifth brother," Yuenung. He too lived with grandmother.

My father's given name was Guangjun; he was the oldest grandson of Zeng Guofan and most favored by Zeng. When father was six years old, Zeng Guofan brought him to the new governor general's quarters at Nanjing. When father saw ancestral tablets and couplets, even then, he could recognize many characters. Father was only fifteen years old when his father died but he was able to handle things like an adult. He could even chant poems and sing duets with those of the older generation. His literary attainments were obvious. He also had a distinguished military record. During the war with Japan (1894–95), when he was twenty-nine years old, father led the Gangwu Army, a force of five thousand, into Manchuria to aid Korea against Japan.

Father first married a Madam Tang. She suffered from poor health and after seven years of marriage and two miscarriages, both due to severe toxemia, father took a concubine, the honorable Ms. Shuai. But she also was childless so, while in Beijing, he married my mother, Madam Chen. Mother's family came from Dianbai in Guangdong and were quite close with the family of Liang Dingfang. My mother's father died early in life after fleeing from an armed uprising. My mother's mother then lived with the Liang family, but she also died young and my mother was brought up by a concubine of the Liang household. Before she died that concubine implored Liang Dingfang, "I love this daughter of mine dearly; you must give her in marriage to an able and personable husband who is successful in the civil-service examinations early in life. I ask this of you from my heart."

After she died, Liang bore her request in mind. He liked my father and resolved to wed the adopted daughter of his concubine to father as a concubine with status as a wife. This type of marital arrangement was commonplace in Guangdong Province. Thus my mother at age sixteen was married into the Zeng family. All of the ceremony and ritual was most impressive, but my grandmother, Madam Guo, did not approve of the Guangdong practice of having a concubine with status as a wife and demanded that my mother return the betrothal gifts, including a pair of blue jade bracelets. Grandmother later gave them to me and I still have them.

My mother was gentle and respectful. In Beijing the three women, Madam Tang, Concubine Shuai, and my mother, lived together quite tranquilly until the autumn of 1890 when Madam Tang died of toxemia during pregnancy. The following day my great uncle Zeng Guoquan also died in Nanjing. Then, the entire family returned to Hunan.

At about the same time, there was great discord in the Liang family following the death of one of the senior women, a Madam Gong. Because of this, grandmother did not allow the women of our family to have anything to do with them. As a result, my mother felt cut off from her family and was terribly distressed. However, she had a gentle and understanding nature; she respected grandmother's wishes, and never complained to my father. She even respected Concubine Shuai's first status and yielded to her in all things.

A year after Madam Tang's death my father went through a middleman and secured a second concubine with the status of wife, Madam Zhao of Hengshan, but she, too, had no children. Grandmother's heart's desire was for grandchildren. Father had had four spouses and no offspring, so when I was born, even though I was not a boy, grandmother was elated. When I was seven, our household had still not produced a son, so father took yet another concubine, Ms. Hua, whom he kept outside the household. She gave birth to the fourth male in my generation, Zhaohang. After Zhaohang passed his first birthday, he and his mother moved into our home. In my fourteenth year, my mother gave birth to the eighth male in our generation, Zhaohua. Grandmother was overjoyed but mother was very sick.

She developed abscesses of the breast that caused her extraordinary suffering and severely weakened her.

My grandmother died in 1916 while Yuenung and I were attending the university in England. Following the birth of Zhaohua, my mother remained constantly with Grandmother, attending to her every need. She frequently had colds and other minor ailments not of a serious nature. On March 12, 1916, grandmother dined with mother and two of my aunts. That evening at about seven she began crying out continuously, complaining of a pain in her heart and perspiring profusely. My Uncle Jirong, his wife, his daughter Baohan, and my mother hastened to dry her with a large towel and change her clothing and bedding. In less than half an hour she passed away. I believe it was heart trouble. Since that generation of our family dwelled in the countryside, there were no Western doctors to care for her. However, Chinese regard death without sickness as a great blessing.

Later when I returned from England, Concubine Hua gave birth to the final son in my generation, Zhaoke; however, ten days later she developed puerperal fever and died. As she was nearing death, she gave Zhaoke to my mother to raise. Mother treated him just as she did her own. She was meticulous about his food and clothing. When he was sick, she would sit with him all night. When he grew up he was deeply appreciative.

By the time I returned from Europe following World War I, my father's branch of the family had grown to include four children, myself and three brothers, Zhaohang, Zhaohua, and Zhaoke. Father had taken a wife, two concubines with the status of wife, and two concubines. Only my mother and Concubine Hua had given birth. However, the solidarity of our extended family provided me with a broad network of relationships.

Chapter 2

Prosperity Hall

I derived many of my values and my outlook as a Chinese woman from the physical surroundings and the social and cultural environment of my childhood home. Our family home was at Xiangxiang in the Hetang District of Hunan Province. The name of the place was Fuyu and our residence was called the Fuhou Tang (Prosperity Hall). Tradition had it that it got that name because my great uncle Zeng Jize had written "they exemplify prosperity" by the listing of famous nobles in the chart of meritorious subjects in the History of the Han Dynasty.

It was a large house built generally on the plan of a noble residence from ancient times. There were two gates: one on the east and one on the west. The buildings and landscaping in the interior resembled the ancient academies of Confucian learning. Over the central interior gate hung a tablet inscribed with the four characters that proclaimed "Home of a brave Marquis." Passing through that gate, one entered a rectangular courtyard surrounded by buildings on four sides, modeled after the "Hall of Four Directions" in Beijing. The building bordering the courtyard included the great halls in which gatherings were held and meals were taken and the apartments occupied by family members: my grandmother, my father, mother and the children, as well as others. There were also servants' quarters and storage spaces and two large verandas, one of which housed our family school. The other had several rooms. One was known as the Yifangguan (Hall of Culture and Virtue), words which I later used in the name of the middle school that I established in Changsha.

On the north and south sides there were two three-story libraries. They epitomized the spirit of learning that pervaded Prosperity Hall. All the cabinets were made of granite to guard against destruction of the books by white ants. The south library housed the books of Zeng Guofan and Zeng Jize. The north library held the collection of books belonging to my grandparents. When we were little, we loved to go to this collection on the second floor where there were all sorts of interesting books. Old Mr. He, custodian of the library, cared for the books; he was very strict. The heavy door was locked tightly for fear that we would get in, but I used to climb from the camelia tree in the courtyard onto the balcony of the building and, from the balcony window, I pushed my way into the library. The library window was covered by a trellis but there was no glass so that fresh air could circulate. In the middle of the trellis there was a square frame that could be pushed in. When I was in the library, if I heard a sound on the steps or if it was time to eat, I would stealthily climb out. One day the teacher of our family school saw me and gave me a severe scolding. After that I was a little more careful.

In 1905, my grandmother gathered the family at our home in Xiangxiang and divided the family property between my father and two of his brothers. Another brother, my uncle Guangquan, was not included in the division because he had been adopted by his uncle, Zeng Jize, and left the main branch of the family. The other family members stayed at Prosperity Hall for eight months. My cousin Yuenung, son of uncle Guangquan, did not, however; he remained in Changsha with his father who was attending the funeral of Madam Liu, his adoptive mother, widow of my great uncle Zeng Jize. While the family was at Prosperity Hall, my cousin Zhaoquan, uncle Jirong's son, was my constant companion. He and I frequently used the tree and window route into and out of the library where we looked at various types of books. This is how, through informal study, I gained some general knowledge of Chinese culture.

Our family did not follow the beliefs of Buddhism or Taoism nor did we hold stage performances, drink alcohol, gamble, or play cards. However, there were a few exceptions. We observed the Buddhist practice of not eating meat on four days each year. We abstained on the nineteenth day of the second, sixth, and ninth months in honor of Guanyin, the goddess of mercy, and on the twenty-fourth day of the twelfth month in honor of all the gods. On these days the entire family, young and old, ate no meat. It was said that this practice was begun by Zeng Guofan. Because of this, my grandmother observed it.

Our family engaged a Chinese opera company to perform on grandmother's birthday and on my father's birthday, but at no other times. These performances were limited to two days. Formerly, during the Qing Dynasty, big families such as ours had a stage in the parlor of their home. If there was an occasion to celebrate, such as a wedding, they would invite guests and have a banquet with wine and a stage performance to entertain them; however, following the teachings of Zeng Guofan, our family eschewed luxurious living so there were few such performances.

The only gambling that grandmother allowed was from the twenty-fourth day of the twelfth lunar month until the fifteenth day of the New Year when she permitted some games played with dice. The adults could also play a little Mahjong.

The New Year was a very festive occasion. On New Year's Eve, there were colored lanterns and red candles set out everywhere, charcoal fires in basins, roasted lotus seeds, red dates, and dried longan tea. The burning in the stoves gave off a tantalizing aroma. We placed food and wine before the spirit temple as an offering to our ancestors. Later everyone ate the ceremonial New Year's meal and the older generation distributed New Year's gifts of money to the children and decorated the doors with New Year's couplets. The servants who managed the household then closed the gate and put up a strip of red paper bearing the four characters "bar the gate, celebration overflows." After a while, the family members who were on the outside of the gate put up another strip of red paper with the four characters saying "open the door to great fortune." Then they set off a great blast of firecrackers, the doors were thrown open, and everyone crowded in with firecrackers and lanterns shouting congratulations, success, prosperity, and other lucky sayings.

When we celebrated New Year's Eve at Prosperity Hall, we also built a tall column with tree branches covered with pine oil, and set it afire—what in ancient times was called "torching the courtyard." Most of the adults would play cards all night. The children all begged to stay up, too. Actually, the adults also stayed up because things got wild on New Year's Eve and, staying up, they could guard against fire or thieves.

The next morning at daybreak, we made offerings to our ancestors and paid New Year's calls. Each branch of the family provided lotus seed tea and candy boxes inside of which there were trays of candied fruit divided into compartments. They brought these to grandmother's quarters. All who came to pay New Year's calls that day would drink lotus seed tea. Those who stayed longer would eat fine noodles and eggs. As soon as the children saw the boxes of candy opened, they started eating. We thought NewYears was lots of fun.

The adults, especially my mother who was caring for grandmother, were very busy before the New Year sending presents to friends and relations. After the New Year, they had to entertain guests and give presents to their guests' children. Each child received between fifty cents and one dollar and all were given a silver dollar in a red paper envelope. Although there were many other married women and male and female servants in our household, grandmother insisted that my mother manage everything.

Gambling and other such pastimes stopped after the fifteenth day of the New Year. The children could play with their lanterns for half a month at the beginning of the year, but when the eighteenth day of the New Year arrived, the custom in our family was that classes began in the family school. The day before school started, we invited the teacher to a banquet. There was a male host and the male students attended. As a female student, I did not eat with the teacher. The next morning, bright and early, we all paid our respects to Confucius and then formally began studying. The adults in the family would rejoice that the children were once again in school saying, "The wild horses have been bridled."

The tending of family graves at the Qingming Festival was, like the teacher's banquet, mainly for boys. I went only to the graves of those ancestors from whom I was directly descended. So I never went to the graves of my most famous ancestors, the great military hero, Zeng Guoquan, or the successful diplomat, Zeng Jize. It was even more strictly forbidden for girls to go traveling for pleasure or to go bathing. Not until I went to school in Hangzhou and lived with my uncle Jirong did I go to the resort at West Lake near Hangzhou and visit the tomb of Yue Fei, the loyalist hero of the Southern Song Dynasty (1127–1278), Lingwen Temple, Mount Gu, and other scenic spots.

At the Dragon Boat Festival on the fifth day of the fifth lunar month, commemorating the tragic suicide of the great poet and patriot, Qu Yuan, we would eat steamed rice dumplings in palm leaves, hang out little satchels of perfume, and call on friends and relatives. These customs are followed in many places but, in Hunan, we also ate salted duck eggs. Everyone had to eat at least two. The popular belief was that they could improve one's hearing.

The night of the seventh day of the seventh lunar month was the festival celebrating the reunion of lovers, sometimes called the laying down of needles. This was a festival principally for girls. Girls of the family would spread melons and fruit in the courtyard to honor the star Vega, the spinning maiden, when it met the star known as the cowherd crossing the Milky Way. In the starlight under a new moon, we would thread red silk thread through an embroidery needle with seven eyes and then fill a large ceramic basin with water and place it in the moonlight. Early the next day, we laid the needle across the surface of the water. If the needle floated and the shadow cast by the sun entering the water made an image of the needle like the pistil of a flower or a pen or the balls on an abacus, this indicated that the girl who had laid it on the surface of the water would have great skill with the needle.

The fifteenth day of the seventh lunar month is the Ghost Festival. It is a time when people all over China make sacrificial offerings to their ancestors. Our family was no exception. From the first day of the seventh month we would make simulated gold and silver ingots from paper to burn for the dead and address packages to them. On the top of each package, we would write that this was for such and such an ancestor in the spirit world and on the bottom we would write that it was respectfully presented by such and such a descendant. Packages bearing the names of individual ancestors could go to ancestors of the past five generations. For the rest we had twenty or thirty packages addressed to "Ancestors of the Zeng family of past generations."

On the evening of the tenth day, we would set out a banquet on two tables in the dining hall as an offering to our ancestors. The skirts around the tables, the drapery on the backs of the chairs, and the chair cushions were embroidered crimson. The banquet was set out on three sides of the tables. On the fourth side facing outward there was a flower vase and four dishes of fruit. There was also a skirt on this side of the table. A little further out in the center, there was another table with an incense burner, a candle-holder, a flower vase, yellow prayer paper, and chimes arranged on it. This table also had a crimson embroidered skirt. Still further out there was a kneeling mat placed on a crimson carpet. At sunset on the evening of the tenth day, the male master of ceremonies and the adult males took lanterns and firecrackers outside the main gate and facing west knelt and offered gifts. At Prosperity Hall, this was outside the West Gate. The meaning of this stemmed from the belief that in earlier times the deceased ancestors returned to the West. Afterwards with the master of ceremonies carrying three sticks of incense in his hands, the men walked straight to the center hall. Behind them strings of firecrackers and lanterns were brought in. The head of the household placed incense in the burner. Those assembled there then said softly one after another, "Our ancestors have returned." Thereupon, the family members—adults and children from the elders on down in that order—knelt before the seat of honor and paid their respects. When we cleared away the banquet the same ritual was followed. After that every day at all the meals, for the remainder of the festival, we would pay our respects in accordance with ritual.

After the evening meal on the fourteenth day of the festival, carrying lanterns and torches, fragrant flowers and firecrackers, the family members bore the packages bearing ancestors' names down to the river's edge. First, they laid out the sacrificial items and after paying their respects, they burned the packages. The sacrifices to ancestors at the Ghost Festival were then concluded. When we were small, we were affected by this atmosphere; sacrificing to the spirits felt like they were actually there. We would not dare play, laugh loudly, or casually eat anything in the central hall when this was conducted.

The Mid Autumn Moon Festival is a women's festival. We have a popular saying, "Men don't worship the moon and women don't sacrifice to the Kitchen God," since the sacrifices to the Kitchen God are restricted to males. Even though the Moon Festival is supposedly only for women, in reality it is one of China's great festivals, often called the Mid Autumn Festival. Friends and relatives present gifts and go calling. It is a more festive time than the Dragon Boat Festival.

In addition to enjoying the moon and eating moon cakes, there is also the custom of presenting melons. If a woman was married for a long time and was still childless, friends and relatives had a small boy present her with a melon. This was a very long melon wrapped up in a child's red silk garment with two golden flowers stuck in it. With the child holding the melon in his arms, gongs and drums sounding, firecrackers going off, and lanterns displayed, they brought the melon to the childless woman's home, placed it on her bed and covered it with a quilt. Then they came out and loudly offered congratulations to the couple wishing them a child very soon. Naturally, those that presented the melon had to be provided with food and drink and received most graciously; the child that bore the melon was given a gift of money.

After the Mid Autumn Festival comes the New Year, which I have already mentioned. Each year, on the fourth day of the New Year, we held a banquet for our tenants. In Qing times we used to have several tens of tables for them and each tenant family could send two representatives; the tenant families in

Xiangxiang and the vicinity were all invited. After the establishment of the republic in 1912, we had only twelve or thirteen tables with six people at each table. They sat on three sides of the tables. On the fourth side, the front, there were dishes of fine quality food. Before each place there were lotus leaves or a sheet of waxed paper so that if the guests wished to take food home they could wrap it up. In addition, before each person there was placed four pairs of cakes—known as baba—made from sticky rice, polished glutinous rice flour, and water stirred together and formed into a cake mold. They were as big as rice bowls and about half an inch thick with designs on them made with vermilion dye. This type of cake had to be made before the twenty-fourth day of the twelfth month. When the first dish was to be served, at the outset of the banquet, there was a great explosion of firecrackers and the young hosts went to each table and offered a toast. Standing in front of the table where the food was placed, they bowed to express their appreciation for the year's labor, for the tenants' service to us.

In our district, on this occasion the person who carried the long tray of food was special. He held the tray up on the palm of one hand above his shoulder about even with his ear, loaded with more than ten bowls of food or soup. His body was a little bent but he trotted smoothly. The bowls of food would not tip over; even the soup didn't spill. A person went before him to clear a path. This person bent from the waist and went backwards waving both arms to the side pushing apart the onlookers on both sides. When they arrived at the dining hall, the man carrying the tray with a turn of the hand lowered it, keeping it level. The man who cleared the way then put the food on the table. Sometimes there was another man who followed behind the tray carrier and helped with the food. I have traveled widely in China and abroad and I have never seen anything like this anywhere else. It is a truly remarkable feat. In my home district there were only two or three men who could do it.

These customs and observances may seem like trifling matters; however, the rituals and the old ways were firmly implanted in our lives. For a girl to ignore or evade them was unthinkable.

Chapter 3

My Early Education

My early education was the subject of a poem by my father that may be found in the *Huantianshi Shiji* (Celestial Studio Collection). My own recollection begins when I was attending our family school. I was just four years old. We were in Beijing then and father's two younger brothers and their wives lived with us. One of my uncles had a daughter and a son who went to school with me. Since they were both older than I, I called them older brother and older sister. I can still remember that I was so small that when I sat on the stool my feet didn't reach the floor and I was afraid that I would fall.

The first book that I studied was the *Thousand Character Classic*, a summary of Chinese history and philosophy in a thousand characters, none of which is repeated. I actually understood none of it but I could recognize quite a few of the characters. Of course, I couldn't write those that had a great many strokes, but when I saw them I recognized them—especially in that book. I rarely made a mistake. At that time my older sister was studying the *Book of Odes* and my older brother, the *Sayings of Confucius*, classics compiled more than two thousand years ago. Before long, I mastered the *Thousand Character Classic* and moved on to the *Book of Odes*. I was very proud because I had caught up with my older sister. Although she was already studying the court poetry in the "xiaoya" section and I was still on "quanquan goes the osprey," the very first words of the book, it was still the *Book of Odes*.

Inevitably, my schooling was affected by the political and social upheavals that accompanied the disintegration of the Qing Dynasty (1644–1912). Our family's affairs were inextricably linked to these changes. While I was attending school in Beijing, the One Hundred Days Reform, an abortive attempt by Confucian intellectuals to reform the Imperial Government, took place. Though I was very small, it left a deep impression. It all started one day in August, 1898. There was a fine rain falling and the members of our household—from grandmother on down—got up early. Father had already left Beijing in July and only my uncles and their wives and the other women of the family remained. All I can remember was that messengers for my uncles kept going in and out and hurrying back and forth, sometimes calling out loudly and at other times whispering quietly. Our teacher didn't even start a new lesson that day. We three children wondered what was happening. We heard that a man from Hunan had been killed in the marketplace. I thought to myself, "Fortunately, father is gone; it can't be he." I didn't know then that my father was a follower of the reform leader, Liang Qichao, and that he had spoken out in support of the young reform-minded Emperor Guangxu. Had father remained in the capital, he might well have suffered the same fate as the six martyrs for political reform who were executed on orders from the Empress Dowager after she directed the Army to suppress the reforms.

There is no doubt that the Zeng family strongly supported the reform party. Quite a few days later, we heard that one of great uncle Zeng Guoquan's family members, my uncle Bohang, had taken poison and killed himself. The day that the Army moved to arrest the reformers, my grandmother very wisely sent uncle Jirong to the Hunan-Hubei Guild Hall to get the register of names and burn it. If she hadn't done this, the government could have identified conspirators from this book. A great many people might have been implicated.

After the six men who led the reform were executed, Grandmother thought the whole family should leave Beijing. By that time my father had been appointed to Guangxi Province in south China as prefect in Wuming and my uncle Jirong had been appointed to Zhejiang Province in east China as a sub-prefect. My other uncle, who was a councilor on the Board of Punishments of the Imperial Government, was unable to leave Beijing. Because it was so cold, grandmother delayed our departure until Spring of the following year, 1899. She sighed saying, "Only a junior branch of our family now remains in the capital. I fervently hope that their family enjoys peace and security and that the nation is spared further turmoil."

Who would have thought that the following year, 1900, the Secret Society of Boxers would terrorize foreigners and Chinese Christians in the capital area and that an army composed of forces from the eight nations whose nationals had suffered at the hands of the Boxers would occupy Beijing? In that year also, my uncle's wife and her son succumbed to diphtheria. Her daughter survived and returned to Changsha in the care of a loyal old servant woman. My uncle remained in Beijing and endured very difficult times.

Taiji Chang, the home my cousin Marquis Zeng Guangluan had inherited from his father Marquis Zeng Jize, was completely ransacked by Boxers. Before the looters arrived, the family members escaped to Shanghai with their lives and little else. The four family servants who remained to guard the property were terrorized by the Boxers and some unruly soldiers of imperial General Dong Fuxiang. They swarmed into the house looting and smashing everything as they came. The doorman and a worker who attempted to resist were murdered before the eyes of an old tailor and his wife. When these two realized the fate that awaited them, they committed suicide by throwing themselves down a well.

While Beijing was occupied by the Eight Nation Allied Force that put an end to the anti-foreign activities of the Boxers, many officials and their families who had shown sympathy for the Boxers took their own lives, protesting foreign domination of China and fearing the victor's justice. The Empress Dowager with the young Emperor Guangxu as her prisoner fled the capital, stopping at Huailai just west of Beijing. There, an uncle on my father's side, Wu Yung, arranged their reception. A full account of this can be found in Wu Yuchuan's *Xishou Congtan* (Collected discussions of the imperial travels to the west). My father admired the enlightened efforts at political reform made by the young Emperor and remained loyal to him but, by the late summer of 1900, he was completely under the control of the Empress Dowager. In that year, father wrote his celebrated poem lamenting the death of the imperial consort, Zhen Fei (1876–1900). She had encouraged Guangxu's political reforms. For doing so, the Empress Dowager had her thrown into a well to perish.

I accompanied my parents, my father's second wife, Madam Zhao, and the concubine, Madam Shuai, back to Hunan. We passed the New Year at Changsha in the home of my father's sister, Madam Yu, my grandmother's only daughter and the mother of Yu Dawei, later a prominent official of the national government. After a while, my father went on alone to his new post in Guangxi and sent the family to our residence in Xiangxiang, Prosperity Hall.

I heard that not long after his arrival in Guangxi, when my father met Governor General Cen Chunxuan, father bowed but did not kneel. At that time, members of the Hanlin Academy, such as my father, were regarded as disciples of the Emperor. When meeting with governors or governors general, they would bow but not kneel. The usual practice had been for subordinates to kneel before superior officials, but by that time the ideas of office holders had changed greatly and they had abandoned the practice. After that assignment, father did not again accept an appointment to office. Instead, he gave himself to the study of calligraphy, poetry, mathematics, and foreign sciences such as acoustics, optics, chemistry, and electricity through translations done by the Society for the Diffusion of Christian and General Knowledge among the Chinese of the missionary scholar, Reverend Timothy Richard.

My father had a very modern outlook. He did three things that helped me greatly in life. First, he did not allow my feet to be bound. He discusses this in one of the poems in the *Huantien Studio Collection*. Second, he did not arrange a marriage for me when I was young. Once a family elder, an older relative of my grandfather, said to father, "Your daughter is almost nine. Why haven't you arranged a marriage for her? When she grows up you'll have to wait for someone's wife to die to find a husband for her."

Father responded, "I won't arrange a betrothal until I have her agreement."

"She is young and doesn't understand these things. What knowledge does she have to base her agreement on?" replied the elder.

My father answered smiling. "When she has the necessary knowledge, she can choose for herself and then I'll just agree." From that time on, no one brought the subject up again.

Third, he didn't stop me from becoming a Christian and he allowed me to go abroad to study. While I was in the third year of the Mary Vaughan High School in Hangzhou, I realized that life in the world could be very difficult. I was encouraged and inspired, however, by the Christianity of Ms. Louise Barnes, the principal of Mary Vaughan, and decided I wanted to receive baptism. I feared that my family would be opposed. My father surprised me; he was not. On the contrary, he was quite understanding. He wrote a long letter responding to my questions, citing the examples of Paul Hsu, a prominent scholar and a convert to Christianity during the late Ming Dynasty (1368–1644), Matteo Ricci, the famed Jesuit missionary at the turn of the sixteenth century, and other Christians who had opened schools for the benefit of the Chinese people. But he also pointed me to Yan Fu's translations of Charles Darwin's theory of evolution, Thomas Huxley's teaching of Social Darwinism and other writings in the same vein. He knew there were many aspects to Western learning. Religion definitely was important, but social science could not be ignored.

Each time I recall the happiness of my school days, I especially like to think of my old home, Prosperity Hall. There were hills and lakes, pavilions and terraces rising above the ponds, and libraries. When spring came, the fields were covered with green grains. In the summer, there were lotus blossoms around our residence and outside the gate. In the autumn, laurel blossoms bloomed on the hill behind our home. The fragrance carried for nearly a mile. In the winter, red and green plum blossoms bloomed before the former study of Zeng Guofan, on the little hill to the north of our home. The reds and greens intermingled and the cool scent touched our nostrils. It was a fabulous home. It was our great fortune to study in such an environment when we were young.

When I studied with our teacher in the family school at Prosperity Hall, I read the *Sayings of Confucius* and the *Yupi Tongjian* (imperial comments on the outlines of the *General Mirror of History*), written during the Song Dynasty (960–1278) with commentary by early emperors of the Qing Dynasty (1644–1912). Each day I read two or three chapters in the *Sayings of Confucius* and learned to recite them from memory. Since, at that time, texts such as the *General Mirror of History* were, for the most part, unpunctuated, I would mark off four or five pages with punctuation marks but I did not have to memorize them. At that time I was the only student except for a little servant girl who read along with me for a few months until she was given to a man from the countryside to be his daughter-in-law. Later, another girl attended for more than a year. They read rhymed summaries of other books and the *Sizi nujing* (Four character women's classic). But these two girls were not very bright; their progress was slow and their memories poor. I was always able to learn their lessons perfectly and prompt them in memorizing and reciting. Then we would go out and play.

Our home at Prosperity Hall was very large. The older people did not want me indoors where I might disturb them but it was all right if I was attending class. But the teacher just listened to us recite our lessons and then dismissed us. My first teacher was a Mr. Yin who was skilled in writing and in art. He taught writing quite scientifically. He drew a nine-square grid on a piece of glass and placed it on the copybook over the model character. Then he had me write the character on nine-square grid paper exactly as the model character appeared through the nine-square grid on the glass. Unfortunately, he smoked opium. He never got up before eleven and he taught very haphazardly. While I studied with him, I responded to his poor teaching with equally poor learning.

As I mentioned previously, our home had two large libraries. One was on the south side of the main residence. It was divided into the official collection and the ordinary collection. The official collection contained the books of Zeng Guofan. It included classics, histories, philosophical works, and literature. Most important, however, were the district and provincial gazetteers. There was a gazetteer stored there from every place where Zeng Guofan had served as an official. So our collection of district gazetteers was very valuable. The ordinary collection contained Zeng Jize's books. It included quite a few collections of poetry and a multi-volume, large character edition of the *Annals of the Grand Historian*, the first comprehensive history of China written in the second and first centuries B.C. Zeng Jize's grandchildren had placed punctuation marks in it. But the most valuable part of the collection were the works in English and French. Zeng Jize had served as ambassador to England and France. During the eight years he was abroad, he collected numerous foreign books, including the *Encyclopedia Britannica* and volumes in French. But what we liked best were the microscope, the telescope, and the double glasses through which we could watch colored glass slides of scenery.

The library in the north of the residence housed my grandparents' books. My grandfather enjoyed studying astronomy, mathematics, English, and astrology. Grandmother preferred books on medicine and divination; there were also quite a few works of fiction. This library had three floors. It held precious treasures—knowledge of the arts and various skills accumulated over the years. Though I was very young at that time, I was interested in medicine, divination, astrology, and physiognomy. There, I could browse through books on physiognomy, fortune-telling, and Buddhist religious discipline. It also held large sets of Buddhist sutras and paintings. Though I appreciated the Buddhist art, I couldn't read the books. I even learned several incantations used to summon monsters and chase away ghosts. Like most country folk, we were quite superstitious. When walking from our quarters to the library, I had to pass through a section of the veranda and a dark lane. When I went through at night, I always recited Buddhist incantations to myself. This may have been the beginning of my interest in religion.

In 1902, my grandmother was in Nanjing. The previous year, my father had gone to Beijing to receive the Empress Dowager and the Emperor Guangxu on their return to the capital following their flight to West China during the Allied

Occupation of Beijing. Afterwards, father also went to Nanjing. Then the entire family moved from Hunan to Nanjing. In Nanjing, I studied with my cousin Yuenung (who I always referred to as my brother), my male cousin, Zhaoquan, and my female cousin, Baoling.

My grandmother was a very fair-minded person. She took the eldest child of each of her sons—regardless of whether the child was a boy or a girl—and raised them herself. I was the oldest child of her oldest son; Baoling was the oldest child of her son, Guangzhong. Yuenung was the oldest child of uncle Guangquan and Zhaoquan was the oldest son of my uncle, Jirong. It was just right; there were two grandsons and two granddaughters.

My grandmother's educational principles were unusual for her day. She did not approve of the "eight legged essay" used for the civil-service examinations and she didn't want her two grandsons to take the examinations for the *xiucai*, the first civil-service degree. She preferred that we study foreign languages. Because, at that time, there were a great many students going to Japan for studies, we hired a Japanese, Mr. Morimura, to teach Japanese. Mr. Chen Moxi was employed to teach Chinese, history, and geography. We had to read the newspaper every day and punctuate it. At that time, articles in the paper were written in literary style without punctuation. If we punctuated the texts with a red pen, the teacher could see whether or not we really understood what we were reading. Baoling and I didn't learn the usual subjects for girls: embroidery, cooking etc.; instead we learned to paint, and read and write poetry. Once every week an art teacher came to instruct us. While Baoling and I were occupied learning art and poetry, our two male cousins had physical training.

Each Saturday we wrote a composition. At that time, teachers did not know much about teaching composition, but they gave us some easy topics—such as "An account of the circus" or "The fish and the bird ask questions of each other and reply"—and then let us expand upon them freely. Then they gave us more difficult ones such as "On Xiang Yu," an essay on the legendary hero of the wars at the founding of the Han Dynasty (207 B.C.–A.D. 220) and "The Postscript to the Earl of Zheng defeats Yin in the State of Yan," an account of interstate warfare during the Warring States period (482–221 B.C.). We didn't know how to compose and write an essay, but before long we progressed from composing essays of from one to two hundred characters to essays of seven to eight hundred characters. We felt this was because we had read the papers, punctuated them and punctuated the *General Mirror of History*.

The time I spent in Nanjing was the period of my greatest development. Unfortunately, after I arrived in Nanjing, I contracted a severe case of enteritis and soon couldn't study Japanese with my cousins. After I recovered I audited the class, but today I have no knowledge of Japanese. However, I was stronger than my cousins in Chinese because I read so much at our home in Xiangxiang. There I had read mostly fiction. When I was ten I was able to read literary works like Pu Songling's ghost stories, *Strange Tales from a Chinese Studio,* and the Qing Dynasty miscellany, *Yeyu qiudenglu* (The record of night rain and autumn lanterns). In

Nanjing, I also read such works as Ji Wenda's *Yuewei caotang biji* (Notes on minutiae from my thatched cottage), a Qing Dynasty collection of stories about the unusual. I especially liked short stories. These books helped me greatly in learning how to write. Each time we had to write compositions, the teacher posted the names of those who did well. Though the others were first sometimes, I was first most often. I quietly became leader of the group and introduced them to Taoist breathing techniques, Buddhist meditation, sacrifices to the gods, and other ideas about the deities.

Before long, in 1903, Grandmother moved the family back to Xiangxiang but Yuenung and his mother stayed in Changsha and my uncle Jirong and his wife went to Hangzhou. Only my cousin Zhaoquan and I went with Grandmother to Xiangxiang. My cousin Baoling had discontinued her studies when she reached her fifteenth birthday since it was considered inappropriate for her to continue under the guidance of a male teacher. Thus when we got to Prosperity Hall only Zhaoquan and I received instruction. By then we had already completed our study of the *Zuozhuan*, a commentary on the historical record of Confucius' home state from 722 to 481 B.C., and begun the study of the *Book of History*, another of the Confucian classics. Because the characters were so antiquated and difficult, we did not learn to recite the *Book of History* from memory. We studied it closely and wrote out one or two sections from memory. To this day I think that was a mistake. The *Book of History* is the history, geography, the written admonitions and the songs and poetry of high antiquity. Since I didn't memorize it, I have no recollection of these things and I am very confused about the culture of ancient times.

Zhaoquan and I passed a very happy period of study. Our teacher was a Mr. Wang Shixiang, a man from the nearby city of Hengyang. He had a great interest in geography; he made a map of Hengyang and wrote the address of his family home in large characters "Humpbacked Song Wang's Lucky Star Hall." Zhaoquan and I admired it greatly and thought we would make a map of Xiangxiang and write on it "Fuyu Tseng's Prosperity Hall," but we lacked the motivation and the perseverance to do it. We never even finished making the map.

The real reason Grandmother had gone back to Xiangxiang was to divide up the family property among the members of my father's generation. In the winter of 1903, she invited the older generations of the family—most important was my fifth great uncle Jieshi. He was Zeng Guohuang's son and the only direct male descendant of my great-great-grandfather (Zeng Guofan's father), of that generation who still lived in Xiangxiang. He divided the monetary documents and the land titles into three equal parts and put them in three separate envelopes marked blessings, wealth, and long life. He also wrote one of those words on each of three strips of red paper. Then he rolled the paper into balls and placed them in a pint-sized rice container and told my cousins, Baoling and Zhaoquan, and me each to pick one out with chopsticks. The child from the senior branch of the family would draw the first lot. I then drew out the character for blessings. Baoling drew second and Zhaoquan got the final lot. I forget now which characters they drew. Perhaps Baoling drew long life. After drawing lots, we sat down to a banquet. Everyone offered congratulations and said something intended to bring good luck.

My fifth uncle, my father's younger brother, Guangquan, did not get a share of my grandparents' estate because he inherited through his adoptive father, Zeng Jize. Here I should say something about the kind of man my fifth uncle was. After he was adopted into Zeng Jize's family; Zeng Jize's wife (the daughter of Marquis Liu Rong, a high level aide of Zeng Guofan) bore two sons of her own, so my grandfather wanted to cancel the adoption and have my fifth uncle come back to his family. Zeng Jize was vehemently opposed to this saying that the matter had been settled by their father, Zeng Guofan, and could not be reversed. When Zeng Jize and Madam Liu were alive they divided their family property into nine shares. Zeng Jize's two daughters each got a share, his three sons got one share each. Zeng Jize and Madam Liu each got a share, one share for the official library collection, and one share for their adopted son, my uncle Guangquan. At that time, the two daughters had passed away leaving no heirs. The oldest and the youngest sons both died in infancy, so their property went to the middle son, Guangluan, as did the shares of Zeng Jize and Madam Liu. The one share for the official library did not go to him. There were many complaints from various family members—especially Zeng Guoquan before his death in 1890—about the inequity of the distribution but there was no way he could change it. However, he did give my grandmother acreage to meet the needs of our family. Uncle Guangquan resolved that he would provide for himself and not use his share from the family estate. He held to this resolve until he fled Beijing in 1937 as the Japanese army approached. He then went to Changsha and his son, Yuenung, used some of the income from the family lands to provide for him in his old age. He eventually died in Hong Kong. He used the inheritance only for the last five years of his life when circumstances forced him to do so. Otherwise, one could say, "He was a proud Chinese man who did not live off his family's wealth."

In the Spring of the following year, Grandmother brought the family to Changsha. Baoling had already stopped her schooling but Yuenung, Zhaoquan and I, together with our cousins, continued our studies in the home of my father's sister, Madam Yu, in the Liu family temple on Baonan Street. There were two girls, one older and one younger than I, and my male cousins, Dawei and Dalun. In the morning we studied Chinese with a Mr. Xiung Juru. Mr. Xiung had studied the classically based reform ideology found in the *Gongyang Zhuan*, a commentary on the historical record of Confucius' home state from 722 to 481 B.C. at the Jiaojing Academy in Changsha. This was a center for educational reform in the province. Mr. Xiung had been greatly influenced by Liang Qichao, the leader of the failed reform movement of 1898 who had fled to Japan. He also taught us history and geography and introduced a collection of editorials from the journal *Xinmin Congbao* (the new citizen) filled with revolutionary ideas. Our Chinese improved greatly with Mr. Xiung.

In the afternoons we studied English. Uncle Guangquan, Yuenung's father, initiated this. He secured a teacher, a Cantonese, Mr. Qian Bolan, who had been a student at the foreign language school associated with the Jiangnan Arsenal in Shanghai. His teaching of English was introductory; he also taught physical education. Each afternoon at four, after school was dismissed, we did ten to twenty minutes of Swedish calisthenics. We were quite taken with this probably because of our special tailor-made exercise clothing.

I and my two female cousins of the Yu family, Yuenung and Zhaoquan, were senior students. My male cousins, Dawei and Dalun, were juniors. We read the *Zuozhuan* and they read the *Shijian Jieyao*, which consisted of extracts from *The Annals of the Grand Historian* and *The General Mirror of History*. Dalun and Dawei were very mischievous. They would climb to a very high branch on the laurel tree behind the Yu's parlor and howl until we thought they would fall out. Though we yelled at them constantly, they paid no attention.

In the fall of 1904, Grandmother received a letter from her son, my uncle Jirong, urging her to let Yuenung and Zhaoquan begin schooling outside the family. They subsequently entered Mingde Academy in Changsha. Baoling and one of my female cousins of the Yu family had already discontinued their schooling. There were only four students remaining: one daughter of the Yu family, Dawei, Dalun, and myself. Not long thereafter, Mr. Xiung also resigned. He was replaced by a Mr. Yang who taught us for less than three months. That was the last of my education in the family school.

Uncle Jirong was a believer in the new education, more so than the others in our family. It was he who had urged that Yuenung and Zhaoquan enter the Mingde Academy and he brought Baoling and me to Shanghai to enroll us in a girl's school there. However when we arrived, at the end of October, all the regular schools in Shanghai had begun classes and were unwilling to admit new students. There was only one school, Ms. Yan Mo's Christian School for Girls, that would accept us. Baoling and I and Uncle Jirong's daughter, Baohe, were admitted. Baohe had been crippled by osteomalacia as a child and had not attended the family school. Uncle Jirong and his wife hoped that, although Baohe was crippled, her life would not be wasted if she could pursue further education.

In Shanghai we must have looked like country bumpkins, right off the farm, as it were. Furthermore, my family had always led a frugal life. Our clothes were very plain. I often felt mortified because of my appearance in this vast metropolis filled with foreigners.

Uncle Jirong's contribution to our education was great. He believed China needed new knowledge to recover from the tragedy that had befallen our country during the Sino-Japanese War. He witnessed this first hand as a troop commander in Manchuria when he was only nineteen. Because of this, he always wanted us to learn new things, especially science and engineering. Later when younger family members studied science and engineering, they received great inspiration from him. We all felt a deep debt of gratitude to Uncle Jirong.

Chapter 4

Life in the Mission Schools

The first time I left home was to attend Ms. Yan Mo's school in Shanghai. Everything there seemed strange; the first few days, I felt like I was in a fog. There were fewer than one hundred students but the levels of the students were very uneven. There was no fixed curriculum, not even a formal classroom, just a few buildings. Small groups of students tried to teach themselves. We sang, prayed, and did handicrafts in one rather large building that served as church, the study hall, the music room, and handicraft classroom. I began to learn how to play the organ, to do handicrafts and to make garments but there was no mathematics, history, or geography. The Chinese teacher liked me and Baoling because our Chinese was much better than the other students. We sometimes wrote compositions and we read a Chinese textbook that had well-known short selections in literary Chinese like "The Source of the Peach Blossom Spring," "Yueyang Tower," and "The Rhapsody on the Battle at Red Cliff." These were very easy for us. At first, three or four students studied with us; however, later it was just Baoling and I.

This was a Baptist school and it was very strict. We had to worship six times on Sunday. Morning worship was like standing an early morning watch. After breakfast, we worshiped again. At ten o'clock we went to the church to worship. After lunch, we could rest for about an hour; then there was Sunday school. At five, we sang hymns and, at seven in the evening, we worshiped once more in the church. On Sunday, we couldn't work or read—except for the Bible. Fortunately, we were permitted to write letters. This was too much for those of us who were not members of the church. While at this school, I gave absolutely no thought to religion. But we did think Christmas was nice; every student received a doll and candy. I liked singing hymns, too, but they were local Shanghai hymns and the word order seemed strange, so I didn't get much out of them.

The Shanghai dialect was another problem for me. When I first entered school, I felt it was impossible. Many words were very difficult to figure out. The same words had entirely different meanings in the Hunan dialect. One time, one of our classmates put a blackboard eraser in water and let it soak. Baoling and I laughed at her and said, "The cloth is stuck together with glue. If it soaks through, the eraser will fall apart. This is as 'stupid as a pig.'" "Stupid as a pig" in Hunan dialect sounds very close to "devil" in Shanghai dialect. A classmate heard us speaking in Hunan dialect and told the teacher on duty who scolded us saying, "How can you call a classmate 'the devil.'" We protested, "We didn't say that. We just said it was as 'stupid as a pig.'" Speakers of Shanghai dialect thought this was very funny. We didn't.

I was not long at Ms. Yan Mo's girls' school. The next year Baoling, Uncle Jirong's daughter Baohan, and I entered the Wuben girls' school near the Shanghai West Gate. Another cousin, Li Yikang, and several Hunanese girls also attended there. Among them the one who left the greatest impression on me was Zhang Mojun, known in the West as Sophie M.K. Chang, (1883–1965). She was also from Xiangxiang and in later life a champion of women's rights, a leading educator and an official of the Nationalist Government. She was in the second year of teacher training, while I was only in the second year of the upper primary school. Despite the difference in our levels, we got on very well. For one thing, we were both Hunanese but also, our outlook on life was similar and different from the other students. She inspired me with revolutionary anti-Manchu fervor.

The curriculum at the Wuben School was much better than at Ms. Yan's. I would have been very happy to study there longer, but several problems prevented me from doing so. First, I had become very nearsighted and the elders in the family did not permit the wearing of glasses. As a result, I couldn't see anything on the blackboard clearly. This affected my grades, which were only mediocre. Second, that year my grandmother turned sixty. Uncle Jirong and his family went to Wuhan in Hubei Province, where grandmother was living with one of her sons, to pay their respects. Naturally, I went along also. When we arrived in Hubei, my uncle didn't approve of me attending the school there. Since my schoolwork had not been very encouraging, I was not enthusiastic about returning to school. That was the end of my study in Shanghai.

When Uncle Jirong and his family returned to Shanghai, my grandmother, my mother, my brother, Zhaohua, and I remained in Hubei. We lived in my uncle's residence at the Opium Taxation Bureau. Since there were so many children in my uncle's household, after a year, my grandmother took my mother, my brother, Zhaohua, my cousin Baoling, and me to Uncle Jirong's home in Hangzhou, capital of Zhejiang Province on the southeast coast. Uncle Jirong was very enthusiastic about the new education and enrolled me and Baoling in the Hangzhou Provincial Normal School for Women. We both passed the examination for the regular teacher's course but Baoling only stayed in school one semester. Then she went back to Hunan with grandmother to be married into the Yao family. My mother and brother went with them.

During the year and one half that I attended the Hangzhou Provincial Normal School for Women, I did well in my Chinese, mathematics, physics, chemistry, music, and physical education classes, but I took an elective course in English and did poorly. I enjoyed reading in the library: the *Mingru Xuean* (Confucian scholarship of the Ming Dynasty) and *Huang Lizhou Wenji* (Collected works of Huang Congxi), both by Huang Congxi, an anti-Manchu revolutionary scholar of the seventeenth century, and the work of the contemporary constitutional reform advocate Liang Qichao, *Yinbing Shi* (Ice water studio). My taste in literature reflected the influence Sophie Chang had upon me at the Wuben School.

There were not many extracurricular activities for students. The principal, Ms. Wang Yingguan, wanted us to go to the primary school attached to the Normal School for practice teaching and observation. She feared that students from provinces other than Zhejiang would not be able to get positions teaching Chinese language or history in Zhejiang because their accents would be unintelligible. We would be limited to teaching subjects such as music, physical training, or writing Chinese. When classmates from Zhejiang did practice teaching in the primary school, we had to observe and try to improve our accents. This kept those of us from other provinces rather busy.

During the year and one half I was there, I never participated in sports, singing, or the debating society. This was surely a shortcoming in my education. However, I made good friends. I learned through informal discussions and had good times with friends my own age. As soon as we got out of class, we would sing, jump rope, or enjoy a snack together. Relaxing like this with friends was fun and I learned to speak the Hangzhou dialect.

Ms. Wang was very close to the students. She taught a class in self-cultivation once a week. She lived and dined with the students; her bed was in my dormitory, at the very head of the room in the center. There were six beds on each side; mine was just inside the door. I had entered school late so I got the last bed, the one that caught the draft from the door. But this didn't bother me; I actually was quite comfortable there. We all respected Ms. Wang. Though she was kind, there was no question of her authority.

There was also a mathematics teacher, Mr. Chen Boyuan, who had a great effect on my education. When I entered Hangzhou Provincial Normal School, I was behind grade level in mathematics. While at Wuben, I couldn't see the blackboard clearly and the teacher spoke the Shanghai dialect, which I didn't understand, so I learned very little. I didn't know how to do fractions and the Normal School students had already studied algebra and geometry, about which I knew nothing. Professor Chen had the best student in our class tutor me. She explained things clearly and had great patience. Before long I began to understand fractions, ratios, and algebraic equations; it all suddenly made sense. By the end of the semester, I caught up to the class. In the second year, I was among the strong students in mathematics. When I graduated, my average grade was above eighty percent.

Professor Chen Boyuan spoke to me at that time, saying, "You have natural ability and your understanding of the different branches of science is very well balanced. I think it would be a waste of your talent to be a primary school teacher. There is a missionary school that is about to open and they have asked me to teach mathematics, chemistry, and physics. If you are interested, I can arrange for your admission. The name is Mary Vaughan High School for Girls. It is run by the Church of England Missionary Society and has a promising future." I was inclined to accept right away but because of my experience at Ms. Yan's mission school, I hesitated. Furthermore, I didn't know how my grandmother and my parents would react. So I told Professor Chen that I would reply after Chinese New Year. Uncle Jirong very much approved of the idea and wrote a letter back to Hunan for me. My grandmother and my father agreed that I should go to the school and, after Uncle Jirong recommended it, my mother did also.

That year I didn't go back to Hunan for Chinese New Year. In 1908, in the first month of the New Year, I took the examinations to enter Mary Vaughan High School for Girls. Because this school was established in memory of Mary Vaughan, when it opened her good friend, Ms. Louise Barnes, was named principal. The highest class had only two students: Ms. Zhou Qingzeng and me. We each studied Chinese individually. She read ancient Chinese literature and I read the Daoist philosopher, Zhuangzi, a text from the third century B.C. My writing of Chinese was superior to hers but her English was better than mine. We used English textbooks in all courses except Chinese, mathematics, and Chinese history. My English gradually improved and by summer vacation, I caught up with Ms. Zhou. In the second year a new English teacher, Miss Weightman, arrived. Her teaching of English was very systematic. I improved greatly studying with her. I could read simple novels and I won the English prize for the school.

My cousins, Baohan and Xiao Xiaowei, as well as other cousins of the Xiao, Li, and Ding families attended Mary Vaughan High School with me. At that time, on the eve of the republican revolution of 1911, there was a feeling of solidarity among us Hunanese. I was the senior student, so naturally they looked to me as a leader.

The English are inclined to cling to the old ways. This was very much in evidence at Mary Vaughan High School. The Church of England Missionary Society was extremely conservative even by English standards, so there were a great many religious ceremonies. On Sundays, we worshiped five times if we were at school but we could go home on Saturday if we were back before five on Sunday. In that respect, it was not as rigid as Miss Yan's school. I was respected at Mary Vaughan; I was the leader of my dormitory. I received a scholarship and an opportunity to study in England, which proved to be a turning point in my life.

Chapter 5

Finding Christ in China

While I was studying in Shanghai, my cousins, Yuenung and Zhaoquan, both enrolled in a mission school, the Wenhua Academy in Wuchang. In their letters to me, they often mentioned that the curriculum was poor. The religious education at the Wenhua Academy was not very stimulating. Not surprisingly, my cousins had no interest at all in Christianity. I had the same feeling during my first year at Mary Vaughan. Although I couldn't help but admire the way these Christians went about their work, the way they preached their faith was greatly at odds with traditional Chinese thinking. So I couldn't readily accept Christianity. I had to acquire the faith very gradually. Since my Christian faith is an important reason for writing this memoir, I'll explain it all in detail.

In the first semester of the second year that I was at Mary Vaughan, I think it was the spring of 1910, one day, one of my classmates was surprised to find that someone—I don't know who—had ripped quite a few pages from her English practice book. The lessons she was to hand in had been destroyed. The instructor inquired and, as might be expected, nobody admitted doing it. Then, Ms. Barnes, the principal, announced that, if by lunchtime, the person who did this did not come forward and admit her guilt, the entire student body would be punished. Noontime came and went and no one confessed; then small groups of students began talking in the dining hall about how to respond. I was rather quick-tempered and I said, "If the school authorities can't find out who did this, how can they punish the entire student body? I think it is very unfair." At that time, we didn't know what kind of punishment the principal would actually impose. When four o'clock came and we were dismissed from class, the whole student body was herded into a large lecture hall where everyone had to copy from a book for one hour and we were not allowed to talk. We just had to sit at our tables and copy. We copied until five o'clock. Then, an English faculty member came in and said, "Form into lines and go outside in the yard and walk back and forth for an hour. Then you can go and have dinner." I looked at her self-satisfied expression, which showed no consideration for the students, and, without getting angry, I stood up and said, "I'm not going out. Copying in here is all right; it has some benefit for us but walking has no benefits." After I spoke up, there were six or seven other students who would not go out either.

This incident was resolved but after that the school authorities considered me a troublemaker. I grew more and more angry and considered myself a rebel leader. Together with some like-minded students, I put out a small paper entitled "Bits and Pieces" to spread the word about the unfairness in the school. The paper also carried revolutionary ideas about national affairs. The principal became aware of this and discussed with the faculty what should be done. There were quite a few who advocated terminating our registration in the school. However, Professor Chen Boyuan argued that we were all good students, and that dismissing us would reflect poorly on the school.

We had heard of the proposal to dismiss us, so when we went home on the next Saturday, we decided not to come back. Professor Chen, however, wrote a letter to my uncle Jirong saying that the school had no intention of dismissing us but wanted us to apologize and discontinue the paper. If the dispute continued, it would damage our reputations and the reputation of the school. My uncle had been instrumental in getting our schooling started. Now he urged us to return to school. So the next day, I and my six cousins from Hunan and a student from Zhejiang who was involved with us went back to school as usual. We went into Ms. Barnes's office, and bowed to her and the two proctors who were also present. When the others left, Ms. Barnes kept me in her office. Weeping freely, she spoke to me straight from her heart: "I know that you are not opposed to the school. It is just the devil in your heart that made you do this." Then she asked me to kneel down and pray with her. Her words were sincere. There was no hatred. It touched me deeply and I replied straight from my heart that I would change and that the paper would not come out again. From this episode I learned the meaning of Christian love. If it were not for the goodwill of Professor Chen Boyuan and the love shown by Miss Barnes, I would have been dismissed and my life after that would have been very different.

After this episode, I came to respect the love that Christians showed and grew to admire them for it. Not long afterwards, Reverend Ding Limei came to Hangzhou to preach. Crowds numbering in the hundreds went to listen to him. I went many times; my heart was seeking the truth. One day I went to the nearby scenic resort at West Lake to relax. As I approached the tomb of Yue Fei, the loyal military servant of the Southern Song Dynasty (1127–1278) who tried to save China from barbarian invasions only to be betrayed by a treacherous minister at court, I thought about the unfairness of life. Then I saw the dikes named for the great Tang poet Bo Zhuyi, and the Song poet Su Shi, and the tomb of the famed courtesan of Song times Su Xiaoxiao and I thought to myself how brief life really is and I wondered, "What does it all mean?" The ancients had a saying, "Life may be filled with great achievements like that of the fathers of Chinese civilization, Yao and Shun, but it crumbles to dust. Or it may be filled with cruelty like that of the infamous brigand of antiquity Daozhi and it will still crumble into dust." So why should man try to do good? What of the philosophy of Cao Cao (A.D. 155–220), protector of the last Emperor of the Han Dynasty (207 B.C.–A.D. 220), "Drink and make merry for life is short?" I also thought about the decline of China's position in the world and wondered what was causing it.

When I returned to school, I discussed my feelings with Ms. Barnes. By that time we had already put aside our differences and become good friends. I had been promoted to be a class leader. Ms. Barnes was very understanding. We read the Bible frequently and prayed together. We studied the Gospel of St. Mark and read the Book of Job. I had great respect for Miss Barnes's warmth and her Christian conduct. I discovered that she was not extremely learned and articulate, simply an ordinary person. This is the wonder of the spirit of Jesus. It can change an ordinary person into someone extraordinary. Ms. Barnes was ordinary but the spirit of Jesus made her extraordinary. By this time, I already felt that China needed the driving spirit of Christianity. Then I began to think about becoming a Christian.

There was another instructor who had a great influence on my Christian beliefs. When I was in the second semester of my second year, my English teacher was Ms. Weightman. She was an excellent teacher and very close to the students. One day, a Ms. Stuart appeared to substitute for her for several classes. Ms. Stuart was lame; she was also very young, friendly, and interesting to talk to. All the students liked her.

One day, after Ms. Stuart left, Ms. Weightman asked us, "Do you want to know how Ms. Stuart became lame?" Of course we did, so she told us. Ms. Stuart's father had been a missionary in Sichuan Province. In 1900 during the Boxer Uprising, when she was a child, Boxers broke into her home and killed her parents, brother, and sisters. She hid under the bed and the Boxers didn't know she was there. But one of the Boxers plunged a bloody sword through the bed and into her leg. She didn't dare make a sound. The man probably thought his sword had struck a small piece of furniture stored under the bed. Anyway, the Boxers left their house. She couldn't walk because of the wound to her leg but, the next day, good-hearted members of her father's church came and found her. She was barely breathing. They managed to revive her and, then sent her to the Mission Society in Hankou. Although she escaped with her life, she would always be lame. As she grew up in England, at first, she despised the Chinese because it was they who had slaughtered her family and made her a cripple. She harbored a fearful hate but, then, one day in church, she was moved by the Holy Spirit. She not only put aside her hate, she resolved to come back to China as a missionary.

As I listened to this, I was deeply moved. Seeing the kind of person Ms. Stuart was made me believe in Christianity even more. However, it was not easy to convert to Christianity at that time. In the first place my family had been followers of Confucianism for thousands of years. From the sacred founders of the Zeng clan down to Zeng Guofan, my grandfather, and my father, all generations were disciples of Confucius. Second, my grandmother's father, Guo Peilin, was killed by the Taiping Christian Army while defending the city of Yangzhou. She was a believer in Confucianism and gave no credence either to Buddhism or Daoism, and of course, none to Christianity. None of our friends or relatives were followers of foreign religions. To have a young woman of the family become a Christian would simply make them a laughingstock.

I attempted to resolve this by writing to my family and explaining in great detail the bitterness and the sadness in my heart and the love and dedication of Christians. I told them that I saw no conflict between Confucianism and Christianity and that Christianity could awaken China from its lethargy. I wished to become a Christian to save myself and others. I asked my grandmother's and my father's permission. My grandmother was not very enthusiastic; however, my father was willing to consider it. He mentioned the contributions of Paul Xu (Xu Guangqi), a convert to Christianity who studied with Jesuit missionaries during the Ming Dynasty. Nevertheless, he wanted me to read some books of other schools of thought before proceeding. He suggested Thomas Huxley's *On Evolution*, Herbert Spencer's *A Study of Sociology*, Charles Darwin's *On the Origin of Species*, Adam Smith's *Wealth of Nations*, and a few rather superficial works on Buddhism. He didn't ask me to read anything on Daoism. By the time I read these books, it was almost Christmas. At Christmastime, I was baptized in the Church of England. The Reverend Yu Xianting conducted the ceremony.

The year I was baptized was also the year of the Chinese Revolution. On October 10, 1911, the tenth month nineteenth day on the Chinese calendar, the revolution broke out at the city of Wuchang in the central Yangzi Valley. Before long, Zhejiang Province declared its independence. Uncle Jirong, then, took the family to Shanghai to take refuge. At the time he was very concerned about family matters and the state of affairs in China; we began talking about religion, especially Christianity. He gradually received the faith.

The road that led Uncle Jirong to Christianity was a long and difficult one. He was my father's youngest brother and was only seven in 1881 when my grandfather died. When he was seventeen, he married a daughter of the Xiao family and a year later she bore their first child, a daughter, Baohe. As a young man Uncle Jirong was known for his skill at swordsmanship and gambling. However, his life changed in the spring of 1895 when he was only nineteen. He led a force of men into Manchuria to relieve my father's Gangwu Army in the struggle against Japan. Though peace talks began before he actually engaged the enemy, he developed an extremely painful condition from long hours of riding horseback. After the war, he resorted to opium to relieve what must have been excruciating discomfort. Before long he was in the clutches of the drug. His acceptance of Christianity gave him the strength to break the habit even before he was baptized. He lay on his bed for seven days and seven nights, eyes watering, nose running, perspiring profusely, writhing in agony of body and spirit; but in the end he triumphed. The habit was broken.

In the fall of 1911, he was baptized and resolved to establish an independent Chinese Christian church. He bought land in Liuyangmen, a poverty-stricken district outside Changsha. There he determined to minister to the needy. By 1921, with the help of contributions from my great aunt, Mrs. Nie Zeng Jifen, and other relatives and friends, he was able to begin construction of a four-sided complex of buildings surrounding a central courtyard. In addition to the church and minister's quarters, there were to be buildings for Bible study, parishioner's lounges, and others. Sadly, in 1922, before the building was completed, Uncle Jirong developed a tumor and passed away. He was only forty-eight. His life was transformed by the power of God's love and my life was directed by his unwavering belief in the power of education.

Part II

To School in England

Chapter 6

On the Way to Study in England

In 1912, Ms. Barnes was eligible for a one-year home leave in England. She wrote to my grandmother and my father to discuss taking me with her to continue my studies in a British school. Uncle Jirong and Uncle Nie Yuntai, Zeng Guofan's grandson and a prominent Shanghai businessman, both strongly supported the idea and they wrote to Hunan urging that I be allowed to go. At the time, I had returned to Hunan. So my mother took me to Shanghai and then on to Hangzhou where we stayed for a week at Ms. Barnes's home. Ms. Barnes also prepared a document stating that even though I had not graduated from Mary Vaughan High School, I was qualified for study abroad. This was another turning point in my life. If I had waited until graduation, two years later, my family might have viewed this quite differently because of the changed political conditions following the revolution. Furthermore, Ms. Barnes would have already taken her leave. It is unlikely that my family would have allowed me to go abroad to study alone. My grandmother stated her position very clearly in her reply to Ms. Barnes's letter. She said that in England I was to be under Ms. Barnes's care and furthermore, if Ms. Barnes returned to China, then I must return also. I was not to remain in England to study on my own.

In mid March 1912, my mother brought me to Shanghai. Uncle Nie Yuntai and Uncle Jirong asked the former Ambassador to the United States Wu Tingfang to arrange my departure. As Ms. Barnes and I boarded the steamer bound for the Manchurian port city, Dalian, I stood on deck and looked at my mother standing silently on the pier. I heard my old wet nurse weeping inconsolably and the blessings and farewells of friends and relatives. Suddenly I realized I was starting down a new path in life. I had no idea what the future held for me, but I was full of hope and faith in God's goodness. I believed that Ms. Barnes would look after me, and I believed in my own determination—my resolve to study and work for the development and welfare of China.

We stopped at Dalian on April 8, 1912, for one night. I had no desire to go about looking at the sights. I actually felt rather angry. I thought of Manchuria under Japanese control, the disputes between China and Russia along the border and the Russo-Japanese War with China as the battleground, and I was sick at heart.

Two days later at Manzhouli on the Russian border, we boarded the Trans-Siberian Railway bound for Europe. At that time, a first-class compartment on a Russian train accommodated two people. There was a bathroom between each two compartments. When one used it, one turned on the light to let the people in the adjoining compartment know that it was in use and then bolted the door. After finishing in the bathroom, one turned off the light and unbolted the door to the next compartment. Everything was very clean on the train. An attendant changed the sheets and pillow cases every day. One bed was along the side of the compartment where the window was situated; it could be pushed up. The other bed was along the wall opposite the door to the lavatory. There was also a small table in front of the window so that passengers could eat in their compartment, but we always went to the dining car. As soon as the passengers got on the train, an attendant came around and asked, "Do you wish to dine in your compartment or in the dining car? The first or the second sitting?" Because there were not enough dining cars, each meal had two sittings. The food was very good, European cuisine. Every day before lunch and dinner, if we came to a large station, the train would stop for an hour and let the passengers stretch their legs on the platform. The local peddlers would try to sell us souvenirs and things to eat. This is how the first-class accommodations were in Imperial Russia. I don't know how things were after the communists seized control of the government.

When we began traveling across Siberia, all we could see was a vast, desolate wasteland. Although it was early April, everything was still covered with ice and snow. I had a strange feeling when the train crossed the ice of Lake Baikal on temporary tracks. I also saw a perfectly round rainbow, radiantly beautiful in the cold clear atmosphere. I think these are rare, even in Siberia.

We stayed a day and a night in Moscow in order to change trains. We visited the museum, the art gallery, and the Kremlin. The church where the coronation of the Tsar took place and the throne used during this coronation are in the Kremlin. This throne was made entirely of gold; the back was very high. The workmanship in the designs on it was extraordinary. At the time, I was still quite small and wore my hair in braids. When I tried to sit on it, the guide smiled and said, "Since you are a child, give it a try, but adults are prohibited."

When the train reached Warsaw in Poland, we had to change trains again. Here the Russian Customs conducted a very thorough inspection, very different from the perfunctory inspection when we first boarded the Trans-Siberian train. Probably, Ms. Barnes had arranged that inspection beforehand and said nothing to me about it. Warsaw at that time was congested with people from many places.

There were Russians with fur hats and long coats, English and Frenchmen dapper in Western style clothing, Germans with high hats and long sleeves and Eastern orthodox priests with long hair half way down their backs and solemn, sanctimonious expressions. Though I only glanced through Liang Qichao's *Bolan miewangji* (The fall of Poland), what I saw in Warsaw brought it to mind and a dark mood came over me. The fall of a nation is a tragic experience.

En route, we received the news that a great English ocean liner, the *Titanic*, had hit an iceberg in the Atlantic and sunk. We heard that it had been built to be unsinkable but the iceberg proved to be too much for it. More than fifteen hundred people lost their lives. It was a bright moonlit night when it sunk, with a calm sea and a gentle breeze. However, since everyone thought the *Titanic* would never sink, the lifesaving equipment was inadequate. Passengers didn't want to get into the lifeboats. Those who were finally persuaded with great difficulty to do so, were too late. When the ship went down, the lifeboats were too close and many were sucked under by the pull of the larger vessel sinking. The water was frigid and many who were not drowned perished in the cold. I thought about the advanced science employed in building this ship and realized, if one concentrates on one aspect of a task and doesn't make provisions for every contingency, it can result in great danger.

When we arrived in Cologne, we changed to a Belgian train. In Brussels, we changed again; this time to a French train bound for Calais where we would board the ferry for England. The French are thrifty to a fault; even a train like this going for a long distance had no dining car. Passengers brought sandwiches with them and very few people even asked about the dining car, but Ms. Barnes and I didn't know this beforehand. Before we got on the train in Cologne we had a little snack but we brought nothing to eat. Then we spent the night on the train. The next day, however, we had no breakfast, no lunch, and not even a drink of water. Not until the afternoon when we arrived in Calais were we able to get something to eat. En route, when we saw people taking out things to eat, we knew we had made a big mistake. The hunger I experienced then made me appreciate the suffering that hunger can cause and to forgive thieves who steal a little food.

We arrived in Calais at about four in the afternoon. After our luggage was inspected, there was only a short wait until we boarded the ferry for England. We had sent a telegram from Brussels to London asking my cousin Yuenung, who was already in England attending the university, to come to the harbor to meet us. When the ferry arrived in Dover, we transferred to the train for London. From the window, I saw Yuenung on the platform pacing back and forth looking for us. I called to him to get on the train and the three of us rode together to London's Charing Cross Station where we changed trains again; then we walked. Finally, we arrived at the home of Ms. Barnes's friend, Mrs. Keith, in Blackheath, a suburb of London, home to the Greenwich Observatory and a well-known girl's middle school.

I was overjoyed to see Yuenung, a familiar face in a foreign land. Mr. and Mrs. Keith looked after us and made us feel right at home. We had dinner with them. Afterward Yuenung returned to London. Ms. Barnes and I stayed with the Keiths. This was my first day in England, April 20, 1912. I laid in bed that night thinking and couldn't get to sleep. I thought of my family and what the future held for me and how I would react in a strange new country. I thought to myself, I must never under any circumstances disgrace the Chinese people.

Chapter 7

Middle School in England

After our arrival in England, we stayed at the Keith's home for two weeks. Then I enrolled in Worthing Church House School, a small boarding school, recommended to Ms. Barnes by the Church of England. The religious atmosphere was intense. I registered in early May. According to the rules, students at Worthing could go home only once each month. However, the principal, Ms. Fisher, sympathized with the fact that I had just come from abroad and allowed me to go home on weekends. In view of this, Ms. Barnes rented rooms in the nearby village of Wapping so that I could go there and stay with her on Saturday nights. Sometimes, Yuenung would come from London and spend the night also. To be together as brother and sister, for he was as close to me as a brother, made us both very happy. I would tell jokes and Yuenung couldn't stop laughing. Although Ms. Barnes could not get the full meaning, she was happy because we were happy. She really liked Yuenung and hoped he would become a Christian.

Worthing was a Victorian style girl's school. The students studied only literature, art, music, and dance. Every day there was worship and Bible study. I received a firm grounding in the Anglican faith and was confirmed by Bishop Lewis. Although I wanted to study science, my English was not good enough so I applied myself to the study of English. Ms. Morter, the dean, helped greatly. She frequently tutored me individually. I studied English literature and some plays of Shakespeare, but I found this very difficult. Still I respected the way Ms. Morter cared for the students. This was one way of expressing Christian love.

After summer vacation, Ms. Barnes and I went to London and made inquiries of Ms. Maynard, the headmistress of Westfield College in the University of London as to how I could enter Westfield. Since I needed to improve my

English, she felt it would be best if I enrolled in Blackheath Upper Middle School for a year before taking the entrance examinations for the university. Ms. Barnes brought me to the younger sister of a friend, a Ms. Kerr, to help me with my English. With Ms. Kerr, I read short stories by Kipling about India and historical novels by Sir Walter Scott. I very much enjoyed the short stories but found the novels long and disjointed. The sentences were confusing and very difficult to understand. The Kerrs were a family strong in their Christian faith. Ms. Kerr's stepfather had a great personality and sang amusing songs. He often talked with me; as a result, my English conversational ability improved remarkably.

In mid September, I returned to London and entered the highly regarded Blackheath Highschool for girls. School regulations were fairly liberal. They didn't want to see a diploma or transcript; everything depended on an oral English examination with the headmistress and the dean. Ms. Barnes introduced me to the headmistress, Ms. Gladston, and the dean, Ms. Frood. The two of them talked with me for about fifteen minutes. My English was very poor but I understood everything they asked me. Though my answers lacked fluency, they were direct and to the point. Without hesitation, the headmistress said, "Put her in the sixth form, upper middle school graduating class. I think she can catch up." This was beyond my highest hopes, and I immediately resolved to work very hard so that they would not be disappointed in me.

I should explain my desire to study science. At that time Chinese students already believed that science could save our country. We were probably even more dedicated to this idea than today's students. We were not seeking to escape from China or to make a lot of money but were resolved, with all our hearts and minds, to use science to serve China. The dean wanted me to choose courses that would prepare me for the University of London entrance examinations. English, mathematics, and a foreign language were required but I could pick two others. I chose biology and chemistry because, at the time, I was thinking of studying medicine and these two courses could fit into the premedical program. Fortunately, Chinese could count as my foreign language. So I had courses in English, mathematics, biology, and chemistry.

The chemistry teacher was the dean; she had a very gentle way with students. After I was at Blackheath for one year, I received the chemistry prize. The mathematics teacher also was a good instructor. Under her guidance my study of mathematics progressed very well. When I took the examinations for the university, I had no difficulties. In English, even though I spoke frequently with Ms. Barnes, I still had problems because my background was lacking. I had had only three years in middle school in China. Sometimes I was unable to reply quickly to questions. The following year, when I took the examinations for the university, English was my weakest subject. Nevertheless, I passed the English oral examination and the other examinations all went smoothly. In September 1913, I entered Westfield College in the University of London.

When I was at Blackheath High School, the facilities were excellent. There were about five or six hundred students, all day students. Ms. Barnes and I lived in a little house that she rented close to the campus. Each morning I got up at 8:30 and went to school for worship led by the headmistress. She first read a passage from the Bible, followed by passages from speeches by famous people. The service was completed with prayers. After the worship service, the leader of each class led the students off to the classroom.

There was one class each for the first, second, and third years. The fourth year was divided into upper and lower classes. The better students were in the upper class of the fourth year. Those who were a little lacking in some respect entered the lower half of the fourth year. So a student could spend two years completing the fourth level. The same arrangement existed for the sixth year. A student could take two years to complete that level. Under this system the three grades of the lower school and the three grades of the middle school could be completed in six to eight years, depending on the student's ability. An intelligent, hardworking student could complete her studies and take the examinations for the university in six years. Those lacking in some respects might take eight years. And there were those who spent eight years but still were unsuccessful. I am not familiar with the current English school system. However, at the time I was there, I felt it was very well structured. It encouraged good students to work hard and progress rapidly while those who were less able had the time to pursue their studies more slowly and receive more help, and they were not made to feel inferior.

Religious education included Bible study that was elective and there was no pressure to take it. There was also morning worship service that was required. I benefited greatly from hearing the words of the great men that were read at the service. There were no classes on Saturday and Sunday. Each day I returned home to the little house that Ms. Barnes rented and prepared my lessons. Ms. Barnes thought my English conversation progressed very well. At first, she and I always spoke Chinese but after half a year I was able to speak English all the time. Yuenung visited us often. When he did, Ms. Barnes would cook rice especially for us—white rice not rice pudding. Yuenung and I spoke to each other in English and it didn't seem strange at all.

I was in the highest class at Blackheath but I was older than the other students. Furthermore, being a foreigner, it was not easy to make friends, but I did make a few and one friendship proved remarkably enduring. In my class there was a student whose older sister was a missionary in Fuzhou. She and I talked occasionally. I became quite close friends with another girl, Ms. Berker. Her parents were friends of Ms. Barnes and we went to their house for tea several times. She never married and cared for her aging mother who lived to be one hundred—for which she received an award from the queen. She visited me in Taibei a few years ago and I returned the visit. We now correspond regularly.

On Sundays we went to church services. The pastor was Canon Lawrence Barnes, a very learned man. We followed the Episcopal liturgy for public prayer, frequently kneeling to worship and referring constantly to the prayer book. At first, I found it awkward but I gradually got used to it. Episcopal prayers were beautiful, brief, and simple but with profound meaning. I felt that compared to the spontaneous prayers in some churches—rambling and disorganized—these were far more solemn and refined. At Blackheath, I was still a neophyte in the faith. Although my beliefs had not changed, I received no great revelations. I felt that Christianity was superior to other religions and the moral character of Christians was also stronger.

Chapter 8

New Friends

Before I entered Westfield College, Ms. Barnes and I visited some of the friends and patrons of Mary Vaughan High School. Mary Vaughan was a member of an eminent and well-to-do English family who dedicated herself to missionary service in China. The reason for China's weakness, she believed, was that Chinese women had not had the opportunity to develop their talents. Her aim was to establish a school offering a modern education for girls to prepare them to enter the university. Alas, Ms. Vaughan, who was regarded by all who knew her as an outstanding Christian, was stricken with a fatal illness and did not live to see the opening of the school. Ms. Barnes then accepted the position of headmistress, a post she held for three years before she took leave and brought me to England.

Ms. Barnes and I first visited the home of Ms. Vaughan's younger sister, Olivia, in Guildford. Ms. Olivia, who was elderly and unmarried, operated a home for working men that offered economical room and board and wholesome recreation such as chess, music, billiards, reading, and handicrafts. She personally led Bible classes and hymn singing and occasionally arranged for outside speakers to address the residents. It was like the YMCA on a smaller scale; everything was very simple and priced economically. The residents all wore working men's clothing; there were no airs about them.

During the two weeks we stayed with Ms. Vaughan, I had the opportunity to talk with these men. They were as pleased and interested as could be to meet a real Chinese girl—at that time I dressed in authentic Chinese clothing. Furthermore, my visit with them was made possible by their generous donations to the China missions. Every Sunday each man donated a few pence. They referred to Ms. Vaughan and Ms. Barnes as "our missionaries."

Though she was traditional in many ways, Ms. Olivia Vaughan's religious thinking was very modern. She didn't advocate strict belief in all points of faith. Rather, her belief was that "we should model ourselves after Jesus in character and actions, then we are Christians." This has had a great influence on my personal beliefs.

We also visited Mary Vaughan's older brother, Edward. A graduate of Oxford, Edward Vaughan was a tutor and professor of Greek at one of Britain's most prestigious institutions, Eton College. He was very learned, having been influenced by the German philosophers during a period of study in Germany. He combined experiential and purely rational learning in his approach to education. A kindly and humorous man, he also had a fascinating personal background. He had tutored King George VI in Greek and the New Testament while the king was still a prince. Once when the prince forgot his books at Windsor Castle, Mr. Vaughan told him to go "home" and get them and not to forget them again.

Mr. Vaughan married late in life a woman from Ireland. Mrs. Vaughan was intensely loyal to the British throne but very proud of her Irish ancestry. One of her forebears had signed the death warrant of Charles I, in 1649, during the English Civil War. I visited the Vaughan's home often; they were always warm and gracious. After World War II, in 1952, during the Coronation of Queen Elizabeth, Yuenung and I stayed at the Vaughan's home for two weeks. Although food was still strictly rationed then, Mrs. Vaughan smiled at me and said, "While you are our guest, I can serve you chicken and rabbit and conversation with an Eton professor. You'll have food for the body and the spirit." She was very kind and, although she didn't speak much about religion, her actions manifested Christian love wherever she was.

We met two other members of the Vaughan family: Philip—a prominent gentleman in Bristol—and his younger sister; they were cousins of Mary Vaughan. Ms. Barnes knew them very well since she previously taught school in Bristol where they resided. They had wholeheartedly supported Ms. Barnes and their cousin Mary going to China as educators.

The Hett family of Sussex were friends of Ms. Barnes and unrelated to Mary Vaughan. Mr. Hett was a prominent gentleman who was enthusiastic about spreading the faith and a very generous contributor to the foreign missions. The first day I was at their home, I was taken ill. My temperature rose quickly to 101 degrees; Ms. Barnes was very worried. Mrs. Hett gave me some medicine. I don't know what it was but after I took it, I fell asleep and perspired freely. The next day I was much better. Though Mrs. Hett was the mistress of a large household, she personally ran up and down stairs bringing water to me, rather than have a maid—and there were many—do it. She was the model mistress of a Christian household; the entire family, including the servants, rose early each morning and prayed together. Helen, the older of their two daughters, could drive an automobile, so she took us sightseeing.

During the summer of 1913, before I took the examinations for the university, Ms. Barnes took me to the home of her friend, Ms. Firth, to prepare for the examinations. Though Ms. Firth was very young, she held a doctorate in literature from Westfield College and had just accepted the post of Secretary of Foreign Missions for the Church of England. I read the plays of Shakespeare with her: a tragedy, *Macbeth*; a comedy, *The Merchant of Venice*; and an historical drama, *Julius Caesar*. I had read *The Merchant of Venice* previously in Chinese so I was already familiar with it. I enjoy tragedy so I also read *King Lear* and *Hamlet*.

We were not far from the former feudal stronghold of the Duke of Norfolk on the east coast of England. Dr. Firth took me to see the Duke's castle and the museum there. She explained that the Duke of Norfolk had originated England's oldest noble family, having come from Normandy with William the Conqueror in 1066, almost a thousand years before. This made me think of my own family; we have only four generations of nobility. China's only really noble line are the "Holy Dukes," the title given to the lineal descendants of Confucius. Other great families have rather brief genealogies. During the Middle Ages and in recent history, China had no feudal system worthy of mention.

Chapter 9

A Difficult Decision

Ms. Barnes had leave for one year when she left China, but she extended it for another half year so she could be with me while I took the examinations for entrance to the university. With the extension, her leave was from April 1912 until October 1913; then it expired. In September 1913, I passed the examinations for admission to Westfield College. At that time, I was residing with Ms. Barnes at Blackheath. Since classes did not commence at the University of London until the middle of October, we had not yet moved to London. Our home was on the side of Blackheath Common at 2 Montpelier Row facing the common. The scenery was lovely, but unfortunately, two doors away was a pub. Every time there was a holiday, there were crowds of drinkers and drunks everywhere. Ms. Barnes often said to me, "You shouldn't look at these bad types. They're the shame of a Christian country. Fortunately, we won't be living here long." At that time, I didn't know what she meant by "won't be living here long."

One day about the middle of September, we arrived home, ate dinner and then Ms. Barnes suddenly said, "Baosun, I have something important to talk over with you."

I said, "What is it? Please, go ahead."

"When I brought you to England, it was the first time I had taken leave in five years. I saw that you had a talent that could be developed and you were a Christian, so I wanted to take you abroad. As it turned out, you didn't disappoint me; you've gained admission to the university and I'm very pleased. Now the Mission Society wants me to return to Hangzhou to be the headmistress at Mary Vaughan again. They haven't been able to find a suitable replacement. Furthermore, I must serve another five years before I will be eligible for retirement with a pension to provide for my remaining years. This year I am sixty. If I serve for another five years, it will just bring me to retirement age and I would have the years required for retirement so I could receive a pension. If I don't return to Hangzhou, not only will I not receive a retirement pension, it will greatly disappoint my friends, especially those in the Mission Society. A number of them have tried to persuade me to return. They said, 'Now, Baosun has been admitted to the university; she should be independent. She has many friends with whom she can stay during summer and winter vacations. When she graduates in four years, she can return to Mary Vaughan High School and serve under you. She has a good course to follow and you have fulfilled your responsibilities. Haven't both of you accomplished what you set out to do?' I thought this over and over again. What they said made sense. But I still was not completely sure, especially since your family entrusted you to me and I must fulfill that trust. How do you feel about this?"

As I listened, I began crying. I had never heard these things before; I had no idea of the importance of Ms. Barnes's retirement. For a moment I was silent as I thought to myself "It will be lonely in England. Fortunately, Yuenung is here. But, if Ms. Barnes leaves, I have no place to go. Furthermore, the remittances from my family could be late. Although Yuenung gets remittances from our family, too, he could count on the person who handles his remittances for an advance. If I were alone here and remittances didn't get through, I have no one to count on for a loan. Also, grandmother will be anxious and angry. What should I do?"

Ms. Barnes looked at me sitting there silently and said, "Don't be afraid. Say what's on your mind. It's only a month until I must return to Hangzhou. I have to make a decision."

"Ms. Barnes," I said, "you understand my position. Since the revolution, things are very different in China. Besides my grandmother told me, over and over again, that when you return to China, I am to come with you. So my wish is to go back with you. Although it's unfortunate that, after gaining admission to the university, I won't go, I want you to qualify for retirement and get your pension. I, also, don't want to go against the instructions of the older generation in my family."

Ms. Barnes looked at me and said with emotion in her voice, "Let's each pray about this tonight and seek the will of God. We can decide tomorrow morning. If we pray fervently, there is no doubt we will know what to do."

Needless to say that evening our innermost feelings bore heavily on each of us. Although I prayed with my whole heart, I was calm. I knew my future was in the hands of God and Ms. Barnes. God would certainly inspire her to take the right path. It was after midnight when I finally fell asleep.

The next morning before six when it was still not daylight, I heard three soft knocks on my bedroom door. I knew it must be Ms. Barnes come to tell me her decision. I felt so uneasy; this was the most important turning point in my life. I dressed quickly and threw open the door. Ms. Barnes was there in her dressing gown. Before I could open my mouth, she said very firmly:

"Baosun, I have decided and I know without a doubt that it is God's will."

"Return to Hangzhou," I blurted out.

"No," she said. "No, remain in England. I feel very firmly that to educate you, a Chinese girl, to return to China and do God's work is ten times more important than my retirement. If I can help you develop your abilities, that is doing the Master's work."

"But your retirement pension. Please don't give it up for me. How can I ever repay you." I pleaded with her.

"Don't worry, the Lord will take care of things. I fully believe that God's will will be done. He will not allow us to sink into an impossible situation."

To be loved so by Ms. Barnes brought tears to my eyes. We prostrated ourselves by the bed and prayed, giving thanks and weeping together. But these were tears of victory and gratitude. Later Ms. Barnes gave me a gold watch; engraved on the inner face were the characters for victory. Her victory and my gratitude were more than my words can convey. This surely is the greatest love there is, a Christian putting aside her own interests to save another. Inspired by Ms. Barnes example, how could I not resolve to do the Lord's work?

At that time, in the summer of 1913, war was threatening in Europe and the political turmoil in China was worsening day by day. Remittances from my family, which were all I had to live on, could easily be interrupted by political or military conditions. When Ms. Barnes made her decision to resign her post and help me, she had no idea of how God would provide the means for her to do so. Hers was the faith of Abraham and the Reverend Hudson Taylor, founder of the China Inland Mission. These men went straight forward, carrying out God's will and not fearing anything that stood in their way. For such faith God will certainly reward them.

Fortunately for us, some time after Ms. Barnes decided on her course of action, Mr. Philip Vaughan heard of this and donated five thousand pounds—and his sister donated three—for Ms. Barnes to use at her discretion, including my educational expenses. During the war when remittances did not get through, these funds made it possible for me to continue my studies. Later my cousin, Mr. Nie Yuntai, and my family repaid the full amount at the official exchange rate; however, had it not been for the Vaughan's generosity and Ms. Barnes faith, it could not have happened.

Chapter 10

Westfield College

The city of London developed gradually—not unlike Beijing, Paris, Washington, and other great cities. It was formed from the aggregation of many smaller towns. Consequently, the streets were not planned. In fact, throughout the city there are ten to twenty different streets called High Street. All were the main avenues in those earlier small towns that grew together to form London. High Street, Kensington, is an example of such a street. So, London University was not like Oxford or Cambridge where the colleges are close to each other and students and faculty can come and go very conveniently. The colleges of the University of London were separated by quite a distance. Moreover, each college had its own instructional regulations but, the curriculum and the faculty of each were approved by the university. The examinations also were uniform and the university, rather than the individual colleges, recruited faculty and graded the examinations. As a result, the level of the students in different colleges was quite similar.

In 1913, the year that I entered Westfield College, Ms. Maynard, who had helped me so much, resigned as principal because of ill health. So, though I was guided by Ms. Maynard, I never actually was instructed by her. Ms. de Selincourt succeeded her as principal. Ms. de Selincourt was originally from an aristocratic French family that had fled to England in difficult times. She received her higher education in England and had formerly served the missions in India. There, she established the University Settlement for Service to Indian Women, to help with such matters as admission to schools, lodging, board, reading, morality, self-development, medicine, and drugs. She contracted malaria in the inhospitable climate and resigned and returned to England. Ms. Maynard then asked her to be the principal of Westfield College. I'll say more about her later and about Ms. Richardson, the vice principal.

Westfield College was in northwest London, not far from Hampstead Heath, a half-hour bus ride from central London. The college buildings were on a small hill. There was an old three-storied building and a new one, also of three stories. A bridge shaped like an "L" connected the second stories of both buildings. Seventy students lived in the dormitory and there were five day students, all of whom were married and from India. Ms. Maynard had been opposed to having too many students, so she established a limit of seventy residents in the dormitory. Her intent was that her philosophy of education should reach each resident and that she could know each student personally.

The vice-principal, Ms. Richardson, was certainly the most effective person in the administration. However, Ms. Dudin Brown, the original benefactor of the college, was a member of the Church of England and the conditions of her gift stated clearly that the principal must be a member of the Church of England. Ms. Richardson was a Quaker, a member of the Society of Friends, so she did not qualify. Soon after I entered Westfield, Ms. Richardson was taken ill so, at first, I saw only Ms. de Selincourt.

The college had divisions of arts and sciences. Offerings in the arts were quite extensive but the sciences included only biology, mathematics, and chemistry. In the first year I elected to take mathematics and chemistry. Since Westfield had no laboratory facilities for the study of chemistry, chemistry classes were held at Bedford College in the Regents Park district. I had to take the bus to Bedford College twice each week to attend lectures in the morning and laboratory classes in the afternoon. Westfield College provided the carfare and lunch money. The Regents Park district was lovely. There was a long, long lake and even though it was in the middle of the city, it was very tranquil, perfect for study.

Westfield College was originally in the suburbs of London but it is now a very busy area that can no longer be considered a suburb. Though the college was not large, each student had two rooms, a bedroom and a study. In the study, there was a fireplace, closet, desk, sofa, and chairs. Students could hang pictures of their own choosing on the walls. I hung four small scrolls of calligraphy that my father had done for me, some Hunan embroidered wall hangings and photographs of my family. The teachers and my schoolmates all liked them very much and they made me feel more at home. My room was on the ground floor of the old building. The window looked out on a rose garden and tennis courts. It was beautiful and comfortable.

I chose biology as my major and mathematics as my minor. But I also selected courses in chemistry, physiology, and health science since at that time I was thinking of studying medicine. However, after the intermediate examinations in the second year, I decided to specialize in the sciences. At first, I thought of majoring in chemistry but Bedford College was so far and it was so inconvenient to use the library there, I decided to major in biology instead. The biology professor, Dr. Delf, guided me gently through the lessons. She was young, with boundless enthusiasm, and did everything in her power to help me understand things. I enjoyed studying with her. Now, a half century later, she still keeps up a correspondence with me.

Ms. Whitby, the middle-aged mathematics teacher, was kindly but very exacting with the students. She also managed non-academic matters such as arrangements for student accommodations, graduation, and ceremonial banquets but not business transactions. At these events, everything went smoothly because she not only knew how each student was doing, she knew who each student's friends were. So in seating for a banquet, she would be sure not to put strangers together. In her specialty, mathematics, she was clear and explicit. Even the slowest student could understand her explanations.

My family had a tradition of excellence in mathematics. My grandfather calculated *pi* to the two hundredth decimal place. On this, the reader may see Ting Quzhong's *Baifu Tang Shuxue Congshu* (White Hibiscus Hall Mathematics Collection.) My father also worked out quick methods for solving mathematical progressions and computing cubes and squares. However, I believe if it were not for Mr. Chen Boyuan in my Chinese middle school, Miss Baldwin in my English middle school, and Professor Whitby, I would never have been able to do two electives in pure and applied mathematics.

English was not required to enter the university but, since my English was poor, I had to seek help frequently from the English teachers. They were all very helpful. Westfield College and the other colleges of the University of London also had extracurricular lectures on special topics. Whenever I could, I attended these. They were a way of expanding my knowledge and improving my English. Later on, when my English—after great effort—became passable, it was because I made an effort to listen. I also joined the college Christian Student Association, the Debating Society, the Reading Society, and the Scientific Lecture Society. These societies usually met once each week. But the Reading Society did not have meetings; the dues were used to buy new books for the members to read. I made a resolution to finish one book each week. Employing the principle of reading rapidly, to understand rapidly, I did not consult the dictionary very often, only when I was completely unable to understand something. In the course of time, I gradually built up my vocabulary. When the vocabulary came naturally, I was more interested in reading. Afterwards I could employ this vocabulary without great difficulty. Furthermore, by reading novels, one can learn English people's customs and practices at home, in society, at court, and among ordinary people. It is really an excellent way of learning about another society.

Chapter 11

Student Life at Westfield College

Life at Westfield College was filled with new experiences for me. The exposure to the way that students were treated at Westfield and the way they responded and conducted themselves afforded me important insights that influenced my direction of women's education in China.

Early every morning, at about 7:00, an hour earlier in the summertime, the morning bell rang summoning us to get up, though some students didn't rise right away. Morning prayers were at 8:00 A.M. but not all the students attended since it was not required. Those who attended had to sign a registration book and wear their cap and gown. At 8:30 breakfast was served; we filed into the dining hall and sat wherever we pleased. There was a long rectangular table along the south side of the dining hall where the principal and the faculty sat. It was referred to as the "high table." At dinner, each evening, some students sat there with the faculty. The names of the students who were to sit at the high table appeared on a list made up by the principal's personal secretary. The first and second names appearing on the list sat on the right and left of the principal. On the occasions I sat in these seats, I felt very honored. The other students were seated randomly around the table. Each evening there were a total of eleven students invited so, every two or three weeks, each student had the opportunity to dine with the principal. Whenever the college had special guests or at vacation time, everything was different.

The women at Westfield were fed often. At 7:00 A.M., a maid brought tea and cookies to the room. This was called "morning tea." It was customary in upper-class English society. I wasn't used to having tea at this time so I told the maid not to bring it to my rooms. At 11:00 there was coffee or milk and lunch was at

12:30 P.M. Those students who went to other colleges to attend lectures did not return for lunch. At 4:00, there was afternoon tea; this was rather informal. Dinner was at 7:00. At 6:30 a bell sounded alerting us to change our clothes. Everyone changed into fresh clothing and jewelry was permitted. If one was sitting at the high table, then one dressed particularly well. At dinner the fare was more plentiful and everything was more meticulous than at the other meals. One did not go to the tea table on the side of the room to fetch tea. There was a person who brought tea to the table. A faculty member sat at each table and acted as host. Although there was talking and laughing, the dining hall was rather subdued, no noisy talking or loud laughing.

The most sociable dining at Westfield was evening tea. After dinner, at about 9:00, a maid brought a great tray with a pot of tea, teacups and pastries to each room. At 9:00, a bell reminded us it was time to stop studying. When the bell rang, laughing and talking began immediately on all floors. Individual students carrying their tea trays went to their friends' rooms to have tea. As soon as new students reported in, they would receive invitations from older students, one or two days in advance, to come to their room for evening tea. Then on the appointed day, they would take their tea tray and go off to the older student's study. The college supplied the tea and pastries but the host provided water and it was considered very nice if the host had several special pastries for her guests. This type of tea party could involve any number of people. The host didn't have to worry about supplying cups and dishes. It gave students an opportunity to chat, tell jokes, discuss school work, and meet new people.

Faculty members also asked students to evening tea. If a student was invited by a faculty member for evening tea, she had to make her apologies to classmates. When faculty members had tea parties and asked students in their own classes, they usually asked only one or two at a time because this gave them an opportunity to learn more about the student's interests and background. However, when they invited students from other departments, the number might run from five to seven students.

In addition to morning prayers, there was a theology class, but attendance was optional. On Sundays, students went out to church or to visit friends. Ms. Barnes still lived in the house she had rented in Hampstead. This was home to me. I went there on Sundays and Ms. Barnes and I worshiped at the Anglican Church. Mr. Howe, a former missionary in Fuzhou, was the pastor.

College regulations required that we return to the campus for dinner on Sunday evening. After dinner we gathered in the common room where the principal gave a report on important happenings in the college or in the surrounding society, such as the positions held by former students or the honors they had received. Afterward, she selected and read aloud poetry or essays by well-known authors, all of a morally uplifting tone. At 9:00 we went to our rooms.

Most classes were held in Westfield College but there were a few students, such as I, who chose classes that required them to travel to other colleges.

Although there were many colleges in the university, they were widely scattered. Only three of these colleges were purely women's colleges: Westfield, Bedford, and Royal Halloway. The Royal Free Hospital was also exclusively for women students. At the University of London, although men and women were equal in most respects, the hospital was still not open to women so we had our own specialized women's facility.

At the time, English society was still very conservative—women could not get degrees at Oxford or Cambridge. Though both universities were opposed to women enrolling for degrees, they were not at all opposed to women pursing studies there. With this purpose in mind, both institutions established women's colleges. Women could attend classes, take examinations, and enter research institutes but they could not receive degrees. The reason for this was that once they received a degree, they became part of the university and had a voice in determining policy. That meant that women could cast a vote to decide controversial issues facing the university. Narrow-minded members of the faculty voiced the opinion that "our university has been for men only for centuries. If we start letting women have a vote, it will put male faculty at a disadvantage." Because of this attitude, it was many years after World War I before Oxford and Cambridge allowed women to receive degrees.

The women at Westfield College were free to leave the college every day but if they were returning after 10:00 P.M., they had to notify the gatekeeper to keep the gate open for them. The gatekeeper had a little book in which the student had to sign her name. Students were required to be in before midnight or to request overnight leave, which could be had only twice each trimester. I chose the University of London because women and men were truly equal there. Unfortunately, the hospital was the exception; it was still very old-fashioned. I think they have changed now

The English academic year was divided into trimesters. The fall trimester was from mid October to mid December; spring from mid January to late March; and the summer trimester from mid April until the end of June. Each trimester was no longer than ten weeks, so that in each academic year there were no more than thirty weeks of classes. Summer vacation was more than three months long so that students of foreign languages, history, geography, and science would have time to visit various countries in Europe for further study and observation. It was an excellent system. Since the academic year was so short, it was difficult for the students to absorb all the material in the lectures. The lengthy vacation period allowed them to do so. This system of trimesters in the academic year would not work too well in China but the longer summer vacation would be an excellent idea to allow students to be out of classes during the extreme heat and have more time for review. It would also be suitable for schools in tropical Asia.

Westfield College had a student association. Its head was called the senior student. If there were problems involving the students and the college, the student association would hold a meeting and after discussion pass a resolution or a request. Then the senior student would present it to the principal to consider and take action. For example, during World War I, in order to conserve electricity, the college required that lights be turned off at ten each night. The students requested an increase of one half hour and the college approved it. The use of fireplaces in student rooms was also restricted. Each day one could not burn more than one small basket of coal. The students requested to increase this at their discretion but the college did not approve the request saying that the restriction was needed to conserve a national resource. The students accepted this. During the three years I was at Westfield, I saw no incidents of student unrest nor did the college ever fail to grant a reasonable request that benefited the students.

Each year during the summer trimester, there was a garden party. Friends and relatives were invited and it was followed by a dance in the evening. There was also a stage performance: a popular drama or a concert. This was arranged by the continuing students to bid farewell to their graduating classmates. They would invite the graduates to take the seats of honor and serve them tea and pastries. The graduating students could ask a few friends to join them.

Each student could also ask guests to the semiannual debates or lectures. The topic for debate was sometimes facetious and sometimes quite serious, for example: "University educated women are not suited for family living," "Teaching false history has benefits for the country," or "Francis Bacon was the author of Shakespeare's plays." The debates would start in the evening about eight o'clock and end at ten. Sometimes the debate topic would be the same as that being debated in the House of Commons, for example "Workers Insurance." Generally, these debates and lectures did much to broaden my understanding. It is still interesting to recall them.

There was a name card in a small bronze frame on the door of each student's room. There were two more cards in each room: a black one and a red one. The word "engaged" was written on them. Putting these cards in the frame meant that the person inside did not wish to be disturbed. If the black card was up, it meant one could still knock on the door. But if the red one was up, the person definitely did not want to be disturbed. Everyone would know that she was writing an examination or a paper that had a deadline.

I wrote my examinations in my room and when the time expired the instructor would come to pick up the paper; there was no proctor. Education at Westfield respected the students' integrity and trusted them completely. I became familiar with a fine educational system. Later when I headed the Yifang School, I adopted many of the methods used at Westfield. Naturally, middle-school students could not be given as much freedom as university students, but Yifang did not proctor examinations. It did not register demerits; nor did we dismiss students for a certain number of demerits. These ideas I absorbed during my years at Westfield. Of course, things inevitably changed there; it is much larger now and admits male students.

Chapter 12

A Modern Girl's School for China

I originally planned to visit Germany in the summer of 1914, but on August 4 of that year England declared war on Germany so I spent my vacation in London. One of the causes leading to the outbreak of World War I was the competition between England and Germany for world hegemony; the assassination of Austrian Archduke Ferdinand was merely the fuse that ignited the final explosion. Regardless of this, the average Englishman sincerely loved his country and once war had been declared, more than 100,000 rushed to volunteer for military service. Many were young men from the upper strata of society and a great number were university students.

There were also those who opposed the war. The most well-known of these were Bertrand Russell and Ms. Royden. Because of their influence, a number of young men became conscientious objectors. Among these, many were Quakers. Because they refused to serve, they endured punishment and physical hardship, but they did not concede. I personally believe that a true Christian cannot take up arms to kill another human being. Furthermore, killing people at great distances, as in this war, amounted to indiscriminate slaughter. There could be no distinction between the old and the young, the good and the bad. If the spirit of Christianity is to prevail, Christians of the world must love and help each other. Since I felt that opposition to the war was reasonable, I often went to the Friends' Meeting House to hear the sermons.

During winter vacation that year, Yuenung and I spent New Year's Eve together. We resolved to dedicate our lives to China and to the world community. We vowed to work diligently together and to help each other toward that goal. As the years passed, he kept this promise; he always loved and protected me and helped me. Whatever success I had as an educator was in large measure due to his help.

In the spring of the next year, I talked often with Ms. Barnes about my determination to return to China and open a school. At first, she thought I should return to Hangzhou and work at Mary Vaughan High School. I didn't completely agree for several reasons. First, Ms. Barnes had left the Church of England Mission that operated Mary Vaughan High School. Second, I felt that since Mary Vaughan was situated in coastal Zhejiang Province there would be plenty of returned students qualified to be teachers and it would be easy for the school to find someone. Third, I wanted to serve in Hunan, my home province. Finally, and most important, I wanted to start a Christian school run entirely by Chinese. Not that mission schools were not good but I felt that Christianity must be completely assimilated in Chinese society before the Chinese people would embrace it as their own religion, as they did Buddhism. Uncle Jirong had also felt this way and started an independent Christian church in Changsha. I would be very willing to accept foreign personnel and financial help but unwilling to accept foreign control or foreign imposed conditions. Ms. Barnes agreed with this idea. These were the worst days of the war and I was still far from graduation; so I put these ideas aside temporarily, but I never again thought of going back to Hangzhou.

My classmates proposed me as the speaker for one of the scientific lectures at Westfield College. I had no choice but to agree. I chose the topic "The Contributions of Science to Man's Life." Generally, it went quite well. The principal, Ms. de Selincourt praised it and asked to speak with me alone. I told her about the problems I was having in my studies and my hope to start a girl's school in Changsha. She was very approving. She said that if Christianity didn't fully adapt to the cultures of China and India, it could not become a great world religion; philosophical explanations of Christianity were by themselves insufficient to spread the faith. I was inspired by what she said and explained it to Ms. Barnes. She then went to Westfield College and met with Ms. de Selincourt and discussed our hopes for a Christian girl's school for China. Ms. de Selincourt was even more enthusiastic. She sought out a number of prominent and zealous Englishmen who would give their support. Among them was Dr. W. Temple, later Archbishop of England. She also enlisted Ms. Richardson and Ms. McDougall to help me present my ideas to other educators. She considered this true missionary work.

In the summer of 1916 I passed the examinations for the bachelor of science degree from the University of London. I believe I was the first Chinese woman to earn this degree. The principal and the faculty were all very pleased. However, the war prevented me from returning to China so I tried to make the most of my delayed departure by enrolling for graduate study at Oxford and Cambridge. Then, in 1917, I returned to the University of London and pursued studies in education.

In the spring of 1917, Ms. de Selincourt fell from her bicycle and broke her wrist. She developed tetanus and within three or four days she was dead. This was a great blow to me. I not only grieved her passing, I feared my plans for the school would suffer a setback. I worried constantly about this. The college was thrown into turmoil and left leaderless by the death of Ms. de Selincourt. Ms. Richardson was named acting principal. She knew of my hopes to establish a modern school for girls in China and when she saw how dispirited I was, she was anxious to help. She and Ms. de Selincourt had been very close friends; their thinking and interests were very similar. Ms. Richardson continued Ms. de Selincourt's efforts on my behalf. So from spring into summer in 1917, she sought help for me. She asked Canon Storr of Westminster to collect donations from English friends and had the secretary of Westfield College, Ms. Child, write letters of thanks. If it weren't for Ms. Richardson, it would have been very difficult for me to realize my hopes.

Ms. Richardson was from a wealthy and philanthropic family in Northern Ireland. She was personally very warm and friendly and, having studied philosophy and literature, was very well spoken. After the Yifang girl's school was established, I kept a little book of my comments on what she wrote to me. Unfortunately, she was not very strong and was often confined to her bed. In 1928, when returning from the Jerusalem Conference of the World Christian Council, I stayed at her home in Ireland for three days. At that time she was already bedridden. Occasionally, she sat up but only to go out in her wheelchair for a breath of fresh air, but her mind was still very keen and she asked about the teachers and students at Yifang.

The three British teachers later invited to teach at Yifang were all selected by Ms. Richardson. They were a fine group of educators. Ms. Madge taught music; Ms. W. Galbraith, who specialized in English, was one of Westfield's distinguished graduates; and Dr. V. Grubb, a Westfield graduate, held a doctorate in science from the University of London. Of course they came after Yifang was established but Ms. Richardson did a great service to Yifang by recommending them.

Alas, while I was occupied with planning and fund-raising, in mid March 1916, my grandmother passed away. Yuenung and I were heartbroken that we were unable to see her one last time. She made the greatest efforts to see that those in our generation of the family received a sound education. She not only allowed us to go abroad for advanced study, she saw to it that our foundation in Chinese was strong so that we did not forget Chinese culture while we were away.

When Ms. Richardson learned of grandmother's death, she was very sympathetic and continued the efforts that Ms. de Selincourt had begun to help me realize my dream of opening a girl's school. By that time Ms. Barnes and I had received the donations of Philip Vaughan and his younger sister so we had some funds for the school. We prayed fervently that with God's help we could return to Changsha, find a good location, and open the school.

Chapter 13

World War I

While I was in middle school in England, I joined the Church and participated in confirmation preparatory classes, but did nothing else to deepen my understanding of Christianity. At Westfield College, however, my thinking gradually broadened and I became quite concerned about Christianity and social problems. This resulted from the many lectures I attended by distinguished churchmen and scholars, such as Archbishop W. Temple, Dr. Richards, Dr. Barnes, Ms. Roydon, and Canon Streeter. Eventually, I got to know Dr. Hodgkin, who was a Quaker. My thinking progressed and, still further, I began to feel strongly that social reform should be inspired by the spirit of Christianity.

I was in the second year of the university when the war began in Europe. On August 4, 1914, following the German invasion of Belgium, the government of England, pursuant to its treaty obligations, sent troops to aid Belgium and declared war on Germany. I recall the day before the declaration of war, August 3: English people assembled for prayer, fervently seeking divine guidance whether England should enter the war and whether the government should make a formal declaration. There were tens of thousands gathered outside St. Paul's Cathedral. At noon they knelt and prayed. The streets and alleys around the Cathedral were filled with people standing and kneeling in prayer. Traffic stopped for ten minutes, in this the busiest section of London, while these people with heavy hearts bowed their heads fervently in prayer. I was one of those people outside the Cathedral. I was deeply moved by their respect, solemnity, and order. I realized that it was the Christian spirit that made this possible. I have mentioned the events of this day before, but I bring them up again here because for me they raised the difficult question of the morality of war. For the sake of one's country or what is right, there are times when there seems no alternative to war, to unleash death and destruction, and take all sorts of inhuman actions. However, Christianity tells us, we should love our enemies as ourselves.

After England entered the war, there was a small group of Christians who came out in opposition to the war. They were, for the most part, Quakers. Their reasoning was quite simple. Yuenung and I discussed it on numerous occasions. First, Jesus did not want men to kill others. Second, Jesus did not want Peter to use the sword to resist. Third, although Jesus had great authority and power, he did not send down fire from heaven to smite the Samaritans. Fourth, Jesus did not defend himself. Finally, Jesus did not take up the sword in defense of his disciples. Thus, the example of Jesus Christ tells us not to wage war. Based on this thinking, Yuenung joined the Quakers. Though I didn't join, I was very sympathetic to their point of view.

In England, during the war, every university had a branch of the Student Volunteer Movement. I joined the movement at Westfield College and twice attended the national meetings. They were held each year in July or August at Swanwick and were attended by one to two thousand university students. There was an assembly each day after which we broke up into small groups to study religious and social problems. When the small groups reached a position, they would report back to the assembly for discussion and possible adoption of their position. I first went in July 1914. At the time, my English was still poor and I didn't speak out. War clouds were already gathering and all the students talked about was war, but they still hoped for peace. The discussion at that point was purely theoretical. Little did we know that World War I would begin in only a few days.

When England first entered the war, the army was all volunteer. Since there was no compulsory service, there were no serious conflicts between military service and religious beliefs. But in the second year of the war when compulsory conscription began, conscientious objectors began to appear. I spoke out on this issue in a meeting of the Westfield College Student Association.

Since China's eight-year war of resistance against Japan, I have discovered that the will to resist the enemy and patriotism are important considerations for the Christian. How can one have an impartial love for all and at the same time maintain the will to oppose a national enemy? To this day, this remains a perplexing problem for me. Recently, many Americans have burnt their draft cards. Was this done out of religious love? I don't know. If it was following the example of Jesus to love your enemy as yourself and not to kill, then I am most respectful of those who did it. But if it was cowardice or a scheme to avoid hardship, then it is certainly not deserving of praise. Communist peace propaganda is misleading and even more dangerous, dishonorable, and frightening.

The Chinese Christian students in England had an association and a publication of their own entitled *East in the West*. Each year after the English students met at Swanwick, we would meet for about a week. Yuenung, Ms. Barnes, and I attended these meetings. We discussed religion, scholarship, Chinese affairs and the war in Europe. Most important for these Chinese students in England was the knowledge of how each felt about these issues. At that time, many of the Chinese students in Europe came from the interior of China. They were quite well organized and had their own publication, but the Cantonese were most numerous and most active.

In addition to the student movement at Westfield College, there was Bible study. I enrolled in a class led by Ms. de Selincourt on the Gospel of John. Her insights were profound, her language precise, and the moral lessons lucid. I thoroughly enjoyed this class. I gained a better understanding of the Resurrection. I also enrolled in a class on reading the New Testament in Greek. However, I was burdened with school work and lacked the determination to study Greek. I was getting nothing from it; so I withdrew.

I attended church at school and with Ms. Barnes, and went to the Quaker Meeting at Hampstead Heath near Westfield College with Yuenung. The surroundings at Hampstead Heath were serene and beautiful. When I was there, I forgot I was in the in the hustle and bustle of London; I was relaxed and happy. I felt I was approaching oneness with nature. In the Meeting, there was no preaching or singing of hymns. Everyone just sat silently, quietly awaiting the guidance of the spirit. Sometimes, someone would stand up and read from the Bible, speak, give testimony, or pray. At other times, no one made a sound. They just sat silently for an hour. At first, I thought that, if I sat quietly for an hour, my mind would wander. But eventually my thinking became focused and I could pray for the nation, for an individual or for the war in Europe. The great Song Dynasty Neo Confucian philosopher, Zhu Xi, advocated quiet sitting and the Buddhists were even stronger proponents of silence, living in isolation for days at a time. There was no minister or preacher in the Quaker meeting, no baptism, no eucharist or ceremonies. Of course there are some who cynically say, "This sitting silently is in itself a ceremony." However, I received great benefit from those times. Moreover, the friends I knew in the Quaker Meeting were well educated and morally uplifting people and their service to society was unequaled: the work of Mr. Fay visiting incarcerated criminals and helping them to reform their lives; George Fox's sincere service to the poor; and Mr. Roundtree's advocacy of cooperation between labor and management. All were pioneering and admirable efforts for social reform. Although I never became a Quaker, I was inclined to do so for a long time.

Besides these formal religious activities, I frequently went to small religious gatherings. By then my English was such that I could fully understand what was going on, so I sometimes preached about the work that the church did in China and the contributions it made. During the worst days of the European war, I frequently made the point that the civilized countries of the world must cooperate to avoid wholesale slaughter and destruction of entire societies. The more science advances, the more sophisticated and fearful the instruments of death. If mankind cannot cling to the loving heart of Jesus and honor Confucius' words that "within the four seas all men are brothers," it will destroy itself and human civilization.

Reverend Timothy Richard, formerly a missionary in Shanxi Province and founder of the "Society for the Diffusion of Christian and General Knowledge among the Chinese" in Shanghai, was retired and living in England at this time. Ms. Barnes, Yuenung, and I visited him several times and I got to know him. He was very kind and gave me an autographed copy of his book *China's Four Hundred Million* which is very sympathetic to Chinese civilization and proposes ways to bridge the gap between China and the West. An appendix contained a plan for cooperation among the world's nations entitled "The Family of Nations," similar to the later League of Nations. His thinking on international organization was ahead of most Europeans of his day. When he learned we were descendants of Zeng Guofan, he told us that he had worked on disaster relief in Shanxi with my great uncle Zeng Guoquan and gave me a small notebook he had kept during that time. Sadly, both books have been lost as I moved about because of wars. To this day, thinking of its loss, I have great regrets.

Though Timothy Richard did not know it, his work had had a great influence in my life long before this. His Society had published translations of Western works on accounting, optics, chemistry, electricity, mathematics, and even literature and geography. My father had avidly consumed many of these. I recall once when I was small, I saw him reading a book entitled *The Essentials of Thermotics*. I didn't understand what was meant by the term "thermotics" or "heat." He explained to me about James Watt boiling water and observing the heat turning into energy that raised the cover of the teapot, and how Watt went on to employ this energy to drive engines and produce motion. Reverend Richard was also well known as the first president of Shanxi University, which was established with funds returned from the Boxer Indemnity paid by China to the nations whose personnel and property in China had been destroyed by the Boxers. Originally these funds were intended to compensate those missionary families in Shanxi who had suffered at the hands of the Boxers.

Paradoxically, wartime Britain provided many opportunities for me to grow in the Christian faith at a time when much of the Christian world seemed to have forgotten the teachings of Jesus.

Chapter 14

Oxford and Cambridge

I graduated from Westfield College in 1916 with the degree of Bachelor of Science. At that time, the final examinations at the University of London were not conducted at the end of June when graduation took place but in October after the next semester had started. This was very inconvenient for most people looking for positions. Those who were going to teaching positions had to take up their duties before October but, since they did not receive their degrees until they passed the examinations, they could not begin teaching when classes began. It was very awkward.

The university had a reason for doing things this way. Quite a few of the students did not completely master their courses prior to graduation. In the three months between graduation and the examinations, they could hire a tutor and prepare. Even though this was a frantic last minute measure, it was not without some benefit. So from the standpoint of those students who weren't quite ready for the examinations, it was not a bad system. Although science students did not have to be examined in English, I wanted to be confident of my understanding of spoken and written English; so I took advantage of this time in the summer of 1916 to get a tutor. My study of science included botany and pure and applied mathematics. I had to take a total of eight examinations: two in botanical theory; two in laboratory botany; and two each in pure and applied mathematics.

These eight examinations dragged on for almost three weeks because they were not scheduled on consecutive days. The theory examination could be in the morning but the laboratory examination for the same course might not be in the afternoon of the same day. Yuenung also took his examinations that year. He was a student at the Royal Institute of Geology and his examinations were also at the University of London. Although we graduated from the same university and took our examinations at the same time, the university was so large and the number of students taking examinations so great that we never saw each other during the examination period. Luckily we both passed, but he passed much higher than I did. This was partly because he had been studying in England longer than I and partly because I was unfocused in my studies. In addition to my required courses, I spent time in the library looking through books on fiction, literature and the arts, politics, philosophy, and even theology. It took considerable time from my required courses and delayed my progress. However, as I look back on it, I have no regrets. This browsing broadened my knowledge considerably.

After the examinations, I was recommended by Westfield College to attend Oxford where I studied English for one semester. I was at St. Hugh's College in Oxford when I received the telegram informing me I had passed the examinations at the University of London. Someone told me, "There's a telegram stuck on the door of your room." At that time it never occurred to me that it might be notification of passing the examinations. I thought it was probably a friend making an appointment. When I opened the telegram, it was from Ms. Barnes. I had passed and been awarded the degree. I was overjoyed. However, I had no one with whom to share my happiness. I wept that I could not be with Ms. Barnes. I had come to Oxford right after my examinations at the University of London and the only people I knew were a history instructor who had tutored me in English and the principal of St. Hugh's, Ms. Jordan. I had very few classmates and everyone else was a stranger to me. I felt my classmates probably weren't interested in my success on the examinations so I told only the principal and my English tutor. Although they were happy for me, I felt that they were just being polite. How I longed to be with Yuenung and Ms. Barnes. They would be so happy and excited and eager to congratulate me.

I returned to London at Christmas time. There was a partial blackout and the mood in the city was somber. But Ms. Barnes, Yuenung, and I invited a few Chinese friends to celebrate Christmas and my passing the examinations. One was an amateur magician who cheered us up considerably. It was a moment of comfort in a world gone mad.

When the Spring semester began in 1917, I continued my study of English, science, mathematics, and education at the London Day Training College and St. Mary's Training College. The students at these colleges had all graduated from university and were pursuing specialized studies in education for one or two more years. Since I was hoping to go back to China as soon as possible, I decided to limit my postgraduate study. In the summer I went to Cambridge for a review of botany. I had attended the summer session at Newnham College in Cambridge twice previously. To return to a familiar place was very pleasant.

The setting of Cambridge differed greatly from Oxford and the University of London. Many of the college buildings are built on both sides of the river Cam and have a bridge connecting them. The name Cambridge is probably derived from this. Each college has a different kind of bridge. St. John's College bridge is built in the style of the Bridge of Sighs in Venice where one of the waterways passes under a bridge on the road leading to the prison. At Cambridge, this bridge leads right into an examination hall. Students joke that "this is truly the Bridge of

Sighs," because their fate is decided there. With the wandering river, weeping willows on both sides, the lofty college buildings and the lawns green throughout the year, Cambridge is serene and beautiful. The common name for the river is "The Backs" because it is at the rear of Cambridge.

At Cambridge, students row for relaxation and train for competition on the river. Each year in May, there is a regatta, but it is not the usual boat race with two or three boats abreast. The bow of the second boat has to hit the stern of the first. If they hit it, they yell "bump" and the boat that was bumped has lost. In May, there is a constant stream of tourists and students having a good time "ragging" the bobbies. If they are able to snatch a policeman's helmet, that is the greatest accomplishment. It was all done in good humor and the bobbies didn't seem to mind. In fact, they were amused.

British universities are renowned for the way they conduct examinations. Each student has an examination credential. However, there is no photograph on it and they don't require the student to give his or her name. It would be very simple to have a substitute take the examination; but I heard of no cases of this happening. If crib notes are found in the examination hall, the examination is nullified. I took many examinations and never saw this kind of thing happen. This is not to say that English students are of better moral character than Chinese students, but the English system does not place as much emphasis on a university diploma as we do in China. For science and engineering students, the English place greater importance on practical experience in factories and mines. University education is a preparation for such experience. After a few years experience in the industry, an apprentice can oftentimes find an even better career path.

In China, we place too great emphasis on diplomas and grades. The motivation to study is not to learn; it is to find a way to go abroad. After graduation from a university, students take the TOEFL (Test of English as a Foreign Language) and go on to get a Ph.D. in the United States, become an American citizen, earn a big salary, and never return to China. Look at the annual statistics on students going abroad, and then look at the numbers returning. There are roughly ten times as many leaving. This is not an exaggeration.

My experiences studying in England were quite varied. I studied in a very small private school; a public middle school; the Universities of London, Cambridge, and Oxford; and a college of education. Although I passed the examinations for graduate school, I did not receive the doctorate because at that time universities, especially Oxford and Cambridge, were not open to women. Women could study and take the examinations but could not receive degrees. Hence, women were not a part of the university. The University of London was the first to remove the restrictions on women students. So I preferred to go there and receive equal treatment with the men, and no discrimination. But the time was inadequate for me to study for the doctorate.

In September 1917, I returned to London. There, Ms. Barnes, Yuenung, and I waited for our exit visas, which were required before we could purchase steamship tickets to return to China. We looked everywhere for more than a month for reservations. Then we learned of a Canadian troop ship returning to Canada with military dependents. Fortunately, the Chinese ambassador in England was able to get us reservations. We were to leave England at the end of October. Before we left, a friend gave a farewell dinner for us. Just as we arrived at her home, the alarm sounded. We all had to take cover in the underground shelter taking with us a gas mask, a hoe, and a shovel to be prepared in case the entrance became blocked and we had to dig ourselves out. Fortunately, it was a false alarm. Our thoughts about returning to China became even more intense.

We were very happy to get our reservations, our exit visas, and our papers for entry into Canada and the United States taken care of. When we boarded the ship, there was a cursory inspection of our baggage and we were asked if we were going home to work for the government. Since we were, the military police confiscated our English personal identification cards. I was really disappointed about that because it had the stamps of all the places we had visited. It would have been an excellent memento. We left England on October 30, 1917.

Part III

The Yifang School for Girls

Chapter 15

Going Home

Ms. Barnes, Yuenung, and I had expended the energy of ten men to get three tickets on the "Scandinavia," transporting military dependents back to Canada. Ms. Barnes, I, and a Ms. Miu, also a missionary, were in one stateroom. I met a Dr. Endicott who had been a missionary in Sichuan. The five of us ate at the same table and talked about the war and about China. The passage from Liverpool to Montreal took ten days. This was longer than usual because we kept to the north and steamed in a zigzag pattern to avoid German submarines. There were eight destroyers protecting us.

Everybody on board carried a life preserver on their person. For the first two or three days, we practiced emergency drills each day. It was very tense. However, every morning at our places at the breakfast table, we found a report received over the ship's radio giving news from the battlefront. If there was special news, an extra edition was published. Measures such as this demonstrated how well organized the English were during World War I. When the ship entered the Arctic Circle, the weather was extremely cold and we shivered incessantly. I was terribly seasick and had to lie down constantly. I couldn't eat, and was too miserable even to talk. It was two days after we arrived in Montreal before I felt right again. This was the worst discomfort I have ever felt while traveling.

When we arrived in Canada, we went to Toronto first and then crossed into the United States. In Toronto, Dr. Endicott brought us to visit the university and a women's college where we stayed for a few days. The principal was a former student at Westfield College. The attitude of the students was very refreshing; their questions to Yuenung and me were uninhibited and spontaneous.

We needed a special permit to enter the United States from Canada. Fortunately, while we were in London, Ambassador Shi Zhaoji had taken care of this for us. When we crossed into the United States, we were asked many questions. Although we had all our papers in order, they still put Yuenung and me last in line before finally releasing us through customs. We felt this was racial discrimination on the part of the American immigration officers. That night, when the train passed Niagara Falls, it stopped and many of the passengers got off to view the great waterfall by moonlight. But Yuenung and I were anxious to get home. We wished only to get to New York and visit several schools and then go back to China so we passed up one of the world's most spectacular sights.

When we arrived in New York, we visited Mr. Wilder, an official of the YMCA, and his wife. We accepted their kind invitation to stay at their home in New Jersey while we visited friends in New York. My uncle Nie Qiying and his wife brought us to Columbia University and introduced us to Dr. Hu Shi (1891–1962), a student of John Dewey and leader of the New Culture Movement that engulfed China following WWI. We also met Ms. Chen Hengzhe and went with her to Vassar College in the Hudson Valley, north of New York City. She later married Mr. Ren Shuyun. I visited them frequently in their home in Beijing. She was the first woman named to a professorship at National Beijing University. Her daughter, E-tu Zen Sun, also a graduate of Vassar and Harvard University, had a long and distinguished career at Pennsylvania State University. Her grandson, Raymond Sun, associate professor of History at Washington State University, has continued the family's dedication to scholarship. More than ten years later, I had a long conversation with Ms. Chen on the night that my father died; it was one of the most emotional moments of my life.

From New York we went back to Canada and took the Canadian Pacific Railroad to Vancouver where we boarded the "Empress of Asia" for the last leg of out trip back to China. Ms. Miu was also returning to China on the same ship. We also met a Mr. Yan Fuqing who was going to Changsha to open the Xiangya Hospital. We talked about how regrettable it was that north and south China were in a bitter civil war.

A very unpleasant incident took place aboard this ship. There were two American girls, who worked for the YWCA and were on their way to Russia, billeted in the same stateroom with a Chinese student. Unfortunately, the Chinese girl was constantly seasick, throwing up every day. The two American women disliked this and wanted her to move out. The conflict between them got so bad that the captain had to intervene. He told the two girls, "This Chinese student has a ticket and a reservation. You can't expect her to move out just because you want her to. Besides, she isn't the only passenger who is seasick." Then, the two American women said they weren't going to live with a colored person. In the end, Mr. Yan and I advised the Chinese student to give in and move in with the female attendants. It is half a century since that happened, but it is unfortunate that, to this day, the racial bias of Americans has not been completely eliminated.

When the ship arrived outside the harbor at Wusung, at the mouth of the Yangzi, I could see the China coast in the distance. I thought of when I left China in 1912, full of hope. Now, things were worse; there was fighting between north and south—and my beloved grandmother had passed away. As I thought of these things, warm tears began streaming down my face. We took a small launch to the Hongkou wharf in Shanghai where my Uncle Nie Yuntai had sent someone to meet us.

We were welcomed at the Nie home by my great aunt, Mrs. Nie Zeng Jifen, and my cousins and their wives. After ten days with the Nies, we went to visit my father's married sister, Mrs. Yu, and her husband and children. It was almost six years since I had seen them. I could not find words to express the sadness over the separation or the joy of reunion that I felt.

While we visited the Nie household, Ms. Barnes lived for the first time in an extended Chinese family. It was an eye-opening experience for her. Her work as a missionary had been directed toward the ordinary people who did not maintain such households. She also had lived at the school that she headed. Now, she saw for the first time the warm relationships between people in an extended Chinese family. Seeing how the children cared for the older people, the respect given to the aged, and the way adults nurtured the youth enabled her to appreciate the great strength of Chinese culture and deepened her love for China.

Later we visited the Yu household again. On that occasion my uncle, Mr. Yu Shouchen, and my aunt were saddened by the recent death of two daughters and a son in their family but they were comforted by our visit. My cousin, Dawei, was just getting ready to go to the United States to study. My other cousins were all attending mission schools but none had any interest in Christianity, probably because at that time the church was out of touch with the lives of ordinary people and the problems of society.

The gulf separating church-sponsored and secular education at that time was great. The New Literature Movement, an aspect of the New Culture Movement that spread through Chinese society during and after World War I, stressed writing in clear language about topics of popular interest. It was favored by students returning from study abroad and was much stronger at Beijing National University than it was at church schools such as St. John's or Hujiang in Shanghai or Jinling in Nanjing. These institutions were more comparable to Southeastern University where the old literature was studied and scholars often drew their subjects and style of writing from remote antiquity. The two educational systems, church and secular, rivaled each other but each had its forte. The church-operated universities inevitably stressed English, Western history and geography, and science. Although they made a considerable contribution in introducing new knowledge, they also missed a great deal concerning Chinese history, customs, and the traditional culture. Because of this, ordinarily, those educated in church-operated universities have found it difficult to have much intellectual influence in Chinese society. Recently, church-operated universities have experienced a great upheaval, and are more disposed toward reform. This surely is a promising development.

Around the twentieth of December 1917, we left Shanghai on a Yangzi river steamer for Hunan. We didn't know until after we got to Hankou that the water in the Xiang River, which flows northward through Hunan and empties into the Yangzi, was so low that no steamships could navigate it. Fortunately, Bishop Root let the three of us stay at the Church of England Mission Society at Hankou to wait for a boat. We stayed at Reverend Lasalle's home and, if I remember correctly, spent Christmas there. Afterwards, we took a boat pulled by a steam-powered tug south on the Xiang River to Lulingtan. But the tug could go no further so we had to pole and row the tow boat upstream. After a day and a night we arrived at Changsha where we found my father and Uncle Jirong and his wife living in very cramped quarters at Wenxingqiao, so Ms. Barnes accepted the hospitality of a Methodist minister and his wife, Mr. and Mrs. Warren.

Yuenung and I stayed in Changsha for two or three days and then rented a small boat and set out up the Xiangshui for Xiangxiang. This boat was tiny. It had a central cabin separated by a board wall from the stoke hole on the stern where the family that lived on board cooked their food. Forward on the bow we had to hang up our own carpet to divide the space with the boat family. From the Empress of Asia that could carry more than 2,000 people, to a Yangzi steamer, to a steam-powered tug pulling a boat, to this tiny row boat was a quick comedown in our mode of transport. But I was yearning for my home and didn't really care. After three days, we arrived at Xiangtan and stayed in an inn for the night. The next day we hired a sedan chair and set out for home, but we had to stay one night in Huashi in a filthy and foul-smelling inn; bedbugs kept me awake all night. The next morning we were up at daybreak. I realized that day I would see my dear mother after such a long separation. I was grateful and happy. Without thinking, I began singing a hymn. Yuenung, in the next room, was startled. He couldn't see that those filthy surroundings were any place to sing a hymn.

From Huashi, my family home was about thirty miles. With an early start, it was a day's journey. On the way we came first to the home of my aunt, Yuenung's mother, at Yangjiawan. She lay sick on her bed. When she saw Yuenung she was overcome with emotion. They looked at each other and wept. She didn't want him to stay at their little farmhouse. She had moved there because she disliked the noise and the humidity at Prosperity Hall. The farmhouse was less noisy and damp. She wanted Yuenung to live at Prosperity Hall and take his meals with my mother. Because the sedan chair-bearers were waiting, we visited for only a little while and then set out again for Prosperity Hall.

When we entered the east gate, family members set off a barrage of firecrackers to welcome us. In the ancestral temple, lanterns and candles flickered brightly. At that time, Yuenung had not yet professed his faith in Christianity so I stepped aside while he kowtowed and offered incense in the temple. I saw that my beloved mother had aged greatly but my younger brother, Zhaohua, was bright-eyed and lively. I was overcome by a torrent of emotions. I thought of grandmother passing away more than a year ago. She had been so kind to us; I really can't find words to express my feelings for her. Her home was there but she was gone. In her quarters the furniture and books all were just as she had left them. When I saw it, a feeling of intense sadness engulfed me. My mother burst into tears and wanted us to go immediately to grandmother's grave and pray for her. The grave was on the side of a hill just across the way, no more than a ten minute walk. We went immediately. Images from the past flooded into my mind as we bowed reverently in prayer. Then I saw a little hut where old Zhao, the gravekeeper, lived. There was also a meeting hall with long benches where my uncle Jirong preached. Grandmother's grave faced toward Prosperity Hall so that she could look out at her children. It reminded me of her boundless love and generosity.

Because I was anxious to get started with the establishment of the school and because Ms. Barnes was in Changsha, I explained to my mother that I couldn't stay for Chinese New Year. Near the end of the twelfth lunar month, I departed for Changsha. Yuenung, however, stayed on in Xiangxiang to look after his aging mother. I took an old woman from our household in the sedan chair with me and went straight to Changsha. Since we didn't bother with the small boat, we made the trip in three days. I had already arranged with my Uncle Nie Lusheng to use two rooms on the second floor of his house at Lexingtian. Miss Barnes and I lived there temporarily while looking for a permanent residence in which to open the school.

We were filled with hope and driven by our dream of a modern girl's school in China. Unaware and uncaring of what difficulties were in store for us, we placed our trust in God and looked to my relatives in the Zeng clan for moral and material support.

Chapter 16

The Yifang Girl's Middle School

After we arrived in Changsha in February 1918, we lived at the Nie residence for four or five months. My cousin, Ms. Xiao Xiaohui, came from Hengyang to help Ms. Barnes and me look at buildings for the school. We finally settled on the Long family home, formerly the residence of the American consul. It was an old style Chinese house with two rows of buildings containing numerous rooms, some quite large. In addition to classrooms, dormitories and a lavatory, it provided an apartment for me and Ms. Barnes, a room for my cousin Ms. Xiao, servants' quarters, separate apartments for my mother, Yuenung, and my little brother, a multipurpose room for dining, visiting and reading, and a kitchen removed from the living quarters. Though it was not large, it was laid out well. We leased it for a year at the rent they were asking.

Yifang was the name of my grandmother's study at Prosperity Hall. Since her teachings influenced me greatly, I decided to name this school the Yifang Girl's Middle School in her memory. We also drew from the thought of Confucius that "one should enjoy the six arts," i.e. ritual, music, archery, riding, writing, and mathematics, so we named each successive entering class for one of the six arts.

Earlier, when I had been in Shanghai, my Uncle Nie Yuntai had wanted me to take over the operation of the Qixiu Girl's Middle School. The Church of England Mission Society also invited Ms. Barnes and me to return to Mary Vaughan High School in Hangzhou. However, we felt that these schools could find qualified teachers easily in the coastal provinces where they were situated, but in Changsha, in the interior, it would be very difficult to find students returned from overseas to serve as a teachers; so we thanked them politely but declined. Now when we compared the facilities at those schools with those at Yifang, surprisingly, we were very pleased. The size naturally was much smaller but it fit our idea of what a Chinese school should be.

That year, on June 6, Yuenung brought his mother from Xiangxiang to Changsha. On the evening of June 8, while en route she suffered a heart attack at Pingtang, about ten miles from Changsha. Yuenung sent a messenger from Pingtang with a letter asking us to send a doctor immediately. The messenger arrived in Changsha on June 9. Dr. Yang and I rushed to Pingtang arriving at three in the afternoon on June 9, but Yuenung's mother had already passed away at noontime.

It was extremely hot just then and we were fortunate that two of my uncles did most of the funeral arrangements. Yuenung's father rushed back from Beijing for the funeral. His mother had the good fortune to be laid to rest at Pingtang on a small hill adjacent to the grave of her ancestor, Zeng Guofan. Shortly after the funeral, Yuenung's father returned to Beijing but Yuenung remained in Changsha to observe the mourning ritual and attend to the grave.

Since Yuenung was in Changsha, we asked him to help us at the school. He had studied geology and was looking forward to a career in that field, never having contemplated teaching in a middle school for girls. My father had gained title to several mines and no doubt would have offered Yuenung an opportunity to put his education to work but the fighting between north and south China had thrown the country into chaos and there was no chance, at that time, of operating these mines. If Yuenung was to use his knowledge of geology, teaching was probably his best option. Accepting the position at Yifang really didn't impede his career as a geologist; the fighting in China did that, and obtaining his services was an invaluable asset for the school. Because he was familiar with my planning for Yifang over the years, he was immediately effective and proved himself a dynamic member of the faculty. He drew up drafts and formulated the regulations for the school.

My father's younger brother, Luchu, had connections with the Changsha gentry. He, my father, and Uncle Jirong secured the grounds of Zeng Guofan's ancestral temple from the local authorities as a future site for the school. In the meantime, the four of us, Ms. Barnes, Yuenung, Ms. Xiao, and I, set about buying furniture, printing regulations, making desks, blackboards and closets for the students' clothes and buying school equipment and books. We began advertising for students in August, first for a college preparatory course and special courses in English and mathematics.

The board of directors of Yifang was organized by my father, Uncle Jirong, and Uncle Luchu. They proved to be most helpful in our initial operation. We filed for registration with the Department of Education and received approval in early June 1918. We opened formally on September 12 with five special students in mathematics and English, including my cousin Ms. Xiao who also was supervisor of the dormitory and business manager. There were also four students in the college preparatory course.

Ms. Barnes agreed to teach English but preferred that I serve as principal. I think this may have been a first in those days in China: an elderly foreigner working under a young Chinese, especially a Chinese who had formerly been her student. Yuenung was dean and taught English, mathematics, physics, and chemistry. I taught English and biology. There were a total of nine faculty, Chinese and foreign, for eight students.

We also invited several well-known people to deliver lectures. Later we established a regular practice of having someone from outside the school speak on a specialized topic every Friday afternoon. On Saturday, I always had a one-hour talk on current events: world affairs or problems related to China, Hunan Province or society at large. We talked about the war in Europe, the May Fourth Movement of 1919, the student uprising that swept across China following the Treaty of Versailles, and the May Thirtieth Movement of 1925, the high point of anti-imperialist protest in China. The students could ask questions and discuss these issues. These activities served to give direction to the students' thinking.

Ms. Barnes was an outstanding Christian and extremely caring toward the students. What is more, she was quite willing to accept our proposals though they might have seemed quite liberal by the standards to which she was accustomed. For example, we proposed that we would not keep a permanent record of every infraction that a student committed; we would not reprimand students publicly nor require them to attend chapel. After classes were dismissed on Saturday until five o'clock on Sunday afternoon, the students could go home. On all these points Yifang differed from church-run schools. Yifang revered Christ but it belonged to no church. Ms. Barnes could understand and accept all this. A sixty-year-old woman, she lived with the Chinese students and shared their joys and sorrows; it is really impossible to give her the credit she is due.

In the spring of 1919, the May Fourth Movement began with student protests in Beijing and moved from city to city throughout China. By that time, the second class of special students had entered and several more joined the preparatory class. They were the earliest students and they understood the difficulties of getting the school started. The feeling between the faculty and the students was very close. We had a reasoned reaction to the May Fourth Movement. We organized a group of ten persons to enforce a boycott of Japanese products to protest the unfairness of the Treaty of Versailles that had awarded the former German holdings in Shandong Province to Japan. This was maintained right down to the final victory in China's war against Japan.

Chapter 17

The Campus at Yifang

The temple commemorating Zeng Guofan was built with a donation of three thousand silver taels from the Court; his disciples, friends, and relatives donated an additional four to five thousand taels; the remainder of the funds were contributed by officials and merchants. It was situated in Changsha at the Xiaowu gate on the main street on a plot of about seventeen acres. Outside the temple was a large level space where sedan chairs and horses could stop. The main gate faced south and a road passed through it directly to the main temple building. On both sides were bell and drum towers. On the main temple building was Zeng Guofan's ancestral tablet. In the sanctuary a horizontal tablet read: "Through toil, he established the foundation of our country." The calligraphy was by Wang Ishu of the Hanlin Academy. Other tablets and pairs of scrolls bearing couplets had long since been destroyed by the ravages of war.

On the east side of the main building was the "Contemplating Virtue" Literary Office in which there was a parlor, a hall fitted out like a cabin on a ship, and a book repository. On the west side was a lecture hall where, in imperial times, holders of the first civil-service degree studied and academic lectures were held. Later, Guo Songtao, China's first Ambassador to the court of Saint James, and Marquis Zeng Jize had the ancestral tablet of Wang Fuzhi, the seventeenth-century Confucian scholar who fiercely opposed the Manchu conquest of China, enshrined in the lecture hall. At the time, the Manchu Court did not permit the veneration of Wang Fuzhi in Confucian temples even if the temple was dedicated to someone else. His anti-Manchu rhetoric was so inflammatory that even his written work was banned. However, Zeng Guofan had arranged for the publication of Wang's writings. Only Zeng, who had rescued the Manchu Dynasty from the Taiping Rebellion, could dare to promote the publication of such openly anti-Manchu tracts. Because Zeng Guofan had so admired Wang Fuzhi, Zeng Jize and Guo Songtao wanted Wang to be venerated alongside Zeng.

Behind the main building of the temple, there was a garden known as the Hao Yuan that became the campus of Yifang. Out the rear door of the main building there was a ridge of green hills beyond which was a large "L" shaped pond. At one end was an octagonal tower crumbling with age. At the corner was a stone hill and a small stone bridge. Atop the hill stood a thatched tower bearing the inscription "The Tower Preserving Simplicity." Close by the octagonal tower, there had originally been a dormitory for students studying for the civil-service examinations. In the same area was the "Listening to the Rain Pavilion," the highest place in the garden. It provided a panoramic view of the city of Changsha. A covered walkway wound through the garden and a foot path led over a stone hill past a large stone bridge. Along the way the flowering trees and bamboos presented a beautiful sight. Each year on the fifth day of the fifth lunar month, the Dragon Boat Festival, following an old practice, we would open the garden to the public.

In May 1919, the Hunan gentry prevailed upon the Northern Army that had been camped in the garden to leave. As soon as they were gone, we moved in. Everything was falling down and in need of repair. While we set about repairing the buildings and installing equipment and furniture, we engaged faculty, recruited students, and gave entrance examinations. We suffered a two-week interruption in May when the Wang Fuzhi Temple Association claimed that, when the Provincial Government had granted them the use of the Lecture Hall, it had included control of Zeng Guofan's ancestral temple. On May 3, Association members turned violent, knocking down the wall between the Association grounds and the campus and attacking the carpenters and masons who were working for us. I halted the work and sought outside mediation which resulted in disallowing their claim to the property. After that, the wall was rebuilt and work on the campus resumed.

The various buildings of Yifang were centered on the pond, surrounding it on the east, north, and west. On the east was the kitchen and the dining hall with a covered passageway leading directly to the "Contemplating Virtue" Literary Office, which later became our elementary school. On the north, there was a large gate within which there was a gatehouse and faculty dormitories. Passing through a second gate there was the principal's office, faculty offices, and classrooms leading to the "Listening to Rain Pavilion." On the first floor of the pavilion were the dormitory supervisor's office, the library, and Ms. Barnes's study. The second floor housed the teachers' bedrooms and the third floor was for storage of literary materials and furniture. It could also be used for observation. On a clear day it was possible to see the far off mountains. On the south side of the lake was a small hill behind which was situated the main building of the ancestral temple.

Going west from the "Listening to Rain Pavilion" there was the academic office, more faculty quarters, the principal's quarters, a large building with student bedrooms on two floors, a two-story classroom building, a court for playing ball, a track and an exercise yard. This was just to the rear of the main building. Before the main temple was forcibly occupied by members of the Wang Fuzhi Temple Association, we held church services there every morning and sang hymns on

Sunday afternoons. All other assemblies were also held there. This was the Yifang Campus in its best days.

The Yifang campus was known as the most beautiful spot in Changsha. We planted flowers and trees and even had two small rowboats for the students to practice rowing on the lake. Sir M. Beauchamp of the China Inland Missions remarked that, "These little oarsmen could navigate on the ocean they are so strong and cautious." We took advantage of the beautiful surroundings in the garden to have garden parties, cooling-off parties—in hot weather, lantern parties, and parties to raise funds for disaster relief: We raised funds for relief of the drought in the Xinhua-Lantian area, the flood in Changsha, and a flood in western Hunan. Each time, the students initiated the idea themselves. They fixed up the pond to look like the famous resort at West Lake with the tower at the center of the lake, the tomb of Yue Fei, the tomb of Su Xiaoxiao, Mount Gu, the Five Willows Restaurant, the Monastery of Retirement and Reflection, and other scenic spots. They were very careful of the proceeds from selling tickets for these parties. Every bit of carfare spent running around to make sales was paid for out of their own pockets. So each time there was a drive for contributions, Yifang was first among all the schools. There was one time—the Hunan drought—that Yifang contributions were second only to relief funds disbursed by the provincial government and, at that time, the student body was about only one hundred. The Christian spirit of saving lives and benefiting society was amply demonstrated.

Chapter 18

An Experiment with Democracy

The organization at Yifang was generally similar to that of other schools. There was the Board of Directors, the Principal, the Dean of Academic Affairs, the Dean of Students, and members of the teaching staff with various specialties. What set Yifang apart was the Student-Faculty Association. In the Spring of 1919, the allies' rejection of China's claims at the Paris Peace Conference triggered student demonstrations throughout China. At Yifang the Student-Faculty Association was organized in response to this unrest.

All students and faculty were members, but the Association functioned through an Executive Committee of five: the chair, the secretary, the bookkeeper, and two staff. Though it had only five members, students at all levels could serve on it, excluding only those in the first semester of lower middle school or the final semester of upper middle school. The academic work during these semesters was especially heavy. The Executive Committee met in plenary session once each month. The Association met twice each semester: once to select members of the Executive Committee and once to conclude Association business. If there was an especially urgent matter, an emergency meeting of the Association could be called to allow students and faculty to voice their opinions.

This Student-Faculty Association made a great contribution to Yifang as a training ground for democracy. Each student and faculty member had one vote per person. If students had a matter they wanted the school to act upon, they had to secure the approval of the Association twice, once in each of two semesters. All important matters such as changing faculty members or adjusting fees were decided this way. When the Student-Faculty Association was established, the rules were drawn up. They served as the constitution and the operating procedures were based on the constitution. The faculty and the principal could not put pressure on this body; even the Board of Directors could not. Since the students greatly outnumbered the faculty in the Association, the real authority in the school lay with them.

The authorization that Yifang received from the Ministry of Education was for a middle school of six continuous years. There was no graduation from lower middle school but, if a student wished to transfer to another school, Yifang could issue her a transfer credential. Students could transfer in at the beginning of the fourth year but Yifang did not accept transfer students in the fifth and sixth years. A maximum of thirty students were admitted each year to the first level of lower middle school. If transfer students were admitted in the fourth year to fill vacancies created by students leaving the school, the total for the class could still not exceed thirty. Because of this, when the upper middle school third-year class graduated, the number was quite small; it never exceeded twenty-four or twenty-five, and once there were only nine.

The students all lived at the school and took their meals there. They ate together with the faculty in one dining hall. Since the faculty and students saw each other frequently, naturally they became quite close. The relationships were similar to those of parents and children. If a student had a minor ailment, it was treated at the school clinic without charge. If there were serious health problems, the school contacted the head of the student's family and discussed what to do about treatment.

The responsibility for character development was shared by faculty and students. Each class and each dormitory selected a leader. These leaders had responsibility for guidance and moral development. If a student's conduct was out of order, the dean of students was notified. If, after speaking with the dean, the student still failed to comply, the dean notified the principal. The principal then spoke with the student individually. Yifang never kept a record of demerits nor dismissed students for a certain number of demerits. Each student who had such a session with the principal went on to mend her ways. The instructors in the various classes gave special help to students who were not doing well in their studies. The principal also gave such special instruction. There were no extra fees for this. I once tutored a student who was very poor in mathematics for a semester. Subsequently, she became one of our best in mathematics.

There was another student who had been in every girl's school in Changsha and left each one after causing some kind of trouble. Her father, the dean of a well-known school in the city, brought her to our school and said to me, "I only hope Professor Zeng that you can get her through to graduation. I will be eternally grateful." One evening, during the first week she was in school, I asked her to come and talk with me. I told her, "No matter what kind of problem you have, whether it is with a classmate, an instructor, even a family member, a financial problem, or one related to marriage, you can come and talk with me about it. I will try to see the problem from your perspective and I will discuss it with you sympathetically." I wanted her to respond but she did not, so I said to her, "If something happens that upsets you, talk to me before you do anything." She agreed to do that. As it turned out, in the three years she was in upper-middle school, she only sought me out twice and both incidents were resolved satisfactorily. This student was from Xiangtian. She graduated in the summer of 1949 when Changsha was already in a state of chaos. I had urged the faculty and students to return to their homes but she insisted on remaining at school for three days in order to see me off on a flight out of Changsha. Our teacher-student bond was that strong.

The school regulations required that the students arise at six o'clock; breakfast was at seven and chapel service at seven forty-five. Classes began at eight o'clock with four classes in the morning. The noon meal was at twelve-thirty followed by a one-hour rest period. Classes resumed again from two until four o'clock, for a total of six hours of class each day. Afternoon classes were, in most cases, science laboratories, music, handicraft, art or physical education: things that did not require intense concentration. Each Saturday in the first class period, I discussed current events: important happenings in the world, in China, or in Hunan. Each Friday afternoon, we invited a well-known person to speak to us. The lecture topics included literature, science, the arts, and religion. By attending these lectures, the students were able to acquire general knowledge apart from their formal study.

The students' academic accomplishments, measured by the examinations for advancement to the next level of study, were very impressive. One hundred percent of our students passed the national examination for university admission. One hundred percent of those who took university examinations for individual universities or examinations to study abroad also qualified.

The best feature, however, was the spirit in which the students undertook their studies. In the evening they studied by themselves without faculty supervision. There were no proctors during examinations and never any crib notes, having a substitute take the examination, or illicit passing of information. Living at Yifang, it wasn't necessary to lock up our drawers; flowers and fruit were not taken from the garden and people didn't use other people's things without asking permission. It wasn't that there was never anything missing at Yifang. In two cases I recall, both students were apprehended: one repented and turned over a new leaf and one left school voluntarily.

There was a case where a fourth-year student lost a gold watch. This was announced many times but the watch was not returned. So the Student-Faculty Association convened an emergency meeting. Someone proposed a search but some of my colleagues and some students were strongly opposed. We feared that, if there were a search, there was the danger of the guilty party putting the watch in another student's things and, thus, shifting the blame to an innocent person. But, since the Student-Faculty Association passed a resolution to have a search, as principal I was powerless to prevent it. I convened students of all classes in the auditorium. Then the Dean of Students, the head of the Student-Faculty Association, and one member of the Executive Committee took the key to each student's trunk, opened it and searched it while the student looked on. While the search was going on, I told the students assembled in the auditorium stories from Pu Songling's *Strange Stories from a Chinese Sudio*, Rudyard Kipling's *The Light That Failed*, and others. The students listened intently. Even those disgruntled association members who had opposed the search became quiet.

When it was so quiet you could hear a pin drop, a worker came in and reported, "The gold watch was found in the garbage can." Everyone was very relieved and no one asked any further questions. I think it unlikely that the person who took that watch, fearing the search, dropped it in the garbage can. She would not have had time after the search was decided upon to do so. Possibly a worker while sweeping the floor carelessly swept it out. It also could have been that the student herself, after eating, wrapped up the scraps of paper and fruit peels, and accidentally included the watch with them as she threw them out. The atmosphere calmed down while everyone was listening to stories. When the watch was found, they went off to class chuckling. The big event of the day seemed like nothing, thanks to the cooperative attitude between faculty and students and the democratic spirit. From that time on, no one lost anything.

Because the number of students at Yifang was so small, we were not strong in competitive sports. At that time in Changsha, Zhou Nan, the alma mater of some of China's prominent women communists, and the First Women's Normal School were the best in sports. One couldn't mention Yifang in the same breath with them. But Yifang had good sportsmanship. Though we lost repeatedly, we never had a losing spirit.

Students could inquire into the financial affairs of the school. They could examine the school's food account once every two weeks. At that time, because there were so few students, they all ate in the dining hall. They could also check the school's financial accounts once each semester. If they compared expenses and income they could see that the income from tuition, board, and miscellaneous fees fell far short of expenses. Expenses did not include salaries for me, Ms. Barnes, Yuenung, or Ms. Xiao since we received none. Foreign faculty members received support from friends abroad. Because of these savings, the annual deficit was not great and the students' miscellaneous fees always had a surplus that was returned to them. Students paid tuition of twenty-five yuan per semester, a boarding fee of twenty yuan, and a miscellaneous fee of ten. The miscellaneous fee included electricity, fuel, and stationery supplies. There usually was a surplus in this account that was returned to the students. The more that was returned to the students the less there was for making up deficits in these areas. If a student withdrew in mid-semester, the boarding and miscellaneous fees were refunded. Tuition was not refundable. The students knew exactly what the school's financial status was and the school enjoyed their trust.

Chapter 19

The May Fourth Movement

As mentioned above, in the spring of 1919, student protests erupted in Beijing and moved from city to city throughout China. These demonstrations and the political upheaval they produced became known as the May Fourth Movement. The students were prompted by patriotism and unwillingness to accept the provisions of the Treaty of Versailles that transferred the former German possessions on the Shandong Peninsula to Japan. China as well as Japan had been part of the alliance against Germany but the allies clearly favored Japan. Angered by the attitude of the powers, students at Beijing National University took to the streets opposing the Treaty of Versailles and calling for the removal of Cao Rulin, Zhang Zongxiang, and Lu Zongyu—the officials of the Beijing government whom they held responsible for China's humiliation. The students at other universities in Beijing rose up en masse in response. Even the merchants in the big port cities closed their businesses in a show of support for the students. Middle school and university students demonstrated throughout the provinces.

By this time, the second class of special students had entered Yifang and several more joined the preparatory class. They were the earliest students and they understood the difficulties of getting the school started. The feeling between the faculty and the students was especially close. Though Yifang had only been open for a year and there were fewer than twenty students, they felt we should participate in some manner. The Student-Faculty Association decided not to take part in the street demonstrations but to do something positive. At the time, a nationwide boycott of Japanese goods was initiated and patriotic teams of ten were being formed to promote the use of Chinese products. The faculty and students of Yifang organized three such teams. Everyone resolved to use domestic rather than Japanese products and not to travel on Japanese ships. The small store that the students operated to sell stationery and foodstuffs stopped carrying Japanese goods.

The ten-person teams were to continue functioning until Japan's attitude toward China changed. Each team selected a leader to direct its activities. Japanese goods that were then in the possession of students were to be registered and stamped but no new goods could be acquired. Then students could continue to use the Japanese things that they already had and would be spared the cost of replacement. I didn't have very many things that were made in Japan, but I did have two or three coats lined with Japanese wool that were registered and stamped by the student team. Each semester we drew lots to determine whom the ten-person team would inspect to see if they had acquired any new Japanese goods. Naturally, if a faculty member or even the principal drew the lot to be inspected, they were inspected in the same way as a student. This was the democratic way things were done at Yifang.

One time during an inspection, the team leader discovered a student who had a new hat with a lining made in Japan. The members of the team decided that it must be confiscated or burnt. The team leader was very cautious. She first cut out a piece of the flannel lining of the hat as evidence and then tore out the lining and burned it in front of a number of people. The student who owned the hat was furious. On Saturday, she went home and told her father. He arrived at the school ready to punish the person who had destroyed his daughter's hat. The team leader said, "We told your daughter that it was not permitted to buy new Japanese goods. She broke the rules and purchased this hat. It was previously decided that purchases that violated the boycott were to be burned. We had no choice but to burn it." He responded angrily asking, "Can you guarantee that not one of your classmates has goods made in Japan?" The group leader replied, "You're free to conduct your own inspection. You can even check the faculty and the principal's things." The offending student's father became highly indignant. He looked all over the students' bedrooms. Though he found several garments made in Japan belonging to faculty members, they all were old and bore the stamp of the ten-person team, authorizing their retention. He then left in a huff. The ten-person teams at Yifang continued for thirty years. They were not dissolved until after Japan's surrender in World War II.

Although our students actively opposed the Japanese policy of aggression toward China, they felt great sympathy toward the Japanese people. In 1923, when Tokyo was struck by a great earthquake, the students, on their own initiative, collected relief funds of more than 500 yuan and gave them to Dr. Hodgkin of the Christian Evangelical Committee to take to Japan. They also asked him to look for a school in Japan similar to Yifang that held to the Christian spirit of loving one's enemies. Our students wanted to correspond with the students and let them know of our fervent desire for peace and the truth of what Japan's militarism was doing in China. Unfortunately, at that time, the Japanese militarists had hoodwinked the Japanese people with propaganda about how the Chinese hated Japan, and inflamed anti-Chinese feelings so effectively that Dr. Hodgkin was unable to find such a school. The Japanese government probably would not allow one to exist.

The students and faculty also took part in the New Culture Movement that had begun advocating clarity in written language and writing about contemporary issues, even before the May Fourth demonstrations. Some strongly opposed the new, simpler writing and insisted on the old literary style; others urged that part of the time in lower-middle school be devoted to the study of the new writing. In lower-middle school, most of our students wrote their compositions in the new style but in the upper middle school they all used the literary style. This continued until 1928; after that either style could be used. Our students also responded to the New Culture Movement by establishing a fortnightly magazine "Miscellaneous Offerings from Yifang." It included various types of writing: essays, poetry, fiction, and notes. Sadly, our school was later disrupted three times by military disturbances and the magazine ceased publication. The students also occasionally put up wall posters, cartoons or humorous essays; they were straightforward and rich in artistic feeling and humor, keenly appreciated by their teachers and elders as well as by their classmates.

The New Culture Movement brought two of the great intellectuals of contemporary Western civilization to Changsha: Bertrand Russell and John Dewey. Bertrand Russell, whose name was known to every school child in China, had left an indelible impression with me for his leadership of resistance to World War I in England. He came from Cambridge to lecture at the invitation of Beijing National University. In Changsha, he was scheduled to speak at the Presbyterian Church and then come to Yifang for a banquet. Ms. Dora Black, who we thought was his secretary, accompanied him to Changsha. However, we learned from his interpreter Zhao Yuanren, a leader of the New Culture Movement and later the Agassiz Professor at Berkeley, that Ms. Black was not Bertrand Russell's secretary but a companion living with him outside of marriage. By the time we discovered this, we had already sent out invitations to the banquet at Yifang to most of the prominent residents of Changsha. Nevertheless, a representative of the Christian schools in Changsha confronted me with the news that the Presbyterian Church would not be available for Bertrand Russell's address and that people from the Christian schools would not be attending the banquet. Ms. Barnes also felt that the example set by Professor Russell and Ms. Black was at odds with the principles that Yifang stood for. I knew, in my heart, they were right.

I wrote to Professor Russell withdrawing the invitation and explained to him why. He sent a letter to me in return explaining that he and Ms. Black were living together because the rigid divorce laws of Great Britain made marriage impossible and left them no other alternative. His address was delivered at another location and Yuenung was asked to interpret. The topic was quite difficult. When Yuenung showed up wearing the traditional mourning garments in observance of his mother's recent death, the audience seemed skeptical of the ability of such an old-fashioned youth to interpret the complex topic of the address. His masterful rendition of Professor Russell's English quickly disabused them of that notion.

Many years later in the mid 1930s while I was in England applying for a grant of Boxer Indemnity funds to assist Yifang, I learned that Bertrand Russell was a member of the Board that would decide whether or not Yifang would receive assistance. Before the Board met, I was introduced to Mr. Russell. It was the first time we had met face to face. He knew who I was immediately and made it clear that he remembered me. My hopes of securing assistance for Yifang vanished. Though we talked for quite a while, he never brought up the awkward events of 1919 in Changsha, and I surely did not. Later, I was surprised to learn that he spoke in support of the award of Boxer Indemnity funds to Yifang. But it all came to naught when the outbreak of war with Japan undermined my plans for the school.

Professor John Dewey and Mrs. Dewey also visited Changsha in 1919. Professor Dewey was very well known in China for his mentoring at Columbia University of Dr. Hu Shi, a leading proponent of the New Culture and clear language. Dewey's pragmatic philosophy advocated education to meet the needs of society. Others felt that education should provide leadership not simply respond to the needs of society. Mrs. Dewey spoke at the YMCA on "The Employment of Women and the Family." Professors Dewey and Russell both have had a profound influence on the youth of China and I feel very fortunate to have known them.

In the months following the May Fourth demonstrations, students became very concerned about national and provincial affairs. In the autumn of 1919 while the northern militarist, Zhang Jingyao, was governor of Hunan, he wanted to allow export of Hunan rice to Japan and impose a tax of one yuan per picul. At that time Hunan was suffering internally from floods and drought and food supplies were inadequate. There were urgent appeals from various quarters opposing the shipment of rice outside the province. Yifang students shared these feelings and joined with students from other schools to encircle the provincial assembly, preventing assembly members from leaving their seats before the issue of rice export was resolved. They were determined that the decision would represent the will of the majority. From noon until seven o'clock they had nothing to eat or drink and no place to rest. Students from other schools began leaving. Finally after the legislators promised our students that they would uphold the ban, the Yifang students also left. Although we gave our best effort to stop the export of rice, it didn't work. The preparations to begin exporting continued.

Then, in an effort to arouse public support for the ban, Yifang students changed tactics. They staged a play entitled "Lu Bo's Hate." It told the story of Lu Bo, the daughter of a rice merchant who repeatedly implored her father not to export rice to aid Japan. Finally, she asked her classmates to go into the streets and do their best to convince the merchants not to harm China by helping the enemy. They tried every way to persuade them but, sadly, a traitorous Chinese devised a plot to murder Lu Bo. In the end she is seen clutching a letter urging the merchants to cease the export of rice. The general effect was to move some merchants to stop doing business with Japan.

The larger significance of the play was to criticize the incumbent governor, Zhang Jingyao, and some traitorous Chinese merchants. Though the stage dialogue and direction may have been a bit amateurish, it was created entirely by the students without any help from the faculty. All direction, stage properties, and lighting were student responsibilities. Furthermore, members of the Student-Faculty Association including the teachers sold ten tickets each, the proceeds going to disaster relief. Not only did the students turn in every cent realized from the ticket sales, they used none of the proceeds for carfare or expenses incidental to the production.

In 1919, I accepted the position of principal of the Provincial First Women's Normal School in Changsha, a post I held from 1919 until 1921. I was reluctant to accept this position since classes at Yifang had just started and we were already experiencing harassment by our radical neighbors from the Wang Fuzhi Temple Association. Nevertheless, at the urging of colleagues in the Changsha educational community who feared the First Women's Normal School would fall under the control of Governor Zhang Jingyao, I accepted.

With the help of a very able staff, I divided my time, for a while, between the two institutions. By the winter of 1920, however, a popular movement to rid Hunan of the oppressive rule of Governor Zhang resulted in government closure of the school and funds were cut off. Financial officers from First Women's Normal and other provincial schools punitively closed by the government responded with boisterous demonstrations at the Provincial Assembly. The school reopened again in the spring of 1921 but, by March and April of that year, the "get rid of Zhang" movement was growing rapidly. In June 1921, with the Southern Army of former Hunan Governor Tan Yankai advancing from Hengyang toward Changsha, Governor Zhang fled and the Southern Army occupied Changsha quite smoothly but provincial funding of First Women's Normal had again been disrupted. Through connections of my father's younger brother, I was able personally to borrow two thousand yuan to provide meals at the schools. The faculty were exceptionally long-suffering and loyal as there were no funds for their salaries.

Moreover, Yifang continued to suffer harassment from radicals from the Wang Fuzhi Temple Association who broke down the wall separating Yifang from the Temple and overran our grounds. I was forced to suspend classes and request police protection. The dispute was settled through the mediation of a group of Hunan gentry including the Changsha District Magistrate. A new wall was erected along a slightly different line, but it was clear to me that I could not do justice to the principalship of the two schools under these trying circumstances. I resigned the position at the First Women's Normal School and devoted my efforts entirely to the development of Yifang, which reopened in the fall of 1921.

From 1922 to 1927, during the high tide of anti-imperialism touched off by the May Fourth Movement, Yifang employed Dr. Grubb, Ms. Galbraith, Ms. Madge, and Ms. Gibson as foreign faculty. The Chinese and foreign faculty lived together and got on very well. Ms. Barnes was the most respected. The students were very cooperative with foreign teachers. The teachers, for their part, lived at the school with the students and took their meals with them. The spirit of cooperation and respect for learning that would become the hallmark of Yifang prevailed.

Chapter 20

April 8, 1927: One Day in the Chinese Revolution

After the May Fourth Movement, prominent members of the newly organized Chinese Communist Party and communist sympathizers surfaced in Changsha. Among them, was Mao Zedong, a native of Hunan who headed the Peasant Department of the Party. In early 1927, Mao assumed responsibility for directing the peasant movement nationwide. Another was Deng Yanda, a Cantonese and a well-known radical though not a communist himself; Deng headed the Political Department of the communist infested Northern Expeditionary Army that occupied Changsha in early 1927. Others included Guo Liang and Liu Zhixun—both Hunanese and early leaders of the party's peasant movement; they organized the 1927 attempt by the Peasant Association to seize Changsha. These and others of similar political leanings operated the Wang Fuzhi Temple Association in the lecture hall on the west side of Zeng Guofan's ancestral temple that housed Yifang. It was a communist base from which they spread lies and attempted to subvert the lawful government.

In the autumn of 1926, the Northern Expeditionary Army under the command of Chiang Kaishek marched northward from Guangzhou. With them came Soviet advisors Galen and Michael Borodin, and thousands of communists who had infiltrated their ranks in the previous few years. The Wang Fuzhi Temple Association members, emboldened by the approach of their fellow radicals, tore down the wall separating Yifang from their temple. They came and went on the campus at all hours of the day and night. There was no stopping them.

A person who went by the name "short stick" chided the principals of Changsha schools everyday in the *Hunan Daily News*. Yifang being privately operated and Christian in outlook, was slandered more than the others; there was even a special edition dedicated to overthrowing Yifang. I saw myself singled out as the target for public derision, and branded a local tyrant, an evil gentry, a landlord, a feudal remnant, and a running dog of imperialism. It got to the point where I thought Yifang might be better off without me. So, before winter vacation in 1926, I announced to the students that I would resign for the sake of the school. At first they were opposed, but after I explained the situation to them several times, they agreed. The Student-Faculty Association organized an administrative maintenance committee and asked several faculty members to join. Yuenung and I served as advisors to discuss general matters involving the school.

I also told the students that things would definitely get worse in the coming year. If anyone wanted to withdraw from school temporarily, they could go home and wait this out quietly. Yifang had already been looted several times and there had been a fight with members of the Wang Fuzhi Temple Association. Though the police had broken up the fight, it was clear that the situation called for great caution.

In early 1927, students from schools in Changsha were either attending political rallies or marching in the streets. They seemed never to attend classes. Ninety percent of the shopkeepers closed their shops and the business district was deserted. A few days before the Women's Festival on April 8, people from the United Students' Association came and said they wanted the whole student body from each school to turn out and march. Our students didn't want to. On April 7, the Student Faculty Association convened a meeting; fifteen staff members and the whole student body were present. A student chaired the meeting. Everyone was emotionally drained and no one wanted to go out and demonstrate. One faculty member suggested, "We don't have to go ourselves; we can send a few of our workers to carry the Yifang banner. This will probably ensure the safety of the school." However, one of the students saw it differently, "We've never participated in this kind of thing and this time should be no exception. Nobody will be fooled if we send a flag to represent our school name. If we don't believe that marching in the demonstration has anything to do with the welfare of women, why should we make a pretext. The worst thing they can do is close our school. It's better to go down gloriously than to survive in dishonor." The result was that the full association passed this proposal with ten faculty votes opposing. The faculty was defeated but the spirit of autonomy and independence at Yifang triumphed. After that, a member of the school's board of directors tried to persuade Yuenung and me to get out of Changsha, even offering to pay our way. We thanked him but declined. He himself was slain by the communists only a few days later.

On Friday, April 8, 1927, I went to class as usual. Although I had resigned as principal, I was still a teacher. In the afternoon, I had a headache and felt dizzy so I went upstairs to rest. Yuenung was still in the office working. Suddenly two people appeared demanding to meet with the school authorities. They had no credentials and were not wearing uniforms but said, "We're from the Peasants' Association and have come to take over the campus. Your school has been closed by the government." Yuenung stood his ground and said, "Show me the official closure order from the Ministry of Education." They said, "Official orders, be damned. Our people are on the way. We're giving you two hours to get out of here."

After a while, forty or fifty people appeared, each carrying a bamboo spear about five feet long with a six or seven inch pointed blade mounted on one end. It could easily be used to stab a person. They swarmed in, running all over the property shouting at the students to get out. Shortly thereafter came troops carrying loaded weapons. The students then rang the bell to call an emergency meeting. At the same time, fearing that I would be harmed, several students escorted me out of the school. Though I and others left at gunpoint, thank God, we were unharmed; the communist party had not yet issued the order to kill us. We took refuge in my aunt's house nearby.

The emergency meeting was attended by both students and faculty. Yuenung reported on the government's closure of the school. The students reacted vehemently. Some said, "We refuse to leave." Others wanted to "petition" the government and try to have it reopened. All this time the spearmen and armed soldiers were standing around the doorway looking in like hungry tigers. I knew how the students felt so I wrote a note and asked someone to bring it to Yuenung to tell the students. "We must get out of the school by dark. We can't forcibly resist; it could result in bloodshed and meaningless sacrifice of life." The students accepted this message and saw that the crowd was growing. In addition to the spearmen and the troops, there were several thousand disorderly onlookers on the street. With that, the deliberations broke up.

The students took a writing brush and wrote on the wall in large bold characters. "The Yifang spirit is not dead." Then they smashed all the glass windows and kitchenware to pieces. Even the spearmen said, "With this kind of spirit, you'll surely be back. Why are you smashing things?" The troops let the students get their personal belongings before leaving but they snatched up important documents and equipment belonging to the school instead. They were angry and bitter but unafraid. They formed into two contingents. One in front led by Yuenung and one bringing up the rear led by my cousin Zhaoquan. They marched through the gate singing the school song and "Onward Christian Soldiers" to the sound of thousands of firecrackers exploding. This put an end to an ugly affair. The hoodlums outnumbered our students twenty to one but they failed to intimidate them.

That evening two of my students held seats for Yuenung and me on a small river boat bound for Hankou. Yuenung brought only one small suitcase with him when he left the school. To avoid arrest, we waited to board until just before sunrise. The other passengers were also fleeing the communists in Changsha. After we got underway, no one dared say a word for a long time. Then some one gave a great sigh of relief. We had escaped, as it were, right out of the tiger's mouth. Only three days later, two of our board members who remained in Changsha were killed by the communists. I'm eternally grateful to those who helped us. Out of Christian love, they put themselves at great risk. Altogether twenty-six of us escaped from Changsha that night.

Chapter 21

Revolution Comes to Yifang

On April 8, 1927, Yifang was in ruins. Yuenung and I escaped to Hankou. There we accepted the hospitality of Bishop Roots of the Church of England Mission Society for ten days. My father had fled to Hankou earlier but we didn't know where he was. It was an open port, teeming with people; we had no idea where to begin looking. We were in Hankou only a few days, however, when an old man appeared at Bishop Roots's door inquiring if a man and a woman, refugees from Hunan, were staying there. He couldn't write our names and wouldn't even speak them out loud, probably for fear that he might be overheard and our enemies would get wind of where we were. We peeked out and saw it was Jiang Wushi, an old man who had served my father. Though illiterate, he was trustworthy, completely loyal, and devoted to my father. When we saw him our spirits soared. "Where is my father?" I asked. "A long way from here in the Hankou Defense Barracks," he replied, "but I can take you there." He led and we followed in a broken-down horse and buggy, through the narrow streets of Hankou.

My father was living in a small house inside the barracks compound where rebels and communists would never think to look for him, "If you live with soldiers," he said, "no one will come looking for you. What's more I've changed my name to 'Cao.'" Why "Cao?" I asked. He replied, "I thought if I forgot and signed my name Zeng, it would be easy to change since the two characters look so much alike." It had never occurred to Yuenung or me to use a different name. Traveling under the name Zeng made it that much easier for our enemies to discover our whereabouts.

After finding my father, we managed to get him a ticket on the steamer to Shanghai. The Chinese riverboats had all stopped operating but there were three foreign lines—Yihe, Taigu, and Riqing—that had ships anchored in the river guarded by gunboats. A foreign guarantor was required to purchase a ticket. With the assistance of Bishop Root, we were able to purchase three tickets: one for my father, one for Jiang Wushi, and one for another relative. To board these ships one had to go out in a small row boat. The day father and old Mr Jiang were to board, there was a torrential rain so there were very few people along the bank of the river. The guards that usually patrolled there to prevent illegal departures from the city were nowhere to be seen. "Good," said my father, "If it weren't raining so hard, we might have to be inspected and that could result in all kinds of trouble." Although he did his best to appear relaxed, his clothing was soaked and I am sure he was terrified. Yuenung accompanied him in the small boat out to the ship. When they arrived, they found there was no ladder. They had to haul father through the hatch used for loading coal. I stood on the bank looking on, fearing that a patrol would come along but, thankfully, none did. I couldn't relax until Yuenung returned. A few days later he and I also took an English steamer to Shanghai. When I saw my father again, I was overcome with emotion.

When we arrived in Shanghai, we had nothing but the clothes on our backs. A former teacher who heard of our predicament generously sent us a hundred pounds. Our cousins, the Nies and the Yus, put us up for about a month. Then we went on to Lushan in the countryside of Jiangxi Province to rest and determine what we would do next. Ms. Barnes, Ms. Galbraith, and Dr. Grubb had fled from the turmoil in Changsha and arrived in Shanghai before us. They hoped to accompany us to Lushan but the British Consul, fearing the anti-foreign violence erupting throughout central China, would not permit them to leave Shanghai. While Yuenung and I were at Lushan, Ms. Barnes suffered a fatal heart attack. The violent closing of our school and the turmoil were too much for her. When we received the news that she had been stricken, Yuenung and I rushed back to Shanghai, but it was too late. She had already passed away. She devoted so much of her life to China and to Yifang; it broke my heart to realize that she would not see it again. I stayed on in Shanghai with a heavy heart and laid my old friend to rest in the churchyard at Baxianqiao in the French Concession.

In Shanghai, we learned of the rash of anti-foreign, anti-bourgeois incidents that had occurred in the Yangzi Valley almost simultaneously with the April 8 takeover of Changsha by the Peasants' Association. Communists and the communist-led Peasants' Association within Chiang Kaishek's Northern Expeditionary Army were attempting to seize control. Beginning on April 12, Chiang retaliated with fierce suppression of communists in Shanghai where his headquarters were. By May, he was in control of the forces in Hunan and Hubei, including the Thirty-fifth Army that was occupying Changsha. On May 21, Regimental Commander Xu Kexiang with the support of his commanding officer He Jian led a force of more than one thousand in a surprise attack on the communist controlled Provincial Legislature, the Peasant Association, and other radical groups. Over one hundred people lost their lives. Shortly thereafter, we learned that order had been restored in Changsha and it was safe to return.

While Yifang was still occupied by troops, our students remembered where the school documents were kept, and every night three students crept over the wall near where the troops were billeted and sneaked out with the files. These included the registration and assignment of land and other important documents as well as the lists of students for each session. If we didn't have these things, it would be impossible to reopen. Thanks to their courage and ingenuity, we were able to start over.

At the same time other Yifang alumnae were planning and working to reopen the school. First they rented a building from the Methodist Church and reopened the elementary school. Everything was set up rather hastily but the enthusiasm they showed was admirable. By mid October they even managed to get back onto the campus. They began restoration work and wired us to return to Changsha. This reopening of Yifang was entirely due to the students' determination and their devotion to their school.

Alas, on Chinese New Year 1928, the "Listening to Rain Pavilion" was burnt to the ground by a fire started by military personnel. Though the students were bitter over the injustice of this, it made them work all the harder to complete the restoration. In the spring of 1928 we began recruiting students for the upper middle school. Yifang's Board of Directors was also having a difficult time managing; they were forced to merge the Yali College, which had been established at Yifang several years earlier, into Huazhong University at Wuhan.

When we reopened, we concentrated our efforts entirely on running a complete middle school, six years uninterrupted by graduation from lower middle school. The Ministry of Education authorized us to do this on a trial basis and it proved to be one of the important reasons for Yifang's success. Students and faculty were together for six years, seeing each other regularly, pursuing their studies and progressing in an orderly and gradual way without the pressure of an examination for advancement to the next level. I feel this is the best system for middle school.

Things went quite smoothly the first year Yifang was reopened. Then, on November 11, 1929, my father passed away. In addition, Yuenung seemed to have something the matter with his lungs so he and my cousin Fubao went to Lushan where he hoped to regain his health. I was troubled by my father's death and Yuenung's sickness but very busy. Since we had stopped operating the college, we provided scholarships for three of our graduates to study in England and one in Jinling Women's University in Nanjing.

In the spring of 1930, the political situation in Changsha went through another upheaval. In mid May, Li Zongren and Bai Chongxi, militarists of the Guangxi Clique, battled their way into the city. He Jian, who had been chairman of the provincial government since he and Xu Kexiang had unseated the communists in 1928, withdrew his forces and the Guangxi troops took up the occupation. Soldiers were billeted in the Sangong Temple at Sima Bridge, very close to our school. Over the years munitions had been stored there by the various armies that had occupied Changsha. The Guangxi troops were careless and a fire started causing an enormous explosion. In an instant, flames lit up the sky and flying projectiles fell everywhere. I felt we had to get the students and the foreign teachers out of the school. We fled to my cousin Zhaoquan's independent church where I learned that on the previous day, Zhaoquan's little boy had found a hand grenade left there by Guangxi soldiers. Not realizing what it was, he began playing with it and it exploded, killing him. We sat there all night, teachers and students, terrified, waiting for the dawn. Then we learned that the school had felt no repercussions from the explosion but the residences on the left side of Sima Bridge sustained heavy damages. No one was hurt but everyone in Changsha was badly frightened.

We resumed classes and luckily, within a month, the Guangxi clique withdrew their forces from Changsha. During summer vacation, Yuenung and I went to Nanjing to petition the Administrative Yuan of the Central Government to return control of all the property of Zeng Guofan's Ancestral Temple, including the Wang Fuzhi Temple, to Yifang. We were successful in this. However, while we were in Nanjing, we heard that not long after the Guangxi army left, He Jian's troops had reentered Changsha. Then in less than a month, on July 28, the communists under Peng Dehuai descended on the city. He's forces were taken by surprise and had to withdraw a second time. Popular wisdom had it that He had lost Changsha twice in forty days. The communist armies ravaged the city. One American friend told me that when she fled Changsha, it was ablaze, the sky darkened by a mantle of black smoke. A great many of our school buildings were damaged or destroyed.

When Peng's communist forces reentered the city, Yuenung and I were still in Nanjing. My cousin Ms. Xiao and two other teachers who were looking after the school hurriedly fled to my mother's home, in Sima Lane, only one street away from the school. They hid there in a very small house for ten days with little food or water. In their haste to get out before the communists arrived, they left everything behind: books, clothing, and personal possessions. Ms. Xiao managed to pick up just one thing, a small astronomical clock that I have to this day. It is on my desk, the only memento I have of the time that Ms. Barnes was at Yifang.

The communists withdrew from Changsha on August 7, and troops commanded by Wang Dongyuan entered the city. Thanks to the efforts of our loyal school workers and the help of neighbors, the school had not been burnt down. Though the troops did a great deal of damage and made a complete mess of things, they left the structures of the buildings and the perimeter wall intact.

My mother, Yuenung, my cousin Ms. Xiao, I, and several others had taken refuge in Hankou where we remained until November before returning to Changsha. Soldiers were again billeted in the school. There was no way to reopen.

Part IV

War with Japan

Chapter 22

The World Christian Council

In the Spring of 1928, when we were rebuilding and making preparations to reopen, I accepted an invitation to attend a meeting of the World Christian Council in Jerusalem; it was convened on the Mount of Olives during the Easter season. I was part of a Chinese delegation of twenty headed by Mr. Yu Rizhang with representatives of various Chinese churches.

We departed from Shanghai. On board ship, there were seminars to study the agenda items for the meeting. After stops at Hong Kong, Singapore and Colombo, we arrived at Port Said, Egypt, where we left the ship and stayed in Cairo for two days. We visited the pyramids and the tombs of the Pharaohs. They impressed me deeply. It was a remarkable civilization that produced such buildings, carvings, and gold and silver work, thousands of years ago in this desert setting.

At midnight, we boarded the train and changed to a ferry to cross the Suez Canal. Night in the desert was bitter cold. The next morning we arrived in Jerusalem. At that time, Palestine was still under the British mandate established following World War I. The Anglican Prelate of Jerusalem, Bishop Meines, invited the leader of our delegation and several members to lunch. Bishop Meines's aunt had known my late great uncle Zeng Jize and his wife as well as other relatives from my father's generation. So he and I had quite a bit to talk about. At the table, we also told stories about Victorian times. I found them very interesting.

During the two weeks of meetings, the most memorable time was Good Friday evening. That night with the landscape bathed in clear moonlight, and a soft breeze moving, Dr. Mott, the chairman of the meeting, led us down the Mount of Olives into the garden of Gethsemane. He first read from the Bible the account of Jesus going into the garden to pray and being betrayed by the Jews. Then, recalling the agony of Jesus, everyone became silent and prayed. After that, a few people led prayers and we sang hymns and then walked slowly back up the mountain. This was the most moving religious experience of my life.

The building where the meeting was being held was the former imperial hostel of Kaiser Wilhelm II. At one time, it had been very impressive but, since World War I, it had been damaged by an earthquake and fallen into disrepair. The structure and the defense works, however, remained intact. Living in this place, my thoughts turned to the fall of a generation of tyrants, the horror of war, and the need for God's love. Two days later on Easter, we all took communion together and joined hands to sing a hymn of farewell. It was difficult for us to take leave of one another. The love of Jesus had made us as loving and close as brothers. It can do this for people the world over regardless of the barriers posed by national borders, race, or language.

After the meeting, I went to Italy to see an old friend from Yifang, Ms. Madge. She took me to visit the expatriate American poet, Ezra Pound, whom T.S. Eliot praised as the greatest poet of the twentieth century. He was a great admirer of Chinese poetry, especially the *Book of Odes*, which he had translated into English. I had a very interesting discussion with him about Chinese culture, literature, and traditional values. He later supported Mussolini's Fascist Party and made propaganda broadcasts for them during World War II. After the war, he was judged insane by the United States and institutionalized for twenty years. Following his release, he returned to Italy. I've had a letter from his wife saying that he was writing poetry again purely for his own enjoyment. He recently passed away.

From Italy, I went to Geneva where I had some business with the YWCA. Mr. Yu, the chief of our delegation, and I then went to England. After a brief stay, he left for the United States but I remained visiting friends and delivering some sermons. At the end of June Mr. Zhao Zichen, another member of the delegation, and I returned to China where I resumed my duties as principal of Yifang.

Chapter 23

The Institute of Pacific Relations

In the spring of 1929, I began receiving propaganda material mailed from Japan and Manchuria stating that the South Manchurian Railroad and other Japanese businesses in Manchuria provided great benefit to China. They also made the case for strengthening cultural relations between the two nations based on the affinity between the Chinese and Japanese written languages. At the time, I scanned these materials but did not pay close attention.

Then, unexpectedly in the middle of May, I received an invitation from the Institute of Pacific Relations to attend a meeting in Japan at the old imperial capital, Kyoto. This organization was originally called "The Pacific People's Committee on International Relations." But since "the people" cannot actually conduct international relations, the name was changed to Institute. This was the third meeting, an earlier one having been held in Honolulu. Institute members came from ten nations: China, United States, Japan, England, Canada, the Philippines, Australia, New Zealand, Indonesia, and Malaya. In addition, the Soviet Union and Korea sent observers. So it was a very important meeting. The central issue was the Manchurian question, the competing claims of China and Japan for control of Manchuria, but there were other issues as well: citizens of Pacific nations residing in other countries, and colonialism. The Soviet Union had sent its observer because of the special interest it had in Manchuria. But all countries on the Pacific Ocean felt that Manchuria was a crucial point of contention between China and Japan that could easily lead to war.

In August 1929, the Chinese delegation held a preparatory meeting in Shenyang (Mukden), the principal city of Manchuria, at the Shenyang Hospital Hostel. After we concluded our discussions of the issues on the agenda, we visited local factories, commercial centers, and schools. I was most impressed by the arsenal at Beidaying; trains could go right into the plant and move weapons directly out. We also toured the Fuxun Coal Mines, which produced a very hard grade of anthracite that could be made into flower vases and tableware. It was reported to be the richest deposit of coal in the world. Our itinerary included a visit to the tombs of the Manchu Emperors of the Qing Dynasty. Huge and unadorned, they were surrounded by stately old trees standing close together. The forests of Manchuria are a treasure and the region yields a variety of products in great abundance. At that time, China relied entirely on the trade surpluses generated by Manchuria to balance the deficit in the rest of the country. How could the Japanese not covet such a treasure?

While attending the preparatory meeting in Shenyang, I had one of the most frightening experiences of my life. One afternoon, a few of us left the hospital hostel on foot and walked across a wooden bridge to a street market. We looked around and bought a few things. As we strolled along, people suddenly began running wildly shouting, "Trouble, the dykes of the Liao River have burst. Hurry and get out of here." The head of our delegation, Mr. Tu Richang, and I ran full speed back across the bridge. Two other delegates, Mr. Bao and Mr. Liang, were right behind us. Just as they stepped off the bridge, it was swept away by the water. If they had been two steps slower, both of them would have been swallowed up by the raging waters. What a close call! Mr. Tu and I got our clothes and shoes soaked but fortunately we were just scared, not harmed. Later we heard that the dikes upstream on the Liao had broken releasing a huge wall of water. The next day, we saw that the small street market was completely destroyed.

After the preparatory meeting was over, I returned to Shanghai and then went to Lushan for a short stay before returning to Yifang. In mid October, I went back to Shanghai and joined the Chinese delegation of ten members headed by Mr. Tu. Besides myself, there were two women delegates: several others including Mrs. Sophia Chen Zen flew directly from Beijing to Japan and joined the delegation in Kyoto.

Our meeting place was at a hotel in Nara Park. Every morning tame deer came to the window or right up to us and ate from our hands. It was truly a place where man and nature co-existed in complete harmony. Kyoto represents Japan's traditional culture; there was an atmosphere of simplicity. I enjoyed it greatly.

There was a plenary session of representatives each morning and small group discussions in the afternoon. In the evening the meeting was opened up to the public. Once, in a discussion of the comparison of Eastern and Western culture, I spoke out: "Eastern culture has morality based on ethical relations." I said, "Each man's thoughts are his own. One does not succumb to the propaganda of newspapers and magazines. It teaches the importance of doing what is right not what is profitable. These principles certainly can strengthen some of the weak points of Western culture: materialism and the excessive concern with personal gain." This received strong approval from the audience.

In the afternoon, the delegation also had ample opportunity to enjoy the scenery and observe the society. We visited Kyoto's great shrines. The images of military figures and civil officials enshrined there were attired in the clothing of the Tang Dynasty (A.D. 618–907) when Japan had borrowed extensively from Chinese civilization. I never thought I would see such a display of old style Chinese garments in Japan. We also observed the tea ceremony, a marriage ceremony, and sacrifices at an ancestral shrine. We visited the imperial university and the rapids and waterfall on the Hozu River. Then we went to the home of a Mr. Nakayama who is said to have been Dr. Sun Yat-sen's landlord when Dr. Sun was in Japan. He had a large garden that he called "The Garden of Hard Work and Happiness" signifying that only through hard work does one gain happiness. He was extremely warm and good-hearted, and supported a number of worthy social causes; he was especially active trying to promote good relations between China and Japan.

The Japanese Emperor invited the delegations to a banquet on November 12. Naturally most of the delegates went; an imperial invitation is not to be taken lightly. But neither Mrs. Chen Zen nor I attended. On the night of November 11, the hotel felt gloomy and dark. I don't know why, but I was distracted and couldn't fall asleep. After I got in bed, I tossed and turned until after eleven. Then I thought I might as well see if Mrs. Chen Zen wanted to chat. Fortunately, she was not asleep yet. So the two of us sat on the side of her bed and talked. Not having seen each other for a long time, we talked about lots of things until two o'clock in the morning. I was embarrassed to stay any longer and returned to my own room but I felt terribly ill at ease. I was anxious about my family and Yifang and didn't sleep all night. The next day I got up and went to Osaka. Together with several other delegates, I returned to China. The remaining delegates went their separate ways returning to where they had come from.

When we arrived in Shanghai, my cousin, who was a doctor practicing in Shanghai, was waiting to meet us. This was odd because she had a very busy practice. She came aboard, threw her arms around me and said, "Your father is gravely ill and wants you to come as soon as possible." I looked at her and said, "Tell me the truth. He died already on the eleventh, didn't he?" We hurried to her pedicab and sat there looking at each other and began weeping. The next day I boarded the steamer for Hunan. At Jiujiang, Yuenung and my cousin Ms. Xiao met the ship. They told me that father had suffered a stroke and passed away at Xiangyang on November 11 at five o'clock in the afternoon. I realized then that the malaise that overtook me in Kyoto was a kind of sympathetic sensory reaction. Many people have had this kind of experience. Although science, at present, cannot provide a satisfactory explanation, we can't deny that such things happen.

In the midst of the tumult at Yifang in 1930, I attended another meeting. This one convened by Justice Robert Feetham under the auspices of the Shanghai Municipal Council to discuss the return of the Shanghai International Concession to Chinese sovereignty. The movement to regain control of the areas in China's port cities previously ceded to the major imperialist powers had begun even before the establishment of Chiang Kaishek's new national government in 1928. But the new government was determined to pursue this issue vigorously. Among those in attendance at the meeting was Mr. Reginald F. Johnston, formerly tutor to the last Manchu Emperor, Henry Buyi. Mr. Johnston had been quite close to the boy emperor. In fact, it was he who had given Buyi the English name Henry. He told me that after Buyi abdicated in 1912, he had tried to persuade him to go to England to continue his education but the two concubines, Jinfei and Yufei, convinced him to stay in China. Buyi, he said, was a good student but entirely lacking in decisiveness. He did exactly what his father Zaifeng, his brother Bujie, or the two concubines bid him. If he had heeded Mr. Johnston's advice, at least he would not have wound up as a Japanese puppet, as he did after Japan seized control of Manchuria in 1932, renamed it Manchukuo, and appointed him emperor.

In October, 1931, the fourth meeting of the Institute of Pacific Relations was held in Shanghai, Nanjing, and Hangzhou. It was less than a month after the Mukden Incident and Japan's invasion of Manchuria. This time Dr. Hu Shi was head of the delegation and the so-called "Liberal Faction" took part. The discussions at different locations were heated and confused. We frequently failed to reach conclusions on important issues. It was not nearly as productive as the Kyoto meeting. We also discovered an "appeasement" faction in our midst. Considering everything, after this meeting, I resigned from the Institute.

Chapter 24

Yifang's Second Rebirth

I was disheartened by the second closing of Yifang in 1930 and exhausted from running around Shanghai during the fourth meeting of the Institute of Pacific Relations in October 1931. After the meeting, I began coughing violently and bringing up blood. My mother rushed up from Hunan. My cousins Baohan, Zhaoquan, and Yuenung were already in Shanghai. They urged me to go to my brother's home at Yantai in Shandong Province to rest. So in late October 1931, my mother, Yuenung, my cousin Ms. Xiao, and I went to Yantai where my brother was assistant director of the Maritime Customs House.

Yantai is on the coast; the scenery is very pleasing, the air clear and fresh. We stayed there altogether nine months. My recovery was slow and complicated by further congestion in the lungs. We were saddened by news from Hunan that Mrs. Zhao, my father's third wife, suffered a stroke and my cousin Fubao and his mother both passed away. While at Yantai I received a telegram from the three Yifang students who had been studying in Britain informing us that they had completed their studies and were returning to China. We hastened to Shanghai to welcome them back and to discuss with them plans for reopening Yifang. The Misses Zuo, Xu, and Chen were intent on getting started right away. So, together with Yuenung, they left for Changsha while Ms. Xiao and I returned to Yantai until I could regain my health and join them.

When they returned to Changsha, they found troops still billeted on the campus. They had caused extensive damage; it seemed as though our school had become their permanent home. Thanks to the efforts of Yuenung, the Board of Directors, and many alumnae, the troops were moved out. A staff was assembled with Yuenung as dean and the returned students assuming key instructional roles. After the school had been open for several months and my condition improved, Ms. Xiao and I left Yantai and returned to Changsha; thus the second reopening of Yifang, in 1932, was entirely the doing of former students and teachers.

From 1932 to 1937, we concentrated on middle-school education, adopting the continuous six-year system that I described previously. Because of this our textbooks, especially in mathematics and English, employed a gradual progress model. We did not use the instructional methods based on a partial overlapping of the lower and upper middle-school curricula. Consequently, we could usually complete the upper middle-school curriculum in the fifth year. The sixth year could then be used for higher studies. Our students were diligent—no poor study habits. Four classes of students completed the sixth year and graduated during this period. Every student qualified in the national examination for university admission and everyone passed the individual university examinations as well.

In the summer of 1936, while things were going smoothly at Yifang, I accepted an invitation from the All China General YMCA to deliver lectures on Christianity in twelve of China's largest cities. Dr. Chen Wenyuan, a YMCA director from Fuzhou, and Dr. Tu Xiqing of Hujiang University in Shanghai were also invited. Our purpose was to bring the message of Christianity to as large an audience as possible, but we especially hoped to reach the educated and students above the middle-school level. Dr. Chen was to focus on religious issues and sign up those who wished to commit themselves. Dr. Tu would concentrate on science and religion and I would address cultural education and religion. With this division of responsibilities, we hoped to avoid redundancy.

After school opened, I left Changsha for Shanghai from where I and my companions began our travel through twelve of China's largest cities. In the north we visited Tianjin, Beijing, and Taiyuan and then headed south into the Yangzi Valley stopping at Changsha, Wuhan, Nanjing, Shanghai, and Hangzhou. Finally we shifted our efforts to south China traveling by coastal steamer to Fuzhou and then on to Xiamen, Hong Kong, and Guangzhou. In every city old friends, former schoolmates, and alumnae from Yifang greeted us and extended lavish hospitality.

Apart from the exhilaration of bringing the Christian message to thousands of young people in China's universities and schools, this trip provided several memorable experiences: visits to places in my homeland that I had not previously seen and meetings with educators and churchmen that left a lasting impression. I will never forget my meeting with the elderly but vigorous President Zhang Boling of Nankai University in Tianjin. President Zhang, a self-made man, rose from the status of a poor scholar to found Nankai. After thirty years, his unceasing efforts had brought Nankai respect throughout China and abroad. Thousands of his students have received national and international recognition.

After our visit to Beijing, we headed south on the Beijing-Wuhan Railroad to Shijiazhuang where we changed trains and proceeded west through the Niangzi Pass in the mountains of Shanxi Province toward the city of Taiyuan. We could see from the configuration of the mountains how readily this pass could be defended. In traditional times, one warrior could literally hold an army at bay. Of course, in these days of airplanes and missiles, this kind of natural defense is no longer effective. As we proceeded into Shanxi, the terrain changed to jagged stone peaks. The hills were bare—neither trees nor grass—and the people lived in cave dwellings in unbelievably harsh conditions. As Dr. Chen explained, in ancient times, these hills were fertile but this was the birthplace of Chinese civilization; deforestation occurred early and gave rise to erosion. Today the hills are practically bare. He made the point, however, that this area is not nearly as barren as Mesopotamia where Middle Eastern civilization originated.

In Taiyuan, I had the opportunity to visit with Mr. Zhao Daiwen, a devout Buddhist. Our discussion focused on similarities between Buddhism and Christianity. Mr. Zhao pointed out that both sought salvation for the individual and benefit for society. While Christianity finds righteousness from faith—thus gaining enlightenment through sincerity, Buddhism reveals the faith through great wisdom—thus gaining sincerity through enlightenment. So, in a sense, the two are complementary.

While in the Yangzi Valley, in Nanjing, I visited the Nanjing Arsenal, and the monument marking the place where the Hunan Army, in 1864, breached the city wall and overran the Taiping headquarters, effectively ending the rebellion. Both sites commemorated the achievements of Zeng Guofan, who had established the arsenal and directed the victory over the Taipings. At the arsenal, I was shown around by my cousin, Mr. Yu Dawei, who was then director. He showed me the former residence of Dr. Halliday Macartney, who was employed at the arsenal as a technical adviser and director in the 1860s and 1870s. Macartney's service at the Nanjing Arsenal was an indication of the efforts of Zeng Guofan and the other great generals of that day to change the prevailing atmosphere and strengthen China. I also visited the huge and stately mausoleum of Dr. Sun Yat-sen and the tomb of the revolutionary martyr of the "Hundred Days Reform," Tan Sitong.

In Shanghai, I departed from the agenda to address a topic requested by the students on "Diplomatic Relations between China and Japan since the Sino-Japanese War (1894–95)." They requested this topic knowing that I had attended a meeting of the Institute of Pacific Relations in Japan but they did not realize, nor did I, how close we were to another war.

In Fuzhou, I visited with retired Admiral Sa Zhenbing, one of the founding fathers of China's modern navy. My travels culminated with a delightful reception in Hong Kong given by returned students from England and a joyous reunion in Guangzhou with my brother Zhaohua who had flown from Guangxi especially to greet me.

Chapter 25

War Comes to Hunan

In July 1937, Yuenung left Yifang to attend a meeting at Lushan. Ms. Xiao, myself, and three other teachers were the only ones living at school. Because the weather was so hot, we all moved into the downstairs classrooms. In the middle of the night on July 7, 1937, we heard someone out on the street yelling "Extra! Extra! The Japanese have attacked. Extra!" We quickly jumped out of bed and sent someone out to buy a paper for us. Then we learned what had happened. Japanese troops had clashed with Chinese soldiers at the Marco Polo Bridge south of Beijing. We never dreamed this one incident would touch off an enormous conflagration leading to World War II. Our officers and men fought for eight bloody years after that and, in the end, they recovered China from the Japanese. But I'll have more to say about this later. On the eighth of July, extra editions of the newspapers came out several times. The atmosphere was extremely tense but the two countries did not declare war; only the military took action. In August, the fighting spread to Shanghai. As more and more of East China came under Japanese control, Yuenung's father returned from Beijing to Changsha where Yuenung could look after him.

The air war began almost immediately. The government warned the people, especially those in schools, hospitals, and other public places, to set up air-raid shelters. The people, however, did not realize the potential horror of air raids and had no understanding of how to prepare. Air-raid shelters and caves were constructed carelessly. Then, on August 15, 1937—the moon was like a picture that night—suddenly the alarm sounded. Many on the streets had nowhere to take shelter. Those in teahouses, restaurants, and theaters crowded together and panicked. I don't know how many lost wallets or were trampled. After that, people began to realize the need for defense against air raids.

We dug an air-raid shelter next to the rock garden at our school. On top we placed pine boards fitted closely together; and on top of them we placed sandbags. The shelter was shaped like a horse's hoof and had six entrances, one for each class. Each class had a faculty member designated to lead them into the shelter when the alarm sounded and a school worker to look after them. Additionally, teachers brought teapots, biscuits, medicines, bandages, and antiseptics for use in the shelter.

After August 15, although we had many alarms, we didn't actually see any more Japanese planes. During this time, our school organized a Red Cross unit with stretchers, medicines, and nurses' aids. The girls' schools in Changsha also began taking turns at night duty at the railroad station to greet and look after sick and wounded soldiers arriving from the front. Some girls were unwilling to go to the station, fearing that it would be a target for bombing. But every time it was Yifang's turn, our students and staff members, including myself, went willingly. Several times while we were there the alarm sounded; we simply took shelter a short distance from the building. When wounded arrived, we gave them tea, changed bandages, and wrote letters for them. They were very appreciative.

It was this way for about two months. Then one day in mid November while I was at the dentist's, actually in the dentist chair, the alarm suddenly sounded—piercing heaven and earth. Fortunately, the dentist had a quick hand and got the drill out of my mouth avoiding what could have been a nasty oral injury. There were three or four alarms right after that. The crowds were shouting, "Bombs are falling—the Japanese devils are bombing us." The streets were instantly jammed with people and vehicles. My companion and I rushed frantically back to the school. When we got there, the alarm had still not been lifted. The students had entered the air-raid shelter by classes. But we had no telephone and information on where the bombs had fallen was slow reaching us. When we learned that the railroad station had been hit, Yifang's Red Cross rescue unit hurried to the scene but the wounded had already been carried off. The first rescue unit to arrive at the station was from my cousin Zhaoquan's independent Christian Church. Units from other churches followed. Casualties were most serious in a nearby hotel where preparations for a wedding ceremony were underway. It is difficult to say how many were killed. Those who were buried in the debris had to be dug out. All we could do that day to help was to distribute food and water.

On December 15, the news of the government's withdrawal from the capital at Nanjing reached us. We were demoralized and decided to dismiss school on December 19. On that morning, my mother suffered a heart attack. When she heard the news of the withdrawal from Nanjing, she felt sure that Changsha would be next. Looking at the ruined buildings and the scenes of tragedy all around her only made things worse. After she was stricken, I asked a German doctor resident in Changsha to look at her. He was with her from five in the afternoon until nine in the evening without even taking time to eat. I realized then how serious it was. When he left, he told us to give her more medicine at midnight, but if she were sleeping, not to waken her. Yuenung, I, and my half brother, Zhaoke, waited until midnight and saw that she was sleeping peacefully. I wrapped myself in a quilt and dozed off in an easy chair outside her door. At two o'clock I heard her breathing irregularly. I looked in on her and found she had no pulse in her wrist. She was slipping away. I cried to Yuenung to get up and told Zhaoke to fetch the doctor. I tried mouth-to-mouth resuscitation but it produced no effect. I heard only the rattle of phlegm, no breathing. When the doctor arrived he said, "She died in her sleep, no suffering at all."

For her whole life mother was sincere and warmhearted. She respected her husband's mother and was obedient to her husband. She educated her children; she did nothing harmful. Yet in the end the terrible times in which she lived claimed her life. How sad! However, later when the Japanese neared Changsha, we took refuge in Hong Kong and our troubles were unending. I feel that heaven spared her these hardships. In that sense her death was a blessing. After going through this, Yuenung thought we had better bring his father to Nanning in Guangxi Province where he would be safer living with my brother Zhaohua.

In the spring of 1938, things got worse. There were frequent Japanese air raids over Changsha and many places were destroyed by bombs. Fortunately, nothing happened to us before the end of the spring semester. Yuenung took his father to Nanning. Then on August 17 at nine in the morning, I was just about to leave for the countryside with Ms. Xiao and three faculty members to escape from the frequent air raids when an urgent alarm sounded. We hurriedly got two students and several workers to gather up important personal belongings and school documents and rushed into the air-raid shelter. At that time the Munitions Office had a great many barrels of gasoline stored in the main building of Zeng Guofan's ancestral temple. There were eighteen officers and men billeted at the school guarding them. Ms. Xiao and I told them they had better get into the shelter. At first they didn't want to; then, as the planes came nearer, they had no choice. When the last soldier got in, the bombs were already falling; a piece of shrapnel struck him in the leg but the wound was not serious. We had medicine in the shelter and quickly bound it up. All we could hear was the roar of the airplane engines and the exploding of bombs. What was really strange was the explosions didn't seem so loud. This went on for about ten minutes and then the sound of the planes faded. It suddenly occurred to me: there was gasoline in Zeng Guofan's ancestral temple and I yelled, "Everybody get out of the shelter." If a bomb had hit the gasoline, there would be a rain of fire and we would be trapped inside. Everybody climbed out and looked to the main temple building where the gas was stored. It had not been hit but many other buildings had been leveled.

Directly across from us the medical-aid station in the Yan family temple had been damaged heavily by bombs. My cousin Baomiao worked there as an aide. I saw her coming down from the wall with blood all over her face, crying "Baosun, Baosun where are you?" Only when she saw that I was unharmed, did she pause to bind up her own wounds.

Altogether fifteen bombs hit the school that day. The bomb craters were about twenty feet in diameter and five to ten feet deep. They filled up with water quickly. The lotus blossoms in the pond were like they had been cut off with a knife. There wasn't a trace of the fragrant cedar tree that had stood next to the entrance to the shelter. But thankfully the students and faculty were all safe. Before long, a student came to look in on us. When she saw the destruction, she almost keeled over. Later on, it was our good fortune that an ambulance from the Xiang Ya Hospital, personnel from the YMCA, and a vehicle sent by a former student came to our aid. They brought us to a small house we had bought for my mother and Yuenung's father to take refuge.

I immediately sent a telegram to Yuenung telling him the school was ruined but the personnel were safe. He hurried back from Nanning and we decided on a plan to merge with the Fuxiang girls' school and move to Yuanling. We got the agreement of Fuxiang's principal quickly, for which I was extremely grateful, and notified our students immediately. Twenty students left for Yuanling in the care of two teachers. Others could not leave Changsha because of family responsibilities. Then Yuenung, Ms. Xiao, Baomiao, and I took three school workers and set out for Nanning.

Chapter 26

Escape to Hong Kong

Not long after we arrived in Nanning, the Japanese occupied Wuhan and then invaded northern Hunan. Fearing that Changsha would soon be in enemy hands, officials torched the city. The fire raged from the night of November 12 until November 14. Over twenty thousand lives were lost and the loss of property was incalculable. But the Japanese did not attack. The Central Government held officials in the Changsha Garrison Command responsible for overreacting; some were even executed.

At the time, Yuenung had gone back to Hunan to get Zeng Guofan's papers and important family documents. Calculating the days it took him to travel, we figured he was in Changsha just when the fire took place. Yuenung's father, I, and other family members in Nanning were out of our minds with anxiety. Also, I had already agreed to attend another meeting of the World Christian Council in India and could not delay my departure much longer waiting for his return. While we were worrying and waiting for him to get back, the Japanese bombed Nanning. Many of our friends' houses were badly damaged. My brother Zhaohua urged us to get out of Nanning as soon as possible and go to Guangzhouwan, the French Concession on the coast of Guangdong Province south of Hong Kong. Since Guangzhouwan was on the way to Hong Kong where I was to join the Chinese delegation bound for the meeting of the World Christian Council, this seemed like a sound course of action. I set out from Nanning for Guangzhouwan in the company of other family members in an automobile and a small truck that Zhaohua had arranged for us. The trip was a nightmare. We narrowly escaped bandits at the border when we crossed into French territory. Two days after our safe arrival in Guangzhouwan, I took the steamer to Hong Kong where I stayed at the home of my aunt Mrs. Yu for three days and then joined up with the Chinese delegation bound for India.

This meeting of the World Christian Council was held at the Christian University at Madras in southern India, over Christmas 1938. The university is near Mount St. Thomas. Tradition has it that Thomas the Apostle traveled to India to spread the faith and that Christianity survived there over the centuries. Even before the modern mission movement, there were Christians in India. They had names such as Thomas, Peter, Martin, etc. Including myself, there were seven in our delegation. Because China was at war with Japan at the time, the delegates straggled into Hong Kong one at a time, making it difficult to prepare for the meeting. Even on board ship, there was little preparatory work accomplished.

When we arrived at our destination, Colombo, the principal port in Ceylon (Sri Lanka), we experienced some difficulties. Ceylon had recently gained independence from India. Our visas were for India, not Ceylon, so the local officials at first were unwilling to let us come ashore. Fortunately, a few members of the delegation were able to persuade the immigration authorities to let us enter. We stayed at the YMCA and the YWCA and the next day took a train across the island and a ferry to southern India.

There were more people at this meeting than at the earlier one in Jerusalem. In addition to the representatives of Protestant churches, there were clergy and faithful of the Greek Orthodox church. President Wu Yifang of Jinling University and several professors flew directly from Chongqing to India and joined our delegation. There was a plenary session daily. The remainder of the day was spent in small group discussions. I joined the group on culture and religion and sometimes met with the group devoted to women's issues.

From the Jerusalem and Madras meetings, two important objectives emerged. First, material civilization cannot be separated from religious morality. Second, previously in spreading the faith, we considered other religions to be our principal adversaries. Recently, materialism has clearly taken over that role. Dr. Mott, who chaired this meeting, as he had the one in Jerusalem, emphasized the theme that scientific knowledge without religion could neither cultivate the individual nor better society.

In addition to the meetings of the Council, we had some other activities. Traveling about, I was able to observe some of India's social problems: The different ethnic groups in India have entirely different languages. Unlike the different spoken dialects in China, in India each is truly a different language with a different script. The caste system was another problem. There was virtually no interaction between people of different castes. The conflict between Hinduism and Islam often led to violence and bloodshed. Women were regarded as inferior and widows often mistreated. The villages were poverty stricken, backward, and filled with superstition and sickness. Finally, the gulf between the wealthy and the poor was enormous. The poverty was beyond anything Chinese can conceive of. Mr. Gandhi led the movement for independence and self-rule to try to address these problems and save India from what promised to be a dismal fate. He acted with great strength, suffering imprisonment and fasting in an effort to inspire the Indian people. I feel great admiration for him.

Dr. Mott proposed that, following the meeting, Mr. Zheng Shaohuai and I go to England to preach on the matters discussed at the meeting. Mr. Yu, the head of our previous delegation to Jerusalem who had gone with me to England in 1928, was not with us this time. He had suffered a stroke while in the United States meeting with Secretary of State Henry Stimson about China's War of Resistance against Japan. After he returned to China, saddened by the plight of the nation and the lot of the Chinese people, his condition worsened and he passed away, truly a great loss to the church and to China.

In England seven representatives from around the world: Africa, India, Southeast Asia, and China, including myself and Mr. Zheng Shaohuai, received a blessing and ordination from the Archbishop of Canterbury in a brief but inspirational ceremony at St. Paul's Cathedral. In his remarks the Archbishop made reference to the church's special responsibilities in Africa and Asia. He later entertained the delegates at tea.

On one occasion while in England, I was a guest at the Soviet Embassy. Among the other guests was Mr. H.G. Wells, the futurist and science-fiction writer. He predicted victory for China in the struggle against Japan. As I talked with him, I realized that he had a very Confucian outlook on life. The Soviet ambassador spoke to the guests at dinner and told us that the utensils and dishes on the table were all made of gold. They represented what the Czars had taken from the labor of the Russian people. I asked him why they didn't place them in a museum where the Russian people could enjoy them or perhaps liquidate them for something that could ease the suffering of the people. He said that they were used to display Russia's artistic heritage to the world. This was clearly a lot of empty talk.

I spoke in many places in England, from north to south, in London, and in Ireland. Most of the time I traveled with other delegates, but I went by myself to the home of Ms. Mary Vaughan's older brother, Edward. He was an instructor at Eton, a prestigious school for the English aristocracy and the sons of foreign royalty. Eton has produced many men of great ability: politicians, scientists, writers, clergymen, and military men. Most famous was the eighteenth-century lexicographer and literary critic Samuel Johnson who was an instructor at Eton. In the library there is a great desk that was his. When famous people are invited to speak there, they stand on that desk while speaking. Those who attend these lectures are the top one hundred students in the highest class, known as the "First Hundred." I had the good fortune to be the first Asian Woman to stand on that desk and speak. My topic was "China's Inevitable Triumph over Japan."

Chapter 27

Japanese Occupied Hong Kong

In early August 1939, my speaking engagements in England completed, I took the P and O Steamship from Britain back to Hong Kong. When I arrived there, I found that Yuenung had brought his father and they were reunited with our aunt Mrs. Yu. My cousin Ms. Xiao, and my cousins Mr. and Mrs. Yu Dawang were also in Hong Kong. Ms. Xiao and I stayed at the home of my cousin, Mr. Nie Guangkun, and took our meals with my aunt, Mrs. Yu. It was a good time with Yuenung and my aunt, and her family. For refugees, unexpectedly, to have a family reunion is a great joy in an unhappy world.

The household of my aunt Mrs.Yu included my cousin, Dawang, and his wife and daughter and my cousin Dawei's wife. Before long, Dawei's wife left for Chongqing, China's wartime capital, to join her husband. I began to feel that it was not right to impose on my relatives for so long, so I rented a small house at number eight Dapu Street in Kowloon and moved in, in September. By this time war had broken out in Europe. Business in Hong Kong was disrupted for a while, but it seemed to recover quickly. Our day to day existence, however, was very difficult. Yuenung had a courtesy appointment as a professor in Hunan University, without pay. He also expedited the import of instruments for the university and taught in a family school to help provide for our needs.

I developed a heart irregularity. Though it was not serious, I had to restrict my physical activity. Sometimes I would be up all night unable to sleep. I was unable to look for employment but fortunately, I had an inheritance from Ms. Barnes, which kept us in necessities. My failing health also prevented me from going to Chongqing to take a seat that had been offered to me in the National Political Council. I stayed there in Hong Kong awaiting whatever fate might have in store for me, worrying about China and wondering when victory over Japan would come. In the winter of 1939, my aunt and her family left for Haiphong, then still under French colonial control.

In the winter of 1940, Yuenung's father suffered a serious heart attack and was admitted to Ma Li Hospital in Hong Kong where he remained for three weeks. While visiting him at the hospital, Yuenung met General Zhang Lingfu, who later helped us greatly in Hunan. The doctor told Yuenung's father that he simply needed rest and did not have to remain in the hospital. Privately, however, the doctor told us that the old man had only a half year to live. We concealed our grief and took him home. He had angina and could hardly eat. Sometimes he couldn't even take liquids for an entire day. Finally, at noon on the twenty-ninth day of the third lunar month, he smiled at us and passed away. In that crazy world, it had to be considered release. I made a pair of memorial scrolls to commemorate him. I tried to express his feelings and my own:

> In youth he extended a great line;
> In adulthood, he held to the family teachings;
> His mourning sash, we gave to the sea;
> To spare his loved ones;
> In old age, his heart ached;
> It could split mountains and part rivers;
> The pain, in the end, took his life;
> Having lost the glory of his home;
> And seen his orchards burned;
> He came here to the south to live out his mortal life;
> And here, were even more warnings of danger;
> Today as we watch him wandering aimlessly,
> Straw sandals and a staff;
> The bamboo grove overflows with sorrow.

After he passed away, I felt more disconsolate with each passing day. Happily a few friends from Guangdong and Kunming visited and raised my spirits. My aunt and my cousin Dawei and his wife also came to Hong Kong and we frequently got together. But we didn't let my aunt know that Yuenung's father had died.

In November 1941, Hong Kong suddenly became very tense. Patrols of Chinese and British policemen were doubled. Leaves for military personnel were canceled and rumors were rampant. Since we didn't understand Cantonese, we were unable to get very much of what was being said. Then in early December the atmosphere seemed to relax noticeably. We heard that a Japanese special envoy, Saburo Kurusu, had gone to the United States to personally negotiate a peaceful solution. Everyone felt relieved. We had no inkling of what was about to happen.

On the morning of December 8, 1941, as I was washing my face, there was a sudden loud report of artillery followed by a long sounding alarm. At first I thought it was a drill but as I listened, I realized it was the real thing. We were actually being bombed. In the streets, the people and vehicles created a deafening din. There were seven air-raid alarms that day. People were at their wits' end. That night there was a blackout and the next day many businesses were closed. All night long the sound of looters, banging on doors, and shattering windows was terrifying. The next morning British troops had already withdrawn from the border with China and hoodlums were running wild in the market area of Kowloon.

That evening we put a big trunk against the inside of our door and sat silently in the dark, hoping no one would bother us. After a while, a knock at the door broke the silence and someone demanded, "Pay your protection fee." We were too frightened to open the door but prayed with all our hearts for God's protection. Just at that moment, when we were overcome with anxiety, someone on the fourth floor of our building fired a shot and the people outside our door fled.

We were no sooner through that crisis when a group of seventy or eighty people with electric torches suddenly appeared across the street headed toward our house. We thought, this time there's no hope. We might as well accept our fate. But the hand of God intervened once again to save us. Just as they were crossing the street toward our place, the last contingent of withdrawing British soldiers marched by. They saw this gang cutting across the street and probably thought they intended to harass British troops. The British fired a volley of shots and the gang scattered and fled. These two events were, in a sense, miraculous. God had answered our prayers.

The next morning, when daylight arrived, we could see Japanese troops streaming into the city. But each contingent was small, ten to twenty men marching slowly, carrying their weapons at port arms. That afternoon the Japanese arrested many of the looters. We were horrified when we saw Japanese soldiers had forced about forty or fifty of them to kneel on the street corner across from us and were preparing to execute them. Our neighbor, Dr. Li Tianyou, had studied in Japan and spoke Japanese. He came forward and pleaded for their lives. Finally, the soldiers let them go.

On December 18, 1941, the Japanese announced that the imperial army was going to invade Hong Kong Island, where all British forces were concentrated, despite British opposition. They warned the civilian population not to come out of their homes after dark and not to go into the business district during the day unless they had urgent business. That night we heard the rumble of tanks, the sound of troops marching and the clatter of horses' hooves on the pavement of Dapu Street. The troops came as far as our house and then stopped. Then we heard a Japanese officer give a command in a soft voice as though it were some sort of a signal. It was repeated and passed on through the ranks down the length of the street. Then they left as quickly as they had come.

These were terrible times. Running water was cut off, and we had nothing to drink. Our rice was used up and we had no way of getting more. Yuenung had a friend, whom hoodlums were threatening with extortion. To elude them, he moved in with us and, to our good fortune, brought some rice with him. So we had something to eat for a few days. On December 23 and 24, there was artillery fire all day. That night British soldiers set fire to the Asia Petroleum oil storage facilities. The sky was filled with flames and black smoke. The artillery fire was incessant. We surmised that the Japanese army had already gone ashore on Hong Kong Island.

Japan had struck almost simultaneously at Pearl Harbor, Singapore, and Hong Kong and declared war on the United States and Great Britain. We were, at once, relieved because we believed this would hasten the withdrawal of Japan's forces from China, and at the same time, we were frightened because we Chinese in Hong Kong and Kowloon were people without a country. We wondered what kind of ill treatment might be in store for us.

Once, when we learned that all of my aunt's family were leaving Hong Kong, Yuenung and I went to see them off. At the time there were no streetcars running, so we walked to their place. After we said our goodbyes, my aunt gave us some rice they had left over, Yuenung put it on his shoulder and we started for home. Worse luck! We came upon some Japanese soldiers firing their weapons and arresting people. It was almost like street warfare. Pedestrians were terrified and dashed frantically for cover. We took cover wherever we could and, with great difficulty, made our way by a roundabout route to our residence. The person who lived on the first floor who let residents in the front gate was too frightened to come out and open the gate for us. Finally our neighbor, Dr. Li Tianyou, let us into his house to get away from all this. Later we returned home, still terrified. This was the first time that I saw an enemy firing at our people. It was also the first time I really feared for my life.

The time we had the greatest luck—actually it was God's goodness—was when we were searched by the Japanese. The occupation government put out an order, early on, that on a certain day they would search civilian residences for munitions or other illegal items. When they came to the home to be searched, they would first have all the people go outdoors and stay on the curb with a Japanese soldier watching them. Then, they would let one person from the family return to the house with the key and escort the Japanese officer as he searched. Naturally, the Japanese soldiers could take anything that they pleased. If they discovered a handgun or something of that sort, it would definitely be confiscated and the owner's life could be in jeopardy. The day we were searched, as luck would have it, the man who was living with us had an appointment with a Japanese officer to show a camera he wanted to sell. He set out two trays of pastries for the officer. Just as he was showing the camera, the Japanese military police came to search our home. When they came into the parlor and saw a high ranking Japanese officer having tea and pastries, they probably thought we were his friends. They never opened our trunks, just took a quick look around and wrote "Inspection

Complete" with chalk on the door. We narrowly avoided a great disaster. If they had found Zeng Guofan's papers that we had stored in those trunks, they would certainly have taken them. They would have realized who Yuenung and I were and forced us to "broadcast for the Imperial Army." This was surely God's special protection, was it not?

Another time, Yuenung was stopped and searched by a gang of street thugs. Thank God, he was able to get away but many who were stopped and searched this way were not so lucky. They were locked in empty rooms and left to starve to death.

Still another time we received God's protection in Hong Kong. When we first arrived, we bought some U.S. dollars and a few pieces of gold jewelry. Fearing that our home might not be safe, we decided to rent a safe deposit box to store them. As it turned out, the safe deposit boxes in all the major banks were rented; so we rented one in the small Wingon Bank. This was God in heaven directing us. On May 1, 1942, the Japanese Army headquarters ordered all safe deposit boxes opened. They started first with the biggest bank in Hong Kong, the Hong Kong and Shanghai Banking Corporation. We heard that the Japanese took all the valuables from the boxes. One of our friends lost hundreds of U.S. dollars. Other losses suffered by close friends were incalculable. The Japanese simply took things and said, "We'll put them in safekeeping for you" and gave the owner a receipt that made no mention of the number of items confiscated or their worth. It even said on the receipt that the owner was "contributing this to the Imperial Japanese Army." Because our box was in a small bank, it was among the last opened. These Japanese jackals had had their fill by then and were not too attentive. Yuenung managed to slip the U.S. dollars and the jewelry into a cloth bag before the inspection began. Incredibly the inspector just glanced at the contents and released the box. Wasn't this the hand of God?

In July and August 1942, Hong Kong was running out of food. Japanese authorities began rationing rice: six ounces, per person, per day of unbearably coarse, dirty, bug infested rice. People were dying of starvation. The corpses lying in the streets were more than one could bear to see. When the food supply got to this point, the Japanese decided to allow people to return to their homes in China. We used to sit upstairs in our house on Dapu Street every day and watch the long lines of refugees returning with their children. They seemed unaware or they didn't care how hard things might be in their new homes.

Yuenung and I were afraid to apply to the Japanese authorities for permission to leave. We knew that, if they found out who we were, they would force us to make propaganda broadcasts. In early August, however, we decided to apply for an exit permit under assumed names: Yuenung as Zeng Zhong and I as Zeng Ping. Friends who went with us, whose names were not so well known, did not need to resort to this trickery. We received our exit permit toward the end of August, packed hurriedly, and gave our furniture and other non-essential items to the landlord.

On August 30, we took the ferry from Kowloon to Hong Kong and, the next day, boarded the Japanese steamer, *Shirogane Maru*, bound for Guangzhouwan then under control of the Vichy government of France. Mr. Yu Liutie, who had been living with us, and his friend Mr. Liao Chuanya from Sichuan helped us to get Zeng Guofan's papers past the Japanese authorities. Mr. Liao offered to precede us and take Zeng Guofan's papers—letters, instructions to the family and the handwritten diary—past the Japanese authorities. He vowed, "not a single sheet of paper will be lost." Somehow, he managed it. If it were not for the remarkable Mr. Liao, we never would have gotten out of Kowloon and certainly couldn't have brought back Zeng Guofan's papers. I am deeply thankful for what he did.

When we boarded the ship, Mr. Yu came to see us off. A friend of his helped us get through customs. As Yuenung was about to board, he was carrying a document case in one hand and a medicine case in the other, both prohibited items. Just as the emigration officer was about to confiscate them, a Japanese friend of Mr. Yu appeared and escorted Yuenung directly up the gangway, by passing the inspecting officer. It was an unbelievable stroke of good fortune. Looking back on that incident, it is clear that we had God's help at every turn, otherwise we surely would have perished. We borrowed money from friends to make this trip. There was never anything in writing, just total reliance and good faith. If it were not for these friends, we could never have gotten out of Hong Kong. They have my deepest gratitude.

After the *Shirogane Maru* weighed anchor, Yuenung took our baggage claim checks to be inspected by a Japanese officer. When he came back, he discovered one was missing. At the same time another passenger also found he was missing a claim check after having it inspected. He went back to the Japanese officer and politely asked if he had it. With no warning the Japanese flew into a rage, striking and kicking this man. When he did, the claim checks he had been holding in his hand fell to the floor. One landed right in front of Yuenung's feet. He looked down and miraculously, it was ours. He picked it up quickly and disappeared. This kind of thing made me realize the hopelessness of a person without a country but I also knew the goodness of God and felt great gratitude.

En route to Guangzhouwan, we stopped at Macao. Unfortunately, several people traveling with us, including my cousin Ms. Xiao, came down with a severe fever. One in our party, a man who had previously worked at Yifang, finally died in Guangzhouwan. Yuenung and several others did not contract the fever but he was really hard pressed to look after those of us who did and at the same time, arrange the burial of the deceased worker. He laid him to rest with great care in Guangzhouwan and arranged for a memorial stone.

My brother Zhaohua sent us money for our return to Hunan but we spent it all while we were recovering from the fever. Fortunately, a friend was able to get some money for us and make rail reservations. When we got to Liaozhou in central Guangxi, we were met by Zeng Fu and Zeng Yuyang of the Zeng clan and they treated us wonderfully. Finally, we boarded the Guangxi-Hunan Railroad for what we hoped would be a peaceful trip to Hengyang in our home province of Hunan.

Chapter 28

With the Guerillas in Hunan

We had some frightening experiences on the Guangxi-Hunan railroad en route to Hengyang. One incident occurred when the train was approaching Guilin in Guangxi Province. The air-raid alarm suddenly sounded; the train stopped and we were ordered to get off immediately and take cover. We were allowed to take only one small piece of hand baggage with us. Thankfully, in about an hour, the Japanese planes left and everyone returned to the train, only to find that all the luggage we left had disappeared.

When we got to Hengyang, we went straight to an inn to rest. Unknown to us, our return had been announced in the local papers; members of the YMCA staff appeared at our inn and asked us to speak on conditions in Hong Kong under Japanese occupation. Old school friends from Yifang also arrived and welcomed us most warmly. They took care of our rooms and meals, even our tips. We were overwhelmed by their hospitality.

The father of one of our students, a banker, was especially helpful. He cautioned us about going on to Xiangxiang, saying: "In these troubled times, traveling through the countryside, you can't be too careful. If you engage five sedan chairs and twenty odd porters and travel in a great caravan, it's very likely that bandits might accost you. Worse yet, if one of the porters is crooked, he might later lead bandits to your home. To be on the safe side, let me send a reliable person from my bank with a letter to your home and your family can send people to bring you back." We did as he suggested. I wrote a letter home to my brother Zhaohang. He sent thirty-two of our tenants to Hengyang to fetch us. Zhaohang thought of everything. He not only had sedan chair-bearers, he even had meat and vegetable dishes prepared for us to eat along the way. It turned out that the food was very much needed. Armies had moved up and down that road from Hengyang to Xiangxiang many times and plundered the villages of almost everything. If you were lucky you could buy a little rice, but there were no vegetables; even salt was in short supply. Thanks to Zhaohang's forethought, we were able to eat while on our way home. We were safe from harm as well. The commanding officer of the Hengyang Garrison Command insisted on sending an escort of eight riflemen and an officer with us in case we encountered bandits.

We set out for Xiangxiang on October 25. Slowed by rainy weather and chair-bearers and porters unaccustomed to their tasks, it was near nightfall on the third day when we arrived at Prosperity Hall. As we drew near, everyone in the family, young and old, came out to greet us. Great salvos of firecrackers announced our arrival. The officer and soldiers who had guarded us and the tenants who had served as porters were rewarded generously for delivering us safely. We felt as though we had come back from the dead, which in a sense we had. In the family in addition to Zhaohang and his wife, his son Xiping and his daughter Rongrong, there were my uncle Guangluan's concubine, Zhou Gongren, and my cousins Baosu, Baoshi, and Baomiao and their children. Though there were few of us, we were very close. The joy of being together again after a long separation was a deeply moving experience. Mr. Yuan, who still lived with his family in Zeng Guofan's former study on the little hill nearby, also came to greet us, as did Zhu Zhusheng, a neighbor boy, who is with us now in Taiwan.

On the next day Yuenung, Ms. Xiao, and I looked around Prosperity Hall. For Yuenung and Ms. Xiao, everything was unfamiliar. For me, this was the place where I had grown up, where I had played and gone to school. I wandered again through familiar places and was nearly overcome by emotion. The gardens were overgrown now and the pavilions in need of repair, their colorful paint peeling and chipped. This was not the picture I had held in my memory over the years. Then I thought of my grandmother, my mother, and myself here, together. Our home was still here but they were gone. Time changes everything; I felt so confused. I wondered for what purpose God had given me life. Life is so short and the things we must do so difficult and so numerous. One lifetime is not enough. I regretted that I had left all this and gone away. My hope was in God's mercy and the power of prayer.

We lived at Prosperity Hall in Xiangxiang for nearly five years. Though much transpired during that time, here I will recount only a few of the most memorable events. The year after we returned home, my cousin Zhaoquan brought his family to live in Xiangxiang. His mother, Uncle Jirong's widow, was paralyzed from a stroke but other members of the household helped her get around. Zhaoquan had three sons and two daughters. The two older sons were away at school. The youngest and the two daughters were at home with the family. Since I had plenty of leisure, I organized an English class for these children. Included were my nieces and nephews, my cousins' children, several neighbor children, and Ms. Wang, who looked after our libraries. They were of different ages and abilities, Ms. Wang being the oldest. Although we used the lower-middle school English text, I followed my own teaching method. I first taught phonetics and then used simple words to ask questions for them to answer, or to make sentences and translate. Their progress was fine, much faster than ordinary lower middle-school students.

When we arrived in Xiangxiang, we asked two workers to find out everything they could about the movements of guerilla forces in the vicinity. If they were within our borders—the lower part of the Hetang District—we would send some men with foodstuffs and wine to let them know we supported them. Some of the guerillas, however, were poorly disciplined; their activities disrupted the lives of the local people. We could understand the guerillas' point of view. As soon as the locals saw them coming, they fled into the hills, taking with them their families, their animals, and everything they could carry. When the guerillas arrived and found an empty village, they would become frustrated, break in the doors and windows, and set fire to things. It was human nature that, if guerillas were made to feel unwanted, they would react violently but, if they were treated well, they would try to get along with the civilian population. Once at the Dragon Boat Festival, the fifth day of the fifth lunar month, we sent seven "sliced up half-hogs" for the guerillas to celebrate the festival.

Another time an officer named Zhao was determined to billet troops in Prosperity Hall. At the time, it was filled with women and children who had fled from Changsha and Hengyang before the approaching Japanese forces. We begged him not to billet his troops there, but he insisted. Then, we learned that Zhao was a subordinate of General Zhang Lingfu, Yuenung's friend from Hong Kong. We explained to Zhao that we knew his commanding officer well and asked for his special protection. He wired General Zhang who replied directing Zhao to extend every protection to us and, if the situation became dangerous, to escort us out of the area. So Prosperity Hall was spared and our relations with guerillas operating in that area became even better. Even the famous Thirty-second Division passed through our lands without breaking the peace.

In the spring of 1944, Commander Peng Weiren of the Fourth Commando asked Yuenung to go on a mission to Loudi. Shortly after he left, the fourth and fifth route guerilla armies decided to hold a meeting at Prosperity Hall to clear up some misunderstandings between the armies and to clarify the defense lines for each. So my brothers and I had to deal with the guerilla leaders without Yuenung's assistance. We set some rules and asked them all to abide by them. First, each commander could bring only five guards and one or two deputies. The guards were to live across the way in the Zhu family temple, or the Xiao family temple, but not in our residence. The deputies could stay with the senior officers in Prosperity Hall. Second, we would accommodate them for a maximum of five days. Third, before leaving they had to agree to send back our chair-bearers who bore them back to their units. Finally, in our home, my brothers and I would be responsible for security. There would be no guards inside the house.

At the end of March the leaders of the armies and their deputies and adjutants arrived one after another. Altogether they occupied seven rooms and it took three tables to seat them for meals. Although we had no gourmet seafood, there was ample meat and fish. On the third day, news arrived that Hengyang had fallen to the Japanese. The guerilla leaders cut their conference short and departed. It happened to be raining when they left and every sedan chair in the district was used to get them on their way.

The next night, to our complete surprise, Zhang Bicun, the commander at Xiangtan, arrived at Prosperity Hall. He was originally to attend the meeting with the others but by the time he arrived, they had all left. We had heard that he was the most powerful of the guerilla leaders, with more troops and more weapons than the others. When he arrived, he had more than one hundred men with him, a deputy, an adjutant and four cavalry scouts. He didn't want to stay in Prosperity Hall. Instead he billeted himself in the thatched hut near the graves opposite our place. We had the cook prepare food and wine and Zhaoquan and some others brought it to him along with enormous quantities of rice and vegetables for his men. The next day Commander Zhang came personally to pay his respects and led his troops in a salute. It was most impressive. At that time we had a twenty man armed self-defense force, under the command of one of the household staff. Zhang gave them a monetary award in pre-war currency; we reciprocated—giving his troops a similar award. At the time, this currency was not totally devalued and could provide something extra for the men. After the guerilla leaders left and Yuenung came back, I breathed a great sigh of relief.

On March 24, 1945, Zhaoquan's mother died. On the same day, Mrs. Shi, the mother of my cousins, Zhenlian and Zhenluo, passed away. We had the funeral for Zhaoquan's mother in our home and everything went smoothly. However, as soon as the funeral for Mrs. Shi was over, Zhenlian and his brother were accused of collaborating with the enemy. These accusations were lodged by a Mr. Wen and a Mr. Xiao, both of Xiangxiang. It seems that Wen and Xiao had a financial interest in a business in Hengyang operated by a Mr. Huang. Huang, who spoke Japanese, was married to a younger sister of Zhenlian. Huang took full control of the business forcing out Wen and Xiao. They retaliated by accusing Huang of being a spy for the Japanese and implicated Zhenlian and his brother for having dealings with the enemy.

Two deputies came from the Investigation Office in Hengyang to arrest them. Zhenlian heard about this on the night of April 15 and came to Prosperity Hall to ask us for advice. He was in a dilemma because the administrator of the Hetang District had received instructions from the Hengyang Investigations Office to be sent on to Zhenlian, summoning him to appear before the deputies when they arrived. But on the back of the letter, the District Administrator had written a confidential message "Don't come under any circumstances." So Zhenlian didn't know if he should go or not, and came to seek our counsel.

Yuenung told him that he must go to meet the deputies—otherwise it would appear that he was guilty. "Don't worry," Yuenung told him. "Go ahead. I'll have our defense force there to rescue you if need be. You just keep your self-confidence and deny emphatically that you have collaborated with the enemy."

The Hengyang Investigations Office sent only two armed guards with the deputies. Besides Zhenlian and Zhenluo, there were five others accused of collaborating, including the District Administrator of the neighboring Tongliang District and the principal of Zhonghua Middle School. I began to wonder what kind of an organization this Investigations Office was and on what grounds they arrested these people.

When the deputies arrived they were surrounded by hostile crowds. People of the Hetang and Tongliang Districts were taking the law into their own hands. The deputies aassessed the situation and decided they had better go along with what the locals wished. When the deputies saw our force of twenty armed men and they had only two, they decided to let Zhenlian and his brother go. The two of them came straight to Prosperity Hall to live.

We had come to know the commander of the Fourth Commando Unit, Wen Yingbing, so we gave him all the facts and asked him to clarify what really happened. We deeply appreciated his help; the investigation cleared Zhenlian and his brother of the stigma of collaboration and they returned to their own home on May 25.

The day they returned home, Japanese troops quite unexpectedly marched through the Hetang District. About seven in the morning, I was awakened by someone yelling, "The Japanese are coming. They're here. Take to the caves." We hastily ate a little breakfast. Then the whole family, young and old, except for Yuenung, set out on foot for my cousin's home, Wenji Hall, a little more than a mile behind Prosperity Hall. We had to climb a steep hill to get there. From the top of the hill, we saw what appeared to be a column of Japanese troops descending a hill opposite ours. We hastily took cover in the underbrush. It was stifling hot and the ants and mosquitoes were biting us—it was really miserable. Finally, two of the men went to find out what they could. An hour passed, maybe more, before they returned. They learned that the people we saw were not Japanese troops but Chinese, like ourselves, fleeing. We then dared to get up and get going again. Since the war against Japan began and we came home from Hong Kong, this was the first time I felt truly like a foot soldier. Though it was only two hours, it was miserable. That day, Yuenung remained at Prosperity Hall, dispensing surplus grain. This seemed to reassure everyone. That evening we also returned to Prosperity Hall.

On another occasion, Yuenung had to mediate a conflict among guerilla units. Three armies were operating where the borders of Hengshan, Xiangtan, and Xiangxiang met, struggling for control of this base area. Open fighting had broken out among them. The local people pleaded with the guerilla leaders not to let this turn into all-out warfare, with all the suffering that would bring. Finally, the parties to the dispute asked Yuenung to serve as a mediator at a meeting to be held in Xiangtan.

Yuenung took my younger brother Zhaoke and they went with the deputy commander of the commandos based in Xiangxiang. The three guerilla leaders talked face to face. Yuenung was there all day and well into the night. Even though darkness had fallen, he decided to come home that night. On the way, the chair-bearers dared not make a sound or speak a word for fear they would be mistaken for the enemy and be fired upon. Finally, when they reached the defense perimeter of the Fourth Commando Unit, they were able to speak and discuss what had happened that day.

Yuenung and Zhaoke had walked right into the lion's den. Surprisingly, they had been able to get these guerilla leaders—who were extremely jealous of each other's power—to cease their squabbling and agree to keep the peace. The sacrifices and suffering of the people would be a little less. It was an amazing accomplishment through God's protection and support. The guerilla leaders, in reality, didn't care much about China or the people, so someone had to step in to bring an end to their incessant bickering and unite their forces against the Japanese.

Four or five American advisers with the commando unit stationed nearby came to our home several times. They were surprised to find so many people who spoke English in a remote place like this. At the time, there were nine of us who had some proficiency. The Americans ate and drank with us and read some of the English books we had. They seemed to enjoy themselves and were reluctant to return to their camp. One big heavy officer got completely intoxicated and had to be taken back in a sedan chair. But he was so heavy that the poles on the sedan chair snapped. So he had to lean on two men all the way back to the camp, singing and hollering along the way. He attracted quite a bit of attention from the country folks.

Yuenung's birthday came in mid October 1945, only a month after the Japanese surrender. Because he had controlled the guerillas and helped his home districts during the war, the people of Hetang and Tongliang Districts decided to present him with tablets inscribed with expressions of gratitude. The Zeng clan also presented a tablet. Three to four hundred guests came, on foot and in sedan chairs, to the presentation. There was the sound of gongs and firecrackers, and a display of banners, parasols and official insignia in a procession along the road—all very exciting. One of the tablets said, "Remembering his ancestors, he caused compassion to prevail." Another said, "You who helped your district, receive our congratulations." I can't remember all the others. When the procession arrived at Prosperity Hall, there was a gathering and speeches. Everything was done according to protocol. Yuenung, as usual, was very humble. But if it were not for him, I hate to think what would have happened to these two districts during the war.

The Hengyang District was an example of how devastating the effects of the war were in Hunan. The capital of the Hengyang District was only about fifty miles from us. The Beichung mountains form the border between our district and Hengyang. On our side are the Hetang and Tongliang Districts. At the end of the war, land in these districts sold for one to two hundred yuan of the wartime currency for a sixth of an acre. On the other side in Hengyang, no one even inquired about buying land. The devastation by the military had been so severe that the land had not been cultivated for five or six years. Heavy underbrush and small trees covered the fields. The ridges between the paddies and the property boundaries were no longer visible. No one wanted such land.

Yuenung not only dealt with the guerillas, he saw to it that there were nurseries for the young, and that the community granaries were filled; he promoted education and settled disputes between the local people. Many places benefited from the things he did.

The general master of ceremonies for Yuenung's birthday was my brother Zhaohang. He directed all the personnel, attended to the guests, tipped our Self-Defense Force and the guests' chair-bearers and attendants. Everything was handled meticulously. There were more than three hundred tables including guests of honor and ordinary guests; there was no fighting, no disputes, and no one lost anything. It was a testimony to his rare talent for arranging this kind of event and a fitting tribute to Yuenung's tireless efforts on behalf of our people during the war years.

Part V

Exile in Taiwan

Chapter 29

The Third Rebirth of Yifang

I lived in my old home in Xiangxiang from the winter of 1942 until the spring of 1946. After the Japanese crossed into our district in May 1945, we sensed that they were exhausted and ready to end the fighting. But we had no idea that the end would come so quickly. I remember, it was August 10, 1945, when the local commando unit received a radio report saying, "Japan has surrendered unconditionally." We immediately sent three workers to nearby neighborhoods carrying signs on long poles saying, "Japan has unconditionally surrendered." They set off strings of small firecrackers to report the good news at the homes of our friends and relatives. Many of them welcomed the news with big blasts of firecrackers. My brothers set some off on the sandy road outside our gate and in the ridges in the paddies surrounding our home. The tenant farmers of the district shouted congratulations joyously.

The months passed and we resumed our peaceful country life. Then, in the spring of 1946, three of my former students came to Xiangxiang and urged Yuenung and me to return to Changsha and reopen Yifang. I told them, "We're too old now. Conditions are unsettled. There's nothing to be gained by us going there." But they persisted saying, "We don't want you to do anything, just provide direction. Besides, we've already got things started; we only want you to give it the prestige and credibility of your name." We couldn't disappoint such enthusiasm, so we agreed that as soon as new leadership for the district was determined, we would go to Changsha.

Efforts to reestablish Yifang were under way but they were slowed by the need to repair damage to the campus sustained during the war and by the lack of maintenance funds. The Chinese government had very generously demanded no reparations for damages caused by the Japanese invasion. As a result, there was no compensation for most of the losses suffered by the Chinese people. This was especially difficult for our school because, in addition to the bombings, looting, and arson by the Japanese, there was damage done by lawless Chinese, resulting in enormous losses, all uncompensated.

The perimeter wall of the campus had been demolished and an army of squatters had taken up residence. When Yuenung, Zhaohang, and I arrived in Changsha on May 24, 1946, a group of our former students had managed to reclaim the southern section but there were about ten families living in the northern, eastern, and western sections who were unwilling to move out. One of the alumnae joked that Yifang had three "too manys": too many doors, too many kitchens, and too many toilets. A group of alumnae continued to work together planning the restoration. They made remarkable progress and ultimately were able to regain control of the entire campus.

One alumna applied to the Changsha branch of the Emergency Relief Agency and got two tons of flour. Using flour as payment in kind, we were able to hire workmen and begin repairs. Rebuilding the wall was most essential. The campus had become a thoroughfare. Everyone coming and going from certain parts of the city took the shortcut through the campus. There were peddlers selling pastries, candy, dumplings, and fried bean curd. Our alumnae pleaded with them to help the school by moving elsewhere and even offered them a small payment if they would leave. Eventually, they succeeded in getting these small businesses and residences to move. Our former students' enthusiasm and perseverance was beyond belief. It was remarkable that so few women could persuade so many refugees to move, but the Yifang girls did it! The details and the names of the former students are recorded in the Yifang Fiftieth Anniversary Volume.

The main building in Zeng Guofan's memorial temple was severely damaged from the bombings. The eight huge stone pillars—it took two people to reach their arms around them—lay shattered on the ground where they had fallen. At a glance, the temple looked like a heap of rubble. I couldn't bear to look at it. On the east side of the temple, the Literary Office still served as the elementary school and on the west side, the Wang Fuzhi Temple Association still occupied the Lecture Hall. The classrooms, bedrooms, and the kitchen were just barely usable. Nevertheless, with the help of our alumnae, we began recruiting students for two classes in the lower middle-school and one in upper middle-school. Most of our faculty were Yifang alumnae who had gone on to higher education. In about six months everything was nearly complete. Some buildings had been repaired and some new ones had been erected. Students and faculty were getting on well and the students were making progress with their studies.

Yuenung was unable to play an active roll in all of this. In 1946, Mr. Wang Dongyuan, Chairman of the Hunan Provincial Government, asked him to take charge of the preparations for the opening of Keqiang College. The first thing he had to do was consolidate the schools of agriculture, engineering, and business. Preoccupied with these tasks, he was unable to teach at Yifang or to take up duties as dean, but he did continue in an advisory capacity and he continued to have a seat in all academic meetings or meetings of the Student-Faculty Association. We were glad to have his suggestions and help.

When we reopened this time, we recruited all new students, unlike our two previous reopenings when we had former students returning. This made it difficult to recapture the traditional atmosphere and the spirit of Yifang. During the war many of these students, especially those in the upper-middle school, fled on foot, as the Japanese forces advanced, to distant districts where they reestablished their schools. Though they were young, they had learned how to care for themselves and had an independence of spirit. When they arrived in Yifang they appeared very self-assured, unlike our old students who came to us like pieces of uncut jade to have their values and characters shaped at our school. Yuenung, the deans, the instructors, and I frequently talked about how to carry on instruction and manage student affairs. Our aim was that current students, like former ones, would be able to get along harmoniously in groups but retain their independence of spirit, follow the school regulations but show initiative and make reasoned proposals, cultivate a love for learning but not be bookworms, appreciate traditional Chinese culture but maintain a scientific outlook, and believe in Jesus but adhere to the teachings of Confucius and Mencius. These were very ambitious goals but we were determined to pursue them.

Chapter 30

The Fall of Changsha

From the reopening of Yifang through 1947, a great deal of reconstruction took place and things seemed to be going quite well. Teachers and students were working together and there was an atmosphere conducive to learning. In 1948, however, things began to change at the national level. Liaoyang Province fell to the communists. Though the Sino Soviet Mutual Non-Aggression Pact was renewed, in actuality, it was nothing more than a concession to the Soviet Communists' intent to infiltrate China. Patriotic Chinese could not help but be concerned by the general trend of events. The Chinese people, however, still felt their rights could be protected and communism could be eradicated.

In this hopeful spirit, the first session of the National Assembly was scheduled for the end of February 1948 in Nanjing. When Mr. Zhang Mochun of our district announced that he would run for a seat in the legislature and would not stand for election to the National Assembly, some citizens of the Xiangxiang District spoke to me, several times, urging me to stand for election. I had never entertained political ambitions, feeling that my talents lay in other directions, nor had I been active politically. I told them, however, if the elders of the Xiangxiang District and my contemporaries selected me, I could not refuse and I would do my best to be effective; but I did refuse to make political speeches or take part in fund-raising.

Friends and relatives of the Zeng clan helped my campaign greatly. From the time of Zeng Guofan and Zeng Guoquan up to the present, the Zeng family had contributed generously to the support of local public welfare institutions, such as grain storage, regulation of the supply and price of grain, care of the aged, infant and child care, bridge repair, and road building. Family members, on their own, had even established public welfare institutions in Hetang and Tongliang. So the Zeng family was greatly respected. In good times, relations were warm and friendly and in emergencies, there was mutual help. Landlord-tenant relations were especially trouble free. Largely because of this kind of public support, I was elected as the representative from the Xiangxiang District to the National Assembly. I didn't spend a penny chasing people's votes. My success was entirely due to the support I received from the elders and my contemporaries in Xiangxiang. After the election was over, I had a party in Changsha to express my thanks to those who supported me.

When the students heard that I had been elected as a representative to the National Assembly, they were jubilant. When it came time for me to leave for the capital at Nanjing, to attend the meeting of the National Assembly, they had an orchestra at the station to see me off. The instructional staff were there also waving their hats and handkerchiefs shouting happily right along with the students. Yuenung, my brother Zhaohua, and Zhu Zhusheng accompanied me.

We arrived in Nanjing on March 10, 1948 aboard a small Yangzi steamer from Hankou. To my surprise, my cousin, Yu Dawei, and a friend were there to meet us. The captain and the ship's personnel seemed to delight in straightening up the ship's parlor and setting out trays of pastries and soft drinks for us, no doubt, because Dawei was the Minister of Transportation in the National Government—the senior agency controlling ship operations. We were overwhelmed.

When we disembarked, we went to the home of my cousin, Zhaoshu, to stay. Though it was less than a month since the birth of their second daughter and the family was still adjusting to the new arrival, they prepared very comfortable accommodations for Yuenung and me in their home. Zhaoshu even lent us his automobile to get around town. Their hospitality was superb and we were most grateful. The greatest inconvenience was that important materials were frequently sent to me in the middle of the night. The knocking at the gate and on the door would wake up the entire family. I was embarrassed by this but there was nothing I could do.

Not long after the preparatory meeting of the Assembly, there was the election of the steering committee. In order to ensure female representation on the committee, there was a proposal to guarantee ten percent of the eighty-one seats for women. I opposed this. I felt that women should be elected in a fair and open election with men, or not at all. Furthermore, women who received fewer votes than male candidates but were placed on the committee because of the ten percent quota for women would feel they had to defer to the male candidates who had received more votes than they. My position was adopted by the assembly. As it turned out, there were only three women elected: Shen Huilian, Zhang Xiwen, and me but we were entirely independent, beholden to no one for our positions. I have to thank my friends, Ms. Yuan Chanying and Ms. Xiao Yunchen, for rounding up votes for me and, of course, those who actually cast the votes.

On April 18, the Assembly passed temporary provisions to the constitution granting the president emergency powers. The next day, Chiang Kaishek was elected the first president of the Republic of China under the new constitution with a total of 2,430 votes. There were three candidates for the vice presidency: Li Zongren, Sun Ke, and Cheng Qian. For some unknown reason, they all withdrew. I was named to a five-person delegation, none of whom were members of the majority Nationalist Party, to persuade them to reenter the race. Eventually they all consented and on April 29, Li Zongren was elected vice president, receiving 1,438 votes.

While the assembly was in session, there was an endless round of banquets, cocktail parties, and teas. Visiting with Cheng Qian, I discovered he was a person of overweening ambition and his beautiful, young wife held some very extreme views. I had serious doubts about him as vice president. Li Zongren and Sun Ke were bitter enemies but Li had the backing of the northern academic community. Sun's newspaper, the *National Salvation Daily*, was attacked. Though I have no idea who was responsible, Li's followers were suspect and the press corps, angered by the attack, turned against Li. This, no doubt, served to reduce his vote total.

The Assembly met day and night. The steering committee had to check the next day's agenda each night and it was often after midnight before I returned home. Consequently, I was unable to visit many of my relatives and friends in Nanjing but I did find time to visit my aunt, Mrs. Yu, on her birthday. I saw some friends and relatives there for the first time since the war. We exchanged fascinating stories of our wartime experiences.

Yifang alumnae, among them my cousin Ms. Zeng Zhaoyu, the distinguished archaeologist and director of the National Museum, invited Yuenung and me to go to Mount Zijin and Mochou Lake. Even though a light sleet was falling that day, we went first to the Sun Yatsen Mausoleum and the tomb of Tan Zitong, martyred hero of the failed 1898 reform movement, and then for a boat ride on Mochou Lake. By then, rain was coming down harder but we were in high spirits— picking lotus leaves, and eating cherries and enjoying each other's company. We had such a good time that we stayed a long time.

After participating in the inauguration of General Chiang Kaishek as President of the Republic of China, Yuenung, Zhaohua, and I traveled to Shanghai to see my cousin Baohan, an orthopedist at the Fenglin Bridge Orthopedics Hospital. She had successfully treated spinal injuries and cured tuberculosis of the hand without amputation. We were very close when we were young, sharing a determination to do something to help people and benefit society. She would often say, "You will heal people's hearts and I their bodies." Yuenung, Zhaohua, and I stayed and visited with her in Shanghai for a while and then returned to Hunan. We didn't know at this parting that it would be many years until our next meeting.

When we arrived back in Hunan, it was nearly the time for summer vacation. The campus at Yifang was refurbished and spruced up in preparation for the thirtieth-anniversary celebration set for September 1, 1948. The day arrived, cool and crisp, and the entire garden was ablaze with chrysanthemums. Even the small hill was layer upon layer of various colored chrysanthemums. The water in the pond was a shimmering jade green. These were truly ideal surroundings in which to pursue one's studies.

A great many people, including friends and relatives of students, attended the thirtieth-anniversary celebration. Remarkably, six of the eight students in the first entering class returned. I was moved by their loyalty and affection for Yifang considering that thirty years had passed since they entered school. The meetings, speeches, music, and parties all went as scheduled. Cheng Qian, Chairman of the Provincial Government, delivered a moving address berating the communists for bringing devastation to China, death to its people, and delivering the nation into the hands of a foreign power. He made an impassioned plea for the people to unite and rid their homeland of communism. As we listened, we never dreamed that, in less than a year, Hunan would be ruled by them.

In the spring of 1949, students in Changsha were caught up in the turmoil caused by the advance of the communist armies into the Yangzi Valley. It was much as it had been in 1927, but there were several important differences. There were two cases of arson at schools that were clearly the work of student agitators. After that, there were other instances of thievery, arson, and even homicide at several schools. There were also some mysterious disappearances. A student leader from Mingde Middle School vanished after participating in a street demonstration. Rumors immediately began circulating that he had been seized by the government and killed. He was later apprehended in Xiangtan and admitted that he had been talked into disappearing to create an incident that would put the local authorities in a difficult position. Of course, he didn't know the identity of the person who had put him up to this.

Another difference with 1927 was the "anti-hunger" movement. Students demanded that the government distribute foodstuffs to them as it had during the war against Japan. This was a totally unreasonable request: the students were not displaced persons as they had been during the war with Japan. They were living at home and could eat with their families. The students were encouraged by communist agitators who were spreading propaganda everywhere. When they heard that a student in Wuhan University had been wounded by a stray bullet, they stepped up their activities and began daily street rallies. A young man from the YMCA was one of the worst. He specialized in sowing dissension between students and faculty. His approach was to appear at a school and request to speak to the student body about youth problems, without the faculty present. Then he would launch into an attack on the faculty. He twice requested to speak at Yifang. I told him he could but we would not bar faculty from attending and he would have to speak in an open auditorium—no private meetings with students. The excellent rapport between our faculty and students was unaffected by this troublemaker.

In most schools, when students went out to demonstrate they didn't request leave or even inform the school authorities about their off-campus activities. Our students not only told us when they left campus, they talked with us about what they intended to do. Unlike other students in Changsha, they kept an atmosphere of cooperation and trust with the school authorities from beginning to end, but conditions were deteriorating rapidly and I could envision more trouble.

There were two major psychological blunders at the time Changsha fell to the communists: the peace talks and President Chiang's leaving office. Both caused a feeling of uncertainty among the people. Foolhardy opportunists who were unwilling to surrender to the communists but felt they would probably gain power through the peace talks, thought up a way of dealing with the situation. They heard that the communists would be lenient with working people. So people started turning their homes into workshops making all kinds of things: stockings, gloves, soap etc. One of the leaders of the YMCA opened a barbershop and a friend of mine began learning carpentry. They didn't realize that the communists did not really support the peace talks and Vice President Li Zongren, who took over the presidency after Chiang Kaishek resigned, did not really have the best interests of the country at heart. When the communists detained our negotiators and issued a list of twenty-four completely unreasonable demands, the talks collapsed and the government moved to Guangzhou. This was the moment of imminent danger for China. Changsha fell instantly.

I had previously accepted an invitation to attend the World Peace Conference being convened in India by Mohandas Gandhi. Since the government had moved to Guangzhou, I had to go there for my passport. On June 30, 1949, after the Middle School graduation, I left Changsha for Guangzhou. Yuenung remained in Changsha but the responsibility for the school was entrusted temporarily to a group of five faculty members. My cousin, Zhaoshu, accompanied me to the airport. As I looked at the friends and relatives assembled there to bid me farewell, a feeling of gloom fell over me.

Chapter 31

The Pavilion of Everlasting Farewell

I stayed in Guangzhou only long enough to make the necessary arrangements to leave China. Then my brother Zhaohua and I went to Hong Kong. At that time, people were flooding into Hong Kong from the interior of China. Landlords were raising rents up to one hundredfold and demanding a transfer fee and a deposit or prepayment of three months rent. Our brother, Zhaoke, had a tiny place in Qingshan Road. He had paid six thousand Hong Kong dollars transfer fee and was paying two hundred Hong Kong dollars per month rent. The prices were frightening. We had no choice but to stay with him for a while and try to figure out what to do.

After a little more than a month had passed, I began to feel quite concerned about Yuenung and my cousin, Ms. Xiao. The situation in China was changing rapidly as the communist armies crossed the Yangzi and advanced southward. One day while I was worrying, I saw a taxi pull up to the curb in front of our place. The driver unloaded a yellow oil-cloth suitcase of the kind made in Changsha. I wondered who could be arriving from Hunan. I never dreamed that the person about to step from the cab would be Yuenung. I was overcome with joy to see him. Originally, he had been reluctant to leave the school even though I urged him to do so time and again. At last he was here and I was greatly relieved.

After he arrived, we sent someone to Changsha to fetch Ms. Xiao. Mr. Zhu Zhusheng from Xiangxiang came out with her. Yuenung went to Guangzhou to meet them. He had written to old Mr. He Yunchang in charge of the library at Prosperity Hall telling him to give Zeng Guofan's papers to Ms. Xiao so she could bring them to us in Hong Kong. As luck would have it, there was a flood in the area between Changsha and Xiangtan, so she could bring only a portion of the papers and draft memorials. We were elated by our reunion in Hong Kong but the death of my aunt, Mrs. Yu, soon after we arrived, saddened us. Fortunately we had been able to get together and talk with her and my cousins, Dawei and Dawang, several times before she passed away.

I had come to Hong Kong as the first step on my journey to India to attend the World Peace Conference announced in 1948 by the Indian holy man, Mohandas Gandhi. Tragically, Gandhi was assassinated in that year before the conference was convened. Nevertheless, his disciple, Mr. Nehru, honored Gandhi's wish posthumously and convened this conference as scheduled in 1949. Both Yuenung and I attended. We left for India in mid November 1949 and spent three months there.

The meeting was held near Calcutta, at Tagore's birthplace and the site of the international college that he founded. There were more than thirty representatives from Britain, the United States, France, Holland, Denmark, Sweden, Burma, Iran, China, Japan, and India. Mr. Nehru attended the opening ceremonies. Since he was an advocate of nonviolence, he had no bodyguards. He ate lunch with us and washed his own dishes and utensils. I later appeared with him as a speaker at a public gathering where an audience of twenty to thirty thousand listened in rapt attention.

I also met his daughter, Mrs. Indira Gandhi, when we visited President Prasad in New Delhi. Since Nehru's wife had died when Indira Gandhi was a small child, she had grown up at her father's side and was wise in the ways of government. She was beautiful, articulate, and charming. When Nehru's successor, Shastri, died in office, India found itself in a dangerous political crisis. Indira Gandhi was selected as prime minister, probably on the basis of her father's reputation, in the hope that she could get the country through the difficult period and then hold elections. As it turned out she showed remarkable political skill both in uniting the battling factions of the Congress Party and in handling the difficult relations with Pakistan after its division into East and West. In the elections that followed, she received a large majority.

At the end of March 1950, we returned to Hong Kong. Only a month or so later, war broke out on the Korean peninsula. We thought the United Nations would surely take decisive action to prevent further spread of communist power. But the United States merely ordered the Seventh Fleet to patrol the Taiwan Straits, thereby preventing a communist attack on Taiwan, but also keeping us from striking back at the Mainland. This kind of appeasement made the enemy stronger and provided no solutions. To this day North and South Korea are bitterly opposed and can't even begin to talk about peace. If the United States had struck at Manchuria and destroyed the communists' strategic industry, Asia would not be in the dire straits that it's in today. There would have been no Vietnam War. This one error turned the whole situation against us. It's time for Asians to get rid of the idea that they can rely on the military might of the United States.

My brothers, Zhaohua and Zhaoke, and my cousin, Zhaoshu, were in Hong Kong. They were trying to start a business to produce T-shirts as a way to make their living. Doing business in Hong Kong was very difficult at that time. The economy was unstable and people were unwilling to invest. Furthermore, with so many people coming from the Mainland competition was fierce. I was never willing to invest in their factory. I didn't have much money and the family depended on me for its day to day expenses. I wouldn't think of risking these funds. They chided me about my refusal to invest, "You know how to cut expenses but you don't understand about tapping new resources." I told them we weren't tradesmen. Unless they were willing to run after the rich and famous, associate with peddlers, and flatter the powerful, it was going to be hard to make a go of it in business.

In the winter of 1950, we received an official invitation to go to Taiwan. We left after the first of the year in 1951. Mrs. Chen Cheng had arranged a very comfortable house for us in Taipei, in Qingtian Street. Everything was just right. We were deeply grateful. There were so many of our friends and relatives in Taipei that it was difficult to see them all. Then, shortly after our arrival, on February 4, 1951, I returned home from church to find a telegram from Zhaoshu in Hong Kong stating simply, "Eighth male of our generation killed in mountains." It was like a bolt of lightning had struck me. Zhaohua was dead. I had no idea what to do; I was paralyzed with grief.

I have never held superstitious beliefs but, in this case, there definitely was a prior indication of tragedy. When I left Hong Kong for Taiwan, Zhaohua brought me to the airport. On the way we passed a public cemetery; it was about half way up a mountain and behind it stood a tower bearing the inscription, "Pavilion of Ever Lasting Farewell." Zhaohua pointed it out to me saying, "Look, the Pavilion of Ever Lasting Farewell." I didn't pay attention at the time and didn't even look at the pavilion. How was I to know that this was our "ever lasting farewell" and that he would die on that very mountain. There are strange coincidences in this world but this was too much to attribute to chance.

Thinking back over those times, I was determined to block my brothers' efforts to go into business. As I feared, they failed and what's more, Zhaohua lost his life. I was heartbroken. He was my brother of the same mother, fourteen years younger. As a youngster, he was very bright with a gentle and affectionate nature. After attending the family school, he entered Yali Middle School and then went on to Boxue College in Hankou. He passed the examinations for the University of Hong Kong where he received the B.A. degree, majoring in English, French, and German, but he also wrote beautifully in Chinese. Poetry was his forte. He took the examinations for the Maritime Customs Service and was named an assistant director, serving in Yantai, Nanning, Guiyang, and Chongqing. When the Mainland fell to the communists, he was stationed in Hankou. He escaped to Hong Kong bringing important documents out with him. His family was there, so he stayed and began looking for a way to make a living. This is how he came to go into business.

He was very loving and respectful of me. He treated me almost like a mother. If I wanted something, he'd find a way to get it for me. He was the same with his brothers and cousins. He practically raised Zhaoke. When he was past forty, someone asked why he hadn't married. "For one thing," he said, "circumstances kept preventing it; for another my mother's dead and I don't need another woman to attend to; and finally nowadays a family is too expensive. So I'll just go it alone."

His death, to me, to Yuenung, and to the whole Zeng clan, was a terrible loss. His writing in Chinese and Western languages was so beautiful; he continued the literary tradition of his Zeng ancestors. Alas, his life was so short.

After Zhaohua's sudden and violent death, Yuenung and I flew back to Hong Kong to make the funeral arrangements. By then Zhaohua's body had been cremated. We purchased a plot in the Chinese Perpetual Care Cemetery, the one below the Pavilion of Everlasting Farewell. After the burial, before we could return to Taiwan, we had to sell Zhaohua's house, the factory had to be closed, the estate probated by a British lawyer, and there were a thousand other troublesome details that took us until the end of August. Yuenung flew back to Taiwan, first bringing with him Zeng Guofan's *Handwritten Diary* and *Letters to his Family*. Zhaoshu followed with his family. Ms. Xiao and I brought Mr. and Mrs. Zhu Zhusheng and their child with us, and Zhaoke and my cousin, Zhenluo, came later by ship.

Our residence on Qingtian Street was secluded and tranquil. In 1951, Xinsheng South Road was practically deserted. There weren't even street lights. The first night we heard roosters crowing and dogs barking. It seemed almost like our old home in Xiangxiang. In Hong Kong for the past two years, there were people and pollution everywhere; we heard no sounds of animals but were awake half the night with the noise of automobiles and people quarreling. This was another world.

We were not in Taiwan very long before Yuenung was asked to take a post as professor of English at Taiwan National University. This provided part of our living expenses. Life was much more comfortable than in Hong Kong. I did not take on any professional responsibilities but became active in the Chinese Women's Prayer Association. Both joy and sorrow lay ahead for us on Taiwan.

Chapter 32

Joys and Sorrows in Taiwan

Yuenung and I have experienced heartbreak and worry since coming to Taiwan in 1951, but we have enjoyed good times and happiness as well. The passing of my dear cousin and close companion, Ms. Xiao, in 1969, following a long struggle with Parkinson's disease left a limitless void in my life. My grief seemed unending. My own battle with cancer, first discovered in my left breast in 1959, was renewed in 1961. It was frightening but thanks to God's mercy, the prayers of my friends and excellent medical care in Taiwan and the United States, I have been in remission for more than a decade. While in Taiwan, the vision in my right eye deteriorated steadily, necessitating cataract removal surgery in 1964. In the course of the diagnosis, it was determined that I was also suffering from diabetes. Nevertheless, the cataract was removed and the vision in my right eye improved remarkably.

Apart from these personal difficulties, the greatest cause for concern in my life here in Taiwan has been the disappointing trend in world affairs that has isolated the Republic of China diplomatically and soured our relationship with the United States. This trend, while disheartening, is by no means a cause for despair. If it has done anything, it has strengthened the solidarity and resolve of the Chinese government and the people of Taiwan.

Representing the Republic of China on the United Nations Commission on the Status of Women in 1952 afforded me the opportunity to speak out on important issues affecting women world wide. I derived a great sense of personal accomplishment from this and remain grateful for the opportunity I had to confront the communist members of the Commission with the truth concerning the Republic of China on Taiwan.

I was nearly overwhelmed with emotion on February 18, 1954 when I watched as 14,000 heroic Chinese prisoners of war from Korea, who chose repatriation to Taiwan rather than the Mainland, met President Chiang Kaishek at Sun Yatsen Hall. Amid cheers and jubilation, the men from each province marched into the arena holding high the map of their province made into a banner. As they entered, as each of us saw the banner of our home province, there was not a dry eye in the crowd. There were tears of sorrow and joy, sorrow from the realization that our native provinces had fallen under the diabolical control of the communists and joy from knowing that we had so many faithful and brave young warriors who chose Taiwan. Furthermore, it demonstrated that the people of the many regions of China, the different levels of society, the various occupational and age groups, were all opposed to communism. These men braved a thousand deaths to seek freedom that all the nations of the world might see that the communists do not have the backing of the Chinese people. Their regime deserves nothing but the contempt of the free, peace-loving nations of the world.

The National Assembly convened the following day, February 19, and accomplished two important political tasks. I felt proud to be involved in both of them. First was the dismissal of Vice President Li Zongren. Li had illegally abandoned his office in 1949 during the final months of the struggle against the communists. On March 10, the National Assembly voted on a Bill of Impeachment against the Vice President presented by the Control Yuan, the watchdog agency of the central government. Of the 1,486 delegates in attendance, 1,403 voted for dismissal.

The second task was the election by the National Assembly of a president and vice president. Though I was scheduled to attend the meeting of the United Nations Commission on the Status of Women scheduled for March that year, I was determined not to give up my sacred right to vote in the election on March 22. I requested the Foreign Ministry to send a substitute to the U.N. On election day, every delegate who could possibly make it was present. Many came from abroad. They came from their sick beds in hospitals, on crutches, wheelchairs and stretchers to cast their votes—a clear demonstration of how seriously the people regarded this election and the affection they felt for President Chiang Kaishek. The outcome was that President Chiang received 1,507 votes and was reelected to a second term as president of the Republic of China. In the election for vice president held on March 24, Mr. Chen Cheng received 1,417 votes and became the second vice president. The voting was without coercion and reflected the consciences of the individual delegates. Li Zongren was not faithful in his duties to the nation; he abandoned his responsibility illegally; the punishment was appropriate. We congratulated the president and vice president on their election. It was a blessing for the Chinese people and a first step toward recovery of the Mainland.

In 1954 President Chiang appointed Vice President Chen chairman of the Planning Commission for the Recovery of the Mainland. Though unworthy of such an honor, I was named a vice chairman. All delegates to the National Assembly and members of the previous planning committee in the Executive Yuan were members of the Commission. It was an organization of more than eighteen hundred members studying plans and policies for recovery of the Mainland, so that when the day arrived there would be no confusion, mistakes, or harmful effects for the Chinese people.

In addition to my service in the National Assembly and the Planning Commission for Recovery of the Mainland, in 1956, I was named a delegate to the meeting of the Asian Anti-Communist League in Manila. I benefited greatly from this and realized how many of the peoples of Asia were opposed to communism.

It was a source of great personal happiness to me when Yuenung was appointed to an academic position at National Taiwan University and subsequently named founding president of Donghai University in Taizhong. Mrs. Moore, sister of *Time Magazine* publisher Henry Luce, contributed the funds to establish Donghai University but there appeared to be no suitable person to serve as president. So the Board of Directors, of which I was a member, invited several Chinese educators who had a background teaching in Christian schools and who were themselves Christians to meet with Mrs. Moore. The intent was to have her select the one she felt best suited to serve as president of Donghai. Each of the people interviewed was asked to make a statement of his views on Christian higher education. Initially, Yuenung was not interested in the position but someone—it certainly was not I—proposed his name. Although he had no church affiliation and was an unbaptized Christian, he was called for an interview. Much to his surprise, Mrs. Moore was very impressed with his views on education and thought him right for the presidency. The Board then offered him the position. Though he initially declined several times, he finally accepted for a period of two years to do the difficult work of getting the school started.

Groundbreaking for the new buildings took place shortly thereafter. Vice President of the United States, Richard Nixon, and Mrs. Nixon were the guests of honor. In his speech, Mr. Nixon urged China to make way for the next generation while preserving its national essence. I had the opportunity to talk with him and Mrs. Nixon at a banquet that evening. He commented on the modernity of life in Taiwan and his firm belief that we represented the authentic tradition of the Chinese people. Mrs. Nixon told me about her daughters. When I mentioned that I was too old to continue teaching, she remarked that "old age is a state of mind."

In addition to construction of school buildings, recruitment of faculty, and establishment of the curriculum, Yuenung set up a system of liberal education and a cooperative education program designed to enable needy students to work to defray their educational expenses. He personally worked several hours each week with the construction workers to demonstrate the dignity of hard work. This won the respect of faculty, students, and workers. They were like one large family. After two years, he resigned and returned to Taiwan National University to provide an opportunity for some other able person to head Donghai. To this day the faculty and students still cherish his memory.

Another great joy was when Yuenung was officially honored as the first person to receive the "Good Man, Good Deeds" award and presented the four character tablet, "Virtuous teacher and human being." Unfortunately, I was in the hospital and unable to attend the ceremony; however, there were many relatives from our family association and former students who did join in honoring him. An orchestra and fireworks display accompanied the presentation of the tablet.

I cherish the memories of the birthday celebration when Yuenung and I turned seventy. The Yifang alumnae and the Zeng Clan Association in Taiwan held a party in a birthday hall at the Taibei Women's Home. Many of the people of Taibei presented congratulatory poems and some well known older scholars gave their commendations. We donated the money given to us on our birthdays to the Zeng Clan Association. We were humbled and grateful beyond words. The celebration given by our former students was even more enthusiastic. We realized that a life given to education returns fellowship and intangible compensation beyond measure.

The celebration that the Taiwan Yifang Alumnae held in the winter of 1968 marking the fiftieth anniversary of the opening of Yifang was yet another moment of great joy. It also marked Yuenung's and my seventy-seventh year reckoned by the traditional Chinese method. Alumnae came from all over Taiwan, from the United States, and from England. Many of them wrote letters and sent us photographs of their families to wish us well. The alumnae association and the Zeng Clan put all these together, pasted up the photographs, and arranged for photo offset reproduction. The celebration was held on December 29 at the Taipei Women's Home.

Miss Shao Menglan, principal of the Shilin Middle School, brought a Chinese orchestra that performed music and dancing. She played the Chinese zither and the flute accompanying me on the lute. I hadn't performed Chinese music for many years and I'm sure my performance was laughable. Everyone was so kind and they insisted that I play; so I forced myself to be the clown. After the music, there was a banquet with six tables. A good time was had by all.

Traditionally, the relationship of teacher and student was like that of parent and child. Yuenung and I have enjoyed the good fortune of having such relationships with our students. We would remind those who would be teachers that the students' respect arises from the teacher's sincerity. This is sometimes no different than the love of a child for a parent. So don't be discouraged; like parents, your rewards will come in the future. Not only did our former students treat us wonderfully, their husbands and children showed great affection. We had the warmth of feeling of a family. This is a true blessing in life.

Also in Taiwan we were reunited with many relatives. There were many more residing overseas and tragically there were many, many close relatives still on the Mainland. We all hope to return there soon, a goal to which we should all give our every effort.

Chapter 33

The United Nations Commission on the Status of Women

The second year that I was in Taiwan, 1952, in the first month of the New Year, my cousin, Zhaocheng, and his wife invited some close friends and relatives to join us for dinner in their home to celebrate my birthday. Madam Chiang Kaishek called to wish me a happy birthday and tell me that she had sent a bouquet of flowers with Secretary T.V. Sung. She also told me that I had been named to head the 1952 delegation to the United Nations Commission on the Status of Women.

I was elated but fearful. I feared that I was not up to the task of representing the interests of the Republic of China on Taiwan in the United Nations, since the communist members and some neutrals bitterly opposed our right to speak for the Chinese people on the communist controlled Mainland. This would be my first dealing with the United Nations. It was also the first time, since coming to Taiwan, that the government had sent a delegate abroad. Furthermore, things were in a state of near anarchy at the U.N. The member states were divided over Cold War issues and I had no idea how this would affect various delegates' positions toward the Republic of China.

Encouragement and assistance from friends and government officials, however, helped me overcome my fears. Governor of Taiwan Chen Cheng, author of the island's successful land-reform program, provided me with materials on Taiwan's reduction of rents to a maximum of 37.5 percent of the crop and the equalization of land rights so that I could respond to inquiries on these matters.

Minister of Economics Ye Gongchao and Madam Chiang Kaishek both encouraged me. With this kind of backing, I made up my mind that I could do it.

Having accepted the position, I set out to attend my first meeting of the Commission accompanied by my brother, Zhaoke. We went first to Hong Kong and then on to Rome where we were met by the ambassador and his wife. We stayed in Rome only two days and then took the train to Paris and from there to Geneva, arriving on March 5. Geneva was an ideal place to hold such a meeting. The scenery, the shining mountains, and clear waters of the lake, were breathtaking. Apart from the United Nations and the World Federation of Labor, there were no other major organizations headquartered there. There was no wild entertainment district and no commercial skyscrapers. The delegates lived in hotels not far from one another and could get to know each other easily. Before the session opened, I met some of the delegates from other nations. Most important among these were the American delegate, Mrs. Goldman, the French delegate, Madame Lefauchere, the delegate from New Zealand, Mrs. Ross, and the Chairwoman from the Dominican Republic. I sought their support in the voting. This proved quite successful.

There were eighteen nations represented on the Commission. Each nation had a regular delegate, a deputy, secretary, and some advisory personnel. The staff sat to the rear of the regular delegate during meetings. There were also experts on special assignments and observers who sat in an outer ring. The delegates' seats were arranged in an oval. Seated at one end were the chairwoman, the secretary, and the deputy secretary. The recorders were seated in the middle. I sat between the Byelorussian and the Cuban delegates. Fortunately, at that time, Cuba was still non-communist or I would have been under attack from both flanks. My brother, Zhaoke, serving as secretary, sat behind me.

Poland was the first delegation to challenge my government's right to represent China. Then the Republic of Byelorussia, a Soviet puppet state, did also saying, "She cannot represent the 700 million people of the People's Republic of China. She is simply the representative of Chiang Kaishek's political faction." I spoke and explained to the chair, "I am not a member of President Chiang's Guomindang Party. Furthermore, the President appoints people to office impartially without respect to personal connections. I'd like to ask those delegates here today from communist nations, if there are any who are not members of the Communist Party?" The communist delegates were silenced and the chair said, "Since the United Nations General Assembly has not rejected the right of the Nationalist Government to represent China, this Commission is not in the position to do so." Subsequently, the chair rejected as out of order several other proposals by communist countries to deny my right to represent China. After gaining this victory, I wired the Foreign Ministry in Taipei asking them to pass the good news to Madame Chiang Kaishek and to Yuenung.

The meeting continued for three weeks. The topics discussed included women in government, economics, law, the professions, and various social problems. All were of great importance. I spoke on each of these issues, reminding the participants that China was there. An unexpected highlight of my stay in Geneva was my meeting with several old friends: Ms. Zhang Hungwei, who had served with me as a delegate to the National Assembly, and three school friends from England, including Ms. Masaryk, daughter of the former Czech President, and two others who had taught at Yifang. They were very warm and friendly. We dined together and viewed the spectacular alpine scenery. I was most grateful for the opportunity to share their company again.

Through my service in the United Nations, I also met Mrs. Eleanor Roosevelt, a member of the Commission on Human Rights, the parent organization of the Commission on the Status of Women. She was very active on the Commission but decidedly left-wing in her politics. She entertained young Chinese leftist writers. This sort of activity by prominent Americans such as Mrs. Roosevelt helped greatly to spread communist influence in the United States.

On another occasion, at a conference of women writers in New York, I had the opportunity to meet the acclaimed American writer, Pearl S. Buck, author of the Pulitzer Prize winning novel about peasant life in China, *The Good Earth*. Ms. Buck had also translated the *Shui Hu Zhuan*, a tale of bandit gangs in north China in the final years of the Song Dynasty (A.D. 960–1278), with the English title *All Men Are Brothers*. We discussed the great influence that the *Shui Hu Zhuan* had on Chinese public opinion in the formation of secret societies and the like. She told me that the translation had been very difficult. Her personal life had been very trying. She had a retarded child who was institutionalized because Ms. Buck was unable to care for her and continue her writing. I found it distressing that such a brilliant mother could not be together with her retarded child.

After the conclusion of the session in Geneva, I went to Paris by train and then on to England. This was my first visit there since the War. I was hosted by the Methodist Church and went about London visiting old familiar places. To see so many of the previously busy sections of the city completely laid waste and many of the great commercial buildings still not rebuilt brought home the horror of modern warfare. I also visited Westfield College and gave a talk and saw many of the older faculty who had been there in my day.

I spent several weeks visiting relatives and friends in Scotland and England before returning to Taiwan. I departed knowing that I had seen Britain fallen from a first class to a second, even a third, class power. I felt even more strongly that mankind must seek the loving heart of God and emulate the loving deeds of Jesus Christ or nuclear war will bring an end to culture and material civilization. The human race will be reduced to less than half its present size and returned to the primitive existence of the Stone Age—a true horror.

Chapter 34

Nixon Resigns from Office

The passage of time and the vagaries of world politics brought a reversal of Taiwan's fortunes in the international arena. In October 1971, the Republic of China withdrew from the United Nations. Though this seemed a setback, the way things had developed it was unavoidable and it strengthened the determination of the Chinese people to work even harder on behalf of their country. It saddened me but it was not a cause for despair. Not since the United Nations sent troops to take part in the police action in Korea has it moved decisively to resolve international disputes. Even when warring nations slaughtered innocent civilians, the United Nations stood idly by, unwilling to violate the autonomy of the states involved. An example of this was when the Chinese communists in 1962 invaded Ladakh and the Northwest Frontier Region of India; another was the war between Israel and Egypt in 1967. In both cases, the United Nations did nothing to halt the hostilities.

The war between Israel and Egypt was actually precipitated by the actions of the United Nations Secretary General, U Thant. Without the permission of the General Assembly, he withdrew the United Nations peace-keeping force in the Gaza Strip separating Israel and Egypt. Seeing this, Israel felt free to take action, and employing its air power, defeated Egypt, Jordan, and Syria within six days. The United Nations applied absolutely no military pressure. Today, if the Republic of China suffered aggression or was bullied by other countries, we could not count on the help, or even the verbal support, of the United Nations.

Furthermore, the Security Council had become the tool of the super powers; the permanent members could employ their veto power arbitrarily to decide any matter they wished. The General Assembly had too many member nations and some small nations voted irresponsibly. They had small populations and very limited national territory; they did not bear great national responsibility and should not have had the power of decision-making in world affairs. Nevertheless, because these small nations were so numerous, their votes could decide the course of world events. It is just as Winston Churchill said, "If the United Nations is to vote with equal representation for all countries of the world, the backward nations will control those that have achieved higher levels of civilization." Unfortunately, he seems to have been right on the mark. There was nothing unreasonable about our withdrawal from the United Nations.

I was bitterly disappointed this year on February 20, only a few short months after our departure from the United Nations, when President Nixon of the United States lowered himself by visiting Communist China. Nixon seemed to ignore the Chinese communists continuing verbal attacks on the United States and followed Henry Kissinger's strategy of rapprochement with Communist China. Their hope was that Communist China could offset the power of the Soviet Union and that the Chinese communists could be persuaded to withdraw their forces from North Vietnam, thereby permitting an orderly withdrawal of American forces from the South. In such a complex state of affairs we must heed the words of President Chiang, "As the situation changes, fear not, but dedicate yourselves solemnly to developing our strengths."

President Nixon's resignation from the presidency only a few years later was fraught with such important meaning for the United States and the world that I ventured this poetic reflection on the consequences of duplicity.

Nixon Resigns From Office*

Richard Nixon was born in a peaceful rural home.
He won a scholarship to law school and after graduation became a
  lawyer.
In the Second World War he entered the Navy and served as a
  lieutenant commander, returning to civilian life with honor.

Nixon married Pat Ryan in 1940.
They had two lovely daughters.

---

*This poem is written in the *jueju* or truncated verse form popular during the Tang Dynasty (618–907) and used frequently to describe themes in everyday life. The stanzas consist of four lines, each containing seven characters with the final character of lines one, two and four rhyming. In an introductory remark, Ms. Zeng explained that Nixon's resignation was of such earth-shaking importance that she provided a vernacular translation so that it could be understood more easily and "politicians may take heed and not abuse their power." This rendition is based upon her vernacular. I have not attempted to rectify historical inaccuracies or distortions since they are essential to the polemical tone of her writing. The poem does not appear in the published memoirs but may be found in *Zeng Baosun nushi jinianj* (Collected materials commemorating Ms. Zeng Baosun) pp. 274–280, held at the Institute of Modern History, Academia Sinica, Nankang, Taiwan.

Nixon made his name as a foe of communism.
In 1948, he used the testimony of Whitaker Chambers to prove that Alger Hiss was a communist sympathizer and that he had deceived the court.
From this, Nixon was able to gain a seat in Congress.

In his 1950 campaign for the senate, he charged that Helen Geohagan Douglas was a communist.
She lost and Nixon triumphed.

In the 1952 American presidential elections, General Dwight Eisenhower was elected by a large majority.
General Eisenhower had selected Nixon to be his vice president.

In 1952, when General Eisenhower first named Nixon as his running mate, there were some who accused Nixon of corruption.
Nixon appeared on television and explained: "I have not taken a bribe only a cocker spaniel puppy for my children."
Since most Americans love dogs, Nixon was forgiven by the voters.

When General Eisenhower was ill, Vice President Nixon represented him in visits to many nations.
In the capital of Venezuela and in Tokyo anti-American feeling was high.
Nixon's car was pummeled with bricks and he was struck in the face.

From Japan, Nixon came to Taiwan where he met with President Chiang Kaishek and broke the ground for the establishment of Donghai University in Taizhong.
Our people held him in great respect.
I was there the day of the groundbreaking.

Because of Nixon's success during his visits to foreign countries, in 1960, General Eisenhower supported him as a candidate for the presidency.
Nixon, having gained greatly from his earlier appearance on television, accepted John F Kennedy's challenge to a television debate.
He did not understand that Kennedy was young and attractive, powerful and wealthy, and Americans wanted somebody new.
In the end, Nixon lost the election.

In 1960, Nixon returned to California and practiced law for two years.
In 1962 he was defeated in the election for governor of California by Pat Brown.
Afterwards he told reporters angrily, "I have no intention of continuing in politics.
You won't have me to kick around any more."

Nixon moved to New York were he practiced law and helped
   Republican Party candidates.
He was especially helpful to Barry Goldwater in his 1964 campaign
   for the presidency.
For this the Republican Party was deeply appreciative.

Nixon seduced the American people with his talk of withdrawing
   American troops from Vietnam, and negotiating instead of
   fighting with the Soviet outlaws in an effort to secure world
   peace.
At that time, Americans were fed up with war.
As a result, in 1968, Nixon defeated Hubert Humphrey by a large
   margin and became President of the United States.

President Nixon's second daughter, Pat, married a well known
   lawyer named Cox.
Julie married David Eisenhower, grandson of President Eisenhower.
Since both weddings were in the White House, they were luxurious
   and with great ceremony as though a princess was marrying a
   commoner.
In 1973, this became one of the considerations during impeachment.

President Nixon employed Henry Kissinger as his secretary of state.
He sent Kissinger to Pakistan.
Kissinger feigned illness for three days, from July 9 to July 11, 1971
   and slipped away unnoticed to Beijing where he met Mao
   Zedong and Zhou Enlai.
The criminal Zhou then invited President Nixon to visit the Chinese
   mainland.
The invitation was not from Mao Zedong.

Unexpectedly on July 15, 1971, President Nixon appeared on
   television and announced that he would visit the Chinese
   Mainland for ten days before May 1972.
The Republic of China on Taiwan and Japan were notified of this
   only one half hour in advance.
It was discussed earlier with the European Allies and the North
   Atlantic Treaty Organization
The whole world protested.

President Nixon and Secretary Kissinger went to Mainland China in
   February 1972 and met with the criminals, Mao, Zhou, and
   Jiang Qing at Beijing.
They talked wildly about a future restoration of normal relations.
They also went to West Lake and then to Shanghai where they issued
   the Nixon-Zhou Communique, completing their mission of
   treachery and deceit.

President Nixon, having kept up United States defenses against the Soviets and drawn close to the Chinese communists, feared the Russians would be suspicious.
So, in May 1972, he went to Russia for high level talks about mutual restraint by the nuclear powers, and a three-sided (U.S., Soviet, and Chinese Communist) and four-cornered (U.S., Soviet, Chinese Communist and Japan) approach to stabilizing world peace.

Peace was hopeless.
India had already allied with Russia.
Japan severed relations with the Republic of China and recognized the Chinese Communists.
Both were great sources of anxiety for the United States.

President Nixon, on the one hand, cultivated better relations with the Communist criminals while at the same time saying that he did not forget old friends.
He advocated two Chinas in the United Nations: the Communist outlaws in the Security Council and the Republic of China as an ordinary member of the General Assembly.
This would violate the United Nations Charter and shake the confidence of the nations of Southeast Asia.
Nothing could have been worse.
The Republic of China angrily withdrew from the United Nations.

After President Nixon went to Beijing, Japan, fearful that its opposition to the communists would isolate it from the United States, became friendly with the Chinese communists.
Japan forgot President Chiang Kaishek's great favors: renunciation of World War II reparations; release and repatriation of prisoners of war; and protection of the Emperor.
In September 1972, Japan foolishly extended formal recognition to the Chinese communists.
Because of Mr. Nixon's actions, other countries were quick to follow suit.

On the night of June 17, 1972, five subordinates of President Nixon forced open the door of the office of the headquarters of the Democratic Party, entered the safe, went through their documents, and installed listening devices in the corners of the room.
They were arrested by police while the crime was in progress.
The leader Mr. McCord was an employee of the CIA.
The public reacted furiously and the Democratic Party called for an investigation.

Nixon Resigns from Office

President Nixon refused to admit prior knowledge or direction of the Watergate affair.
But the five who were charged confessed to being accessories.
They were all jailed or paid heavy fines.

The congressional investigation committee demanded the tape recordings concerning this matter.
President Nixon at first refused to hand them over.
In the end the democratic constitutional system gave him no choice.
On July 28, 1974, he handed over sixty-four reels of tape.
Then the truth became known.
President Nixon had committed crimes.

The congressional impeachment proceedings were scheduled.
The House of Representatives passed a bill of impeachment by a two-thirds majority.
Of the thirty-eight senators on the impeachment committee (seventeen of whom were Republicans) there were twenty-seven who favored impeachment.
Included among these were six Republicans.
President Nixon realized that resignation from office was the only way he could avoid a criminal conviction.

President Nixon had influenced Vice President Agnew to resign in an effort to lessen public resentment against his administration.
Then he named Speaker of the House Gerald Ford as Vice President hoping that, after Ford became president, he would grant a special pardon.

On August 6, 1974, President Nixon explained to his daughters and sons-in-law that he had no alternative but to resign.
They embraced each other and wept.
The two women were extremely upset.

On the night of August 8, 1974, President Nixon spoke on television to the whole nation concerning his resignation, saying, "Because I regard the interests of the United States as most important, and cannot place my personal interests above those, I am resigning so that a new president, who can devote himself entirely to the needs of the country, can take office.
He must continue to give himself entirely to the search for world peace."

Mr. and Mrs. Nixon and their older daughter and son-in-law went through the south garden of the White House and boarded a waiting helicopter.
When they were about to leave, Mr. Nixon raised both hands in the victory sign.
His daughter and son-in-law gave the thumbs-up sign with their right hands.
The White House staff were in tears.

Nixon's photograph had been displayed in all United States embassies and in public places of respect.
After his admission of wrongdoing and resignation from office, these pictures were all removed.

Nixon got his start in politics through his opposition to communism.
When he was elected President of the United States, the people of the Republic of China were elated, feeling that he would certainly support what was right.
They never expected that he would soon be soft on communism.
Then, try to appease the communists and finally, turn toward them.
He was motivated entirely by self-interest.
As a result, he was ruined personally and his name was blackened.
How regrettable!

Nixon's schemes and devices were all in his own selfish interest.
His so-called peace negotiations and restrictions on nuclear capabilities were insincere.
They led to untold disasters.
Let this be a warning to politicians everywhere.

Afterword

The events that I have discussed have been written down at random. There is no literary form and there are many redundancies. What I have encountered in life: early education in the family school; elementary education in missionary schools and higher education in England; all came at a time when education for women was in its infancy. I have witnessed the changes as China passed from empire to republic; two world wars; long years of struggle against Japan and final victory. We were sacked by the communists three times. They seized control of the Mainland, oppressed our people and scorned the intellectuals. One could say that I have exhausted the possibilities for experience in a lifetime. So it is difficult to exhaust it all in one writing. I hardly knew where to start. Furthermore, many of my personal papers have been lost during military disturbances. All my diaries and records no longer exist. It has only been since I have enjoyed the peace and security of life here on Taiwan that I felt I could begin writing, but I have had to rely entirely on memory. Inevitably, this resulted in many errors and gaps. I hope that friends, relatives and schoolmates will catch these and correct them.

In my lifetime I have also suffered considerable travail: several times I was in fear for my life but I always received help from the Lord and was able to escape. Recently many educators, overlooking my shortcomings, have asked me to speak at universities, at middle schools, and to the armed forces. I always do my best to explain spiritual education, traditional culture, and religious morality; I pray that God's brilliance, through me as His instrument, will make these things a little clearer to these young people.

I also want to take this opportunity to thank those who have encouraged me. Mr Xuan Cheng and my brother, Yuenung, corrected the text. Mrs. Liu Yunzhang, some schoolmates and my nephew, Xianqi, drafted it for me. They each have my thanks. I beg the forgiveness of the many others who have aided me whom I have not mentioned by name. They have my deep gratitude. I will always remember them.

Some Thoughts after Reading the Memoirs of Zeng Baosun

How can the memoir of one Chinese woman, exceptional though she may have been, assist the reader to unravel the complex web of wars, revolutions, and social movements that mark the development of twentieth-century China? As Ms. Zeng observed in the Afterword to her memoir, her experiences were so numerous and so varied, it is difficult to imagine how she could have crammed more living into one lifetime. From her recollection of China's failed reform movement of 1898 to her reaction to the dramatic shift in United States-China relations in the 1970s, she reveals the views of a genuinely bicultural observer to the momentous events that shook Chinese society, sometimes reverberating throughout the world. Still, she harbors a certain reserve, both personal and cultural, jealously guarding her feelings about marriage and family and glossing over serious social and economic problems of early twentieth-century China. So, this is not a "warts and all" confession nor an informed exposé, the "inside story" of twentieth-century China. With these reservations in mind, the reader who does not seek too much can find plenty.

First, and perhaps most important, Ms. Zeng's life makes an unambiguous statement about contemporary Confucian thought and practice. She also speaks volumes about her personal faith in Christianity and her view of the relationship between contemporary Christianity and Confucianism. In one account after another, she gradually unveils to her readers her vision of equality for women and her reconciliation of that vision with a culture traditionally hostile to it. Finally her embrace of conservative nationalism inspired by her deep-seated distaste for the communist alternative is clarified by her background and life's experience. The values she espoused: Confucianism, Christianity, equality for women, and nationalism continue to shape the clay of Chinese society on Taiwan and on the Mainland. Their effects are uneven from time to time and place to place. In the way she engaged these issues, Zeng Baosun was a woman of her time and for later times.

Throughout her life she followed the Confucian Way. She took it as her duty to be informed of the traditional teachings of Confucianism and to put them into practice in daily living. This is demonstrated in many ways: the importance she placed on loving relationships within her extended family and with her many close friends; her unwavering faith in the power of education to strengthen the moral fiber and wisdom of those who place their trust in it; her lifelong intellectual reliance on the classic literature from which the teachings of Confucianism are derived; and her determination, when faced with choices, to do what was right rather than what was profitable. It is also clear that she did not question the hierarchical structure and the authoritarian leadership of Chinese government and society, both essential features of the Confucian state. This led her to extol the paternalistic relationship that the Zeng family enjoyed with its tenants while ignoring the widespread landlord abuse upon which communist revolution fed; and to endorse uncritically the evolving military dictatorship of the Guomindang that arose in reply to that revolution.

Zeng Baosun considered her belief in Jesus Christ as the defining characteristic of her life. The aspect of her Christianity that set her apart from millions of devout Christians of her day, however, was her genuinely ecumenical respect for other religions. She regarded other Christian denominations and Buddhism as catalysts that could mobilize the spiritual energy of their followers and elevate the moral standards of the societies in which they flourished. Confucianism was a special case. Consciously or unconsciously, she dealt with it as such. In the most fundamental way, her Christian beliefs were influenced by Confucianism. Religious mysticism, abstruse theological questions, and the like receive little attention in her memoir. Clearly, she was principally concerned with the application of Christian values: faith, hope, and charity, to cultivate the individual and improve society. The convergence of this perception of Christianity with the aims of Confucius to improve the individual and life in society through education and the practice of virtue is unmistakable. Similarly, at every turn of her adult life, her memoir discloses her dedication to the Christian principle of moral rectitude expressed as the Confucian ideal of the *Great Learning*: "Exemplify virtue, love people, and rest in the highest good."

The issue on which she parted company with her Confucian peers was the matter of life after death. Zeng Baosun surely believed Jesus Christ, the Saviour, would reward her with a life of eternal happiness. She declined to take part in the veneration of ancestor's spirits in the Zeng family temple but she respected the genuine feelings of filial piety and family solidarity that ancestor veneration engendered.

Another matter on which she differed with the conventional dictates of Confucian society was the equality of women. Certainly it would be reasonable to assume that Zeng Baosun's self-confidence and dedication to equality for women resulted from her experience with revolutionary women in the Shanghai mission school, or her association with female missionaries and educators, but there is more to it than that. If there was one person who Zeng Baosun looked to as a model throughout her life, it was her grandmother. Her grandmother directed the lives of her family members along paths that prepared them for leadership in a rapidly changing society. She was open-minded and accepting of new ideas and beliefs on their merits rather than their point of origin. Traditional Chinese culture posed no intellectual or psychological barriers for her; perhaps that is why she embraced it so intensely. In this model, and in the encouragement of her father and uncles, Zeng Baosun saw the compatibility of traditional Confucian values with the emergence of strong, independent womanhood. In the life of her mother she saw the modesty, self-control, and subordination that epitomized the role of a daughter-in-law in the Confucian tradition. Admiring her mother, she drew her strength and creativity from her grandmother.

Her struggle for women's equality sometimes overlapped with the women's movement in twentieth-century China: she remained thankful into her old age that her father spared her the agony of bound feet. At other times, however, she trod an independent path: she stubbornly refused the idea that a quota of ten percent female membership should be imposed in the Steering Committee of the National Assembly, insisting on fair and open competition between male and female candidates. The statement that she made through her own life, eschewing marriage and family for a life dedicated to education, religion, and public service was, no doubt, the clearest message concerning her vision of the role of women that she could send in twentieth-century China.

Zeng Baosun's ancestry and upbringing endowed her with a feeling of pride in Chinese culture and a sense of mission to preserve and advance it. The commitment to the Empire that embraced this culture was strong with her great grandfather, Zeng Guofan. During Zeng Baosun's childhood, the Zeng family called for fundamental reforms designed to preserve the imperial system. Nevertheless, when the republican revolution of 1911–1912 overtook the reform movement, the Zengs adapted effortlessly. Zeng Baosun, like other family members, saw it as the shedding of an outdated and ineffective form of rule unrelated to the sense of cultural pride and mission bequeathed by Zeng Guofan. Because of her commitment to Chinese culture and her indomitable faith in God, Zeng Baosun accepted a republican government as the new vessel that would hold the culture that she prized so highly.

She had no patience, however, with those who would destroy the traditional social order through which the culture was expressed, be they communists or warlords. The depredations visited upon the Yifang Middle School by communist revolutionary groups seem to be what drove her to an irreversible stand against the communists. If there was a precise moment when this happened, it was probably April 8, 1927. What happened after that was a progressive turning toward the Nationalist Government of Chiang Kaishek as the best alternative to support the traditional social order that gave expression to the culture she loved. Eventually she came to embrace the dictatorship and the exaggerated nationalism that communist revolution and Japanese aggression evoked in Chiang's regime.

It has been a pleasure for me to meet Ms. Zeng through her memoirs. I have found them always interesting, sometimes controversial, occasionally I felt them wrong-headed, but never did I feel that she gave her readers less than total sincerity about those matters of which she spoke. Through the life of this one remarkable Chinese woman, I hope that Ms. Zeng's English Language readers will gain new insight into contemporary Confucianism, Christianity, and the complexities of twentieth-century Chinese civilization.

A Note on Materials

In preparing this translation, I have worked from an edition published in Taiwan, *Zeng Baosun Huiyilu* (Memoirs of Zeng Baosun) Taipei: Longwen Chubanshe, 1989. This is a reprint of the original edition published by the Chinese Christian Literature Council, Hong Kong, 1976. An edition published in the Peoples' Republic of China, *Zeng Baosun Huiyilu fu/Chongde Laoren Ziding Nianpu*, (Memoirs of Zeng Baosun with the Chronological Autobiography of Mrs. Nie Zeng Jifen) Changsha: Yuelu Shushe, 1986, is missing passages dealing with Ms. Zeng's political views regarding the communist movement, her involvement with the United Nations, and her activities as a National Assembly Person in the Nationalist Government.

Certain reference works and research studies were very useful in translating and adapting Ms. Zeng's memoirs. Most useful was the *Cihai* (Encyclopaedic Dictionary of Chinese) Cihai bianji weihuanhui Ed., Shanghai: Cishu chubanshe, 1979. Of equal importance is the earlier edition, *Cihai*, Taipei: Taiwan zhonghua shuju, 1965 which differs substantively from the later edition with respect to coverage. Most of the literature mentioned by Ms. Zeng as well as many of the personalities, places, historical figures and incidents can be found in one or the other of these two works. With respect to personalities, the popular reference works were useful to augment the *Cihai*. These include: Arthur W. Hummel, Ed. *Eminent Chinese of the Ch'ing Period*, Washington D.C.: Government Printing Office, 1941; Howard L. Boorman, Ed. *Biographical Dictionary of Republican China*, 4 vols., New York: Columbia University Press, 1967; Donald Klein/Anne B. Clark, Eds., *Biographic Dictionary of Chinese Communism*, 2 vols., Cambridge: Harvard University Press, 1971; The China Weekly Review, *Who's Who in China 1918–1950*, 3 vols., Hong Kong: Chinese Materials Center, 1982. Also useful for identification and location of place names is Zang Lihe et. al. Eds., *Zhongguo gujin diming dacidian*, (A dictionary of ancient and recent Chinese place names), second printing, Taipei: Taiwan shangwu yinshuguan, 1966.

Other dictionaries used primarily for clarifying terminology include: Lin Yutang, *Lin Yutang's Chinese-English Dictionary of Modern Usage*, Hong Kong: Chinese University of Hong Kong Press, 1972; Beijing waiguoyu xueyuan yingyuxi (English Department of the Beijing Foreign Language Institute) *A Chinese English Dictionary*, Beijing: Shangwu yinshuguan, 1982; Liang Shiqiu, *A New Practical Chinese-English Dictionary*, Taipei: The Far East Book Co., Ltd., 1972; Kanagae Nobumitsu, *Zhongguoyu Cidian* (Chinese-Japanese Dictionary) Tokyo: Daigakusyorin, 1973; and Zhongguo shehuikexueyuan yuyanyanjiusuo cidian bianjishi (Chinese Academy of Social Sciences, Language Research Institute Dictionary Section) Ed., *Xiandai Hanyu Cidian*, Beijing: Shangwu yinshuguan, 1978

Research studies and collections that have a direct bearing on the background of Ms. Zeng's life include: Chang Pengyuan, *Zhongguo xiandaihua quyu yanqiu Hunan Sheng 1860–1916* (Modernization in China, 1860–1916: a regional study of social, political and economic change in Hunan province), Taipei: Institute of Modern History, 1983; Thomas L. Kennedy Trans., Thomas L. and Micki Kennedy Eds., *Testimony of a Confucian Woman The Autobiography of Mrs Nie Zeng Jifen, 1852–1942*, Athens and London: The University of Georgia Press, 1993; Charlton M. Lewis, *Prologue to the Chinese Revolution The Transformation of Ideas and Institutions in Hunan Province, 1891–1907*, Cambridge: Harvard University East Asian Research Center, 1976; Li Yuning Ed., *Chinese Women Through Chinese Eyes*, Armonk N.Y.: M.E. Sharpe, Inc. 1992; *Zhongguo funu zishu shiwen xuan* (Autobiographical writings and poems by modern Chinese women) Taipei: Lianjing chuban shiyegongsi, 1980.

INDEX

Anglican Church.
  See Church of England
Annals of the Grand Historian, 18, 22
Anti-foreignism:
  Communists, 93
  Peasants' Association, 93
Asian Anti-Communist League, 145

Baifu Tang Shuxue Congshu (White Hibiscus Hall Mathematics Collection), 51
Barnes, Louise:
  Accompanies Zeng Baosun to England, 35–38
  Beginnings of Yifang School, 74–76, 78, 83, 88
  Death of, 93
  Encourages Zeng Baosun to go to England, 35
  Memento of, 95
  Participation in Christian student meetings in England, 60
  Principal at Mary Vaughan High School, 17, 26–29
  Recommends Zeng Baosun's enrollment at Worthing Church House School, 39
  Refusal of Mission Society's request for her return to China, 46–48
  Return trip to China, 65–71, 73
  Role in Zeng Baosun's plans for opening Christian school in China, 57
  Shares Hampstead home with Zeng Baosun, 53
  Zeng Baosun's enrollment at Blackheath Upper Middle School, 40–41, 46
Beijing National University:
  Compared to church-operated schools in China, 71
  May Fourth Movement, 84
  New Culture Movement, 71
Blackheath Upper Middle School, 40
Book of History, 20
Book of Odes, 14, 100
Borodin, Michael, 89
Boxer Uprising:
  Attack on Christian missionaries, 29
  Boxer Indemnity and establishment of Shanxi University, 62
  Christian mission movement following, xiii
  Foreign nations' occupation of Beijing, 15
  Ransacking of Taiji Chang (home of Zeng Baosun's cousin Marquis Zeng Guangluan), 15
  Terrorizing of Chinese Christians, 15.
    See also Richard, Reverend Timothy
Buck, Pearl S., 149
Buddhism, 61, 107

Cambridge University:
  Compared to Oxford University, 64–65
  Compared to University of London, 49
  Curriculum compared to Chinese educational system, 65
  Discrimination against women, 54, 65
  Postgraduate studies of Zeng Baosun, 57, 64
  Student recreation, 65
Celestial Studio Collection.
  See *Huantianshi Shiji*
Chang, Cai, xii
Chang, Sophie M.K.
  See Zhang, Mojun
Changsha:
  Air raids by Japanese, 110
  Destruction of, 112
  Invasion by communists, 94–95
  Lectures of Zeng Baosun, 106
  Provincial capital of Hunan, xii
Chen, Cheng, 147
Chen, Madam:
  Death of parents, 6
  Early life, 6
  Escape to Hankou, 95
  Greets Zeng Baosun upon return to China, 72
  Illness and death of, 6–7, 109–110
  Marries into Zeng household, 6
  Marries Zeng Guangjun, 6
  Mother of Zeng Baosun, 6
Cheng, Qian, 136–137
Chiang, Kaishek:
  Commander of Northern Expeditionary Army, 89, 93
  Elected first president of Republic of China, 135–36
  Elected to second term as president of Republic of China, 144
  Establishment of Nationalist government, 103–104
  Leaves office of president, 138

Chiang, Kaishek (*Continued*)
   Peasants' Association within Northern Expeditionary Army, 93
   And repatriation of Chinese prisoners of Korean war, 144
   Suppression of Communists, 93
China Inland Mission, 79
China's Four Hundred Million, 62.
   See also Richard, Reverend Timothy
Chinese Communist Party, 89.
   See also Communists
Chinese Women's Prayer Association, 142
Chongqing, 115
Christianity:
   Chinese Christian students in England, 60–61
   Compared to Buddhism, 107
   In girlhood home of Zeng Baosun, xiii
   Mission activities and schools, xiii
   Zeng Baosun at Mary Vaughan High School for Girls, 27
   Zeng Baosun's conversion to, xiv, 29–30.
   See also *East in the West*
Church of England:
   Anglican Church and Zeng Baosun's worship, 53
   Chinese Christian students, 60
   Christian Education in, 59
   Confirmation of Zeng Baosun, 39
   Episcopal liturgy, 41
   Louise Barnes and Mission Society, 46–48
   Louise Barnes' resignation from Mission Society, 57
   Mary Vaughan High School, 43–45
   Recommends Zeng Baosun's enrollment at Worthing Church House School, 39
   Religious education at Blackheath Upper Middle School, 41
   Westfield College, 50, 61
   World War I, 59–60, 62.
   See also YMCA
Church of England Mission Society, 26, 46–48, 72, 74, 92
Communists:
   Asian Anti-Communist League, 145
   Chiang Kaishek's suppression of, 93
   Chinese Communist Party, 89
   Hunanese opposition to, 137
   Invasion of Changsha, 94–95
   Victory over Nationalist China, xiv
   Zeng Baosun's criticism of propaganda of, 60
Columbia University, 70

Deng, Yanda, 89.
   See also May Fourth Movement
Dewey, John, 70, 86–87
Donghai University, 145

East in the West, 60
Egypt, 99, 150
Eight Nation Allied Force, 16.
   See also Boxer Uprising

Eliot, T.S., 100
Empress Dowager:
   Flees Eight Nation Allied Force, 16
   Suppression of One Hundred Days Reform, 15
Encyclopedia Britannica, 18
Essentials of Thermotics, 62

Fascist Party, 100.
   See also Mussolini
Feminism:
   Zeng Baosun's Confucian feminism, xiv–xv.
   See also United Nations Commission on the Status of Women
Fuhou Tang.
   See Prosperity Hall
Fuzhou, 106

Gandhi, Indira, 140
Gandhi, Mohandas:
   Convenes World Peace Conference, 138, 140
   Indian independence movement, 113
Gangwu Army, 5
General Mirror of History, 17, 19, 22
Gong, Madam, 6
Guangxi Province, 120–121
Guangxi-Hunan Railroad, 120–121
Guangxu, Emperor:
   Flees Eight Nation Allied Force, 16
   Supporter of One Hundred Days Reform, 15
Guangzhou, 106, 138
Guangzhouwan, 120
Gongyang Zhuan (Commentary on historical record of Confucius' home state), 21
Good Earth, The, 149
Guerrillas, 123–126
Guo, Peilin, 4, 29
Guo, Yun:
   Confucian principles of, 4
   Death of, 7
   Departure from Beijing in wake of One Hundred Days Reform, 15
   Education of, 4
   Encouragement of Zeng Baosun and Zeng Yuenung's study abroad, 58
   Family of, 4
   Grandmother of Zeng Baosun, 4, 15, 24
   Literary preferences, 18
   Rearing of grandchildren of, 5
   Return to Xiangxiang, 20
   Sets conditions for Zeng Baosun's education in England under Louise Barnes, 35
   Sixtieth birthday, 24
   Widow of Zeng Jihong, 4

Hangzhou, 106
Hangzhou Provincial Normal School for Women, 24–25
Hengyang, 121, 126–127
Hong Kong:
   And bombing of Nanning, 112
   And bombing of Pearl Harbor, 116–117
   Conditions under Japanese occupation, 119

Lectures of Zeng Baosun, 106
Zeng Baosun's trip to World Christian Conference, 99
Hu, Shi:
  Institute of Pacific Relations, 104
  Meeting with Zeng Baosun, 70
  New Culture Movement, 70, 87
Hua, Ms. (Concubine):
  Concubine of Zeng Guangjun, 6
  Mother of Zeng Zhaohang, 6
Huang Lizhou Wenji (Collected works of Huang Congxi), 25
Huantianshi Shiji (Celestial Studio Collection), 14
Hunan Army, 107.
  See also Taiping Rebellion; Zeng, Guofan
Hunan Daily News, 89–90
Hunan Province:
  Home of Qu Yuan, 3
  Home of Zeng family, 3, 57
  Hunanese, conservatism of, xii
  In war with Japan, 112, 120

Institute of Pacific Relations:
  Invites Zeng Baosun to Kyoto meeting, 101
  Meeting at Shanghai, Nanjing, and Hangzhou, 104–105
  Zeng Baosun's lectures on relations between China and Japan, 107
  Zeng Baosun's resignation from, 104
Israel, 150

Jerusalem Conference of the World Christian Council, 58
Jirong.
  See Zeng, Guangrong

Korean War, 140, 150
Kowloon:
  Zeng Baosun residence at, 115
  Under Japanese occupation, 117
  Escape from Japanese, 119–120
Kyoto, 101–103

Li, Zongren:
  Becomes president of Republic of China, 138
  Dismissed as president, 144
  Invasion of Changsha, 94
  Vice presidential candidate for Republic of China, 136
Liang, Qichao:
  Followed by Zeng Guangjun, 15
  Leader of One Hundred Days Reform, 15
  Zeng Baosun's study of, 25
Liaoyang Province, 134
Library of Prosperity Hall, 8, 18
Liu, Madam:
  Adoptive mother of Zeng Yuenung, 9
  Daughter of Liu Rong, 21
  Widow of Zeng Jize, 9
Liu, Rong, 21
London Day Training College, 64.
  See also Zeng, Baosun

Luce, Henry, 145.
  See also Time Magazine

Macao, 120
Manchuria:
  Discussion of at Kyoto meeting of Institute of Pacific Relations, 101–102
  Invasion by Japanese, 104
  Japanese interests in, 102
  Mukden Incident, 104
  Zeng Baosun's visit to, 101–102
Mao, Zedong:
  Beginnings of Chinese Communist Party, 89
  Birth of, xi
  Mobilization of peasants, xi, 89
Marco Polo Bridge, 108
Mary Vaughan High School:
  Invites Zeng Baosun to return, 74
  Requests Louise Barnes' return, 46–48
  Zeng Baosun's admission to, 26
  Zeng Baosun's exposure to Christianity, 17
  Zeng Baosun's opposition to returning to as teacher, 57
  Zeng Baosun's studies at, 27–31.
  See also Vaughan, Mary
May Fourth Movement:
  Beginnings of Chinese Communist Party, 89
  Chinese nationalism, xiv, 84–88
  Yifang Schools' participation in, 76.
  See also Beijing National University
May Thirtieth Movement, 76
Methodist Church, 149
Mingde Academy, 22
Mingru Xuean (Confucian Scholarship of the Ming Dynasty), 25
Ministry of Education, 91, 94
Miscellaneous Offerings from Yifang, 86.
  See also New Culture Movement
Montreal, 69
Mussolini, 100.
  See also Fascist Party

Nanjing:
  Arsenal established by Zeng Guofan, 107
  Chinese government's withdrawal from, 109
  First session of the National Assembly, 134
  Lectures of Zeng Baosun, 106
  Mausoleum of Sun Yat-sen, 107
  Petition to restore Zeng Guofan's Ancestral Temple, 95
  Yifang School graduates' study at Jinling Women's University, 94
Nanning, 112
National Assembly, 144.
  See also Zeng, Baosun
National Beijing University.
  See Beijing National University
National Salvation Daily, 136
Nehru, Jawaharlal, 140
New Culture Movement:
  At Beijing National University, 71
  Led by Dr. Hu Shi, 70

New Culture Movement (*Continued*)
   Miscellaneous Offerings from Yifang, 86
   And New Literature Movement, 71
   Yifang School's participation in, 85–86
New Literature Movement.
   See New Culture Movement
New York, 70
Newham College, 64
Nie, Guangkun, 115
Nie, Lusheng, 73
Nie, Yuntai:
   Encourages Zeng Baosun to take over Qixiu Girl's Middle School, 74
   Grandson of Zeng Guofan, 35
   Repayment to Philip Vaughan, 48
   Uncle of Zeng Baosun, 35
   And Zeng Baosun's return to China, 71
Nie, Zeng Jifen:
   Great aunt of Zeng Baosun, 31, 71
   Youngest daughter of Zeng Guofan, xiii
   And Zeng Baosun's return to China, 71
1911 Republican revolution:
   Effects on Zeng family, 13, 30
Nixon, Richard:
   Reversal of U.S. China policy, xiv
   As Vice President of the United States, 145
   Visit to Mainland China, 151
   Zeng Baosun's criticism of, xiv, 151–156
Northern Expeditionary Army, 89

On Evolution, 30
One Hundred Days Reform, 14–15
Ouyang, Ms., 3
Ouyang, Ningzhi, 3
Oxford University:
   Compared to Cambridge University, 64–65
   Compared to University of London, 49, 54
   Curriculum compared to Chinese educational system, 65
   Discrimination against women, 54, 65
   Zeng Baosun's postgraduate study, 57, 64

Pakistan, 140
Paris Peace Conference, 80
Peasants' Association:
   Chiang Kaishek's suppression of, 93
   Closes Yifang School, 90–91
Peng, Dehuai, 95
Planning Commission for the Recovery of the Mainland, 144
Pound, Ezra, 100
Prosperity Hall (Fuhou Tang):
   Childhood home of Zeng Baosun, 8
   Description of, 8
   Library of, 8–9
   In war with Japan, 122–124
Protestant Missions, xiii
Provincial First Women's Normal School, 88

Quakers:
   Meetings of, 61
   Opposition to World War I, 56, 59–60
   Zeng Baosun's sympathies with, 60
Qing Dynasty, 14

Qixiu Girls' Middle School, 74
Qu, Yuan, 3, 11

Republic of China, 143, 150–151.
   See also Chiang, Kaishek
Richard, Reverend Timothy:
   Author of *China's Four Hundred Million*, 62
   First president of Shanxi University, 62
   Founder of Society for the Diffusion of Christian and General Knowledge among the Chinese, 61
   Influence on Zeng Baosun, 62
   And Zeng Guofan, 61–62.
   See also Boxer Uprising
Roosevelt, Eleanor, 149
Royal Institute of Geology, 63
Russell, Bertrand:
   At Changsha, 86
   New Culture Movement, 86
   Marital scandal, 86–87
   Opposition to World War I, 56

St. Hughes College, 64.
   See also Oxford University
St. Mary's Training College, 64.
   See also Zeng, Baosun
Sayings of Confucius, 14, 17
de Selincourt, Ms.:
   Bible study class of, 61
   Death of, 57–58
   Encourages adaptation of Christianity to Chinese culture, 57
   Principal at Westfield College, 49–50, 57
   Service in India, 49
Security Council.
   See United Nations
Seventh Fleet, 140
Shakespeare, William, 45
Shandong Province, 105
Shanghai:
   Chiang Kaishek's suppression of Communists, 93
   Christianity in, 61
   Lectures of Zeng Baosun, 106
   Zeng Baosun's trip to World Christian Conference, 99
Shanxi University:
   Establishment of, 62.
   See also Richard, Reverend Timothy; Boxer Uprising
Shaoshan, xi
Shijian Jieyao, 22
Shi, Mrs., 124
Shuai, Madam (Concubine), 6, 16
Shui Hu Zhuan (All Men Are Brothers), 149
Sichuan Province:
   Boxers' attack on Christian missionaries, 29.
   See also Boxer Uprising
Sino Soviet Mutual Non-Aggression Pact, 134
Sizi Nujing (Four character women's classic), 17
Society for the Diffusion of Christian and General Knowledge among the Chinese, 61

Stimson, Henry, 114
Strange Tales from a Chinese Studio, 19
Study of Sociology, 30
Sun, Ke, 136
Sun, Raymond, 70
Sun, Yatsen, 136

Taibei Women's Home, 146
Taiping Rebellion:
  Hunan Army, 107
  Nanjing Arsenal, 107
  Pseudo-Christianity of, 4
  And Qing (Manchu) Dynasty, xii, 77
  Zeng family history during, 4.
  See also Guo, Peilin; Zeng, Guofan
Taiwan:
  Diplomatic relations of Republic of China, 143
  Donghai University, 145
  National Assembly, 144–145
  National Taiwan University, 145
  Opposition to Republic of China representation in United Nations, 148
  Presidential and vice presidential elections, 144
  Repatriation of Chinese Korean War POWs, 144
  Taibei Women's Home, 146
  Taiwan Yifang Alumnae, 146
  United Nations Commission on the Status of Women, 147
  Withdrawal of Republic of China from United Nations, 150–151
  Zeng Baosun as spokesperson for Christianity, xiv
  Zeng Baosun's seclusion on, 142
  Zeng family reunions, 146.
  See also Chiang, Kaishek; Zeng, Baosun; Zeng, Zhaohua
Taiwan Straits, 140
Tang, Madam, 6
Thousand Character Classic, 14
Tianjin, 106
Time Magazine, 145.
  See also Luce, Henry
Toronto, 69
Trans-Siberian Railway, 36–37
Treaty of Versailles, 84.
  See also May Fourth Movement

United Nations:
  Commission on Human Rights, 149
  Commission on the Status of Women, 143, 147–149
  Security Council, 150
  Zeng Baosun's criticism of, 150–151
United Students' Association, 90
University of London, 57, 63, 65.
  See also Westfield College

Vancouver, 70
Vaughan, Edward, 114
Vaughan, Mary, 43–44
Vaughan, Philip, 48, 58

Vichy Government, 120
Vietnam, 140

Wang Fuzhi Temple Association:
  Emboldened by Chinese communists, 89
  Harrassment of Yifang School, 88–90
  Third reopening of Yifang School, 132
  Violent protest on Yifang School campus, 78.
  See also Zeng, Guofan
Wealth of Nations, 30
Wells, H.G., 114
Wenhua Academy, 27
Westfield College:
  Academic calendar, 54
  Compared to Oxford University and Cambridge University, 49
  Curriculum, 50
  Daily routines, 52–53
  And death of Ms. de Selincourt, 58
  Faculty, 50–51
  Graduation from, 63
  Louise Barnes' inquiries on behalf of Zeng Baosun, 39
  Physical description, 50
  Student association, 54, 60
  Student life, 55
  Zeng Baosun passes entrance examinations for, 46
  Zeng Baosun passes examinations for bachelor of science degree from University of London, 57, 63
  Zeng Baosun's matriculation at, 49
  Zeng Baosun's participation in societies of, 51
  Zeng Baosun's studies at, 40–42.
  See also University of London
World Christian Conference, 99
World Christian Council, 12–113
World Peace Conference, 138, 140
World War I:
  Beginnings of, 59
  Declaration of war, 56
  Opposition to war, 56
  Zeng Baosun's equivocations about, 59.
  See also Quakers
Worthing Church House School, 39
Wuben School, 24
Wuhan:
  Japanese invasion, 112
  Lectures of Zeng Baosun, 106

Xiamen (Amoy), 106
Xiangxiang:
  Birthplace of Zeng Baosun, xi
  Family home of Zeng Baosun, 8
  Guerillas in, 123–124
  Home of Zeng Guofan, xii
  In war with Japan, 122–123
  Zeng Baosun wartime residence, 131
Xiao, Xiaohui:
  And beginnings of Yifang School, 74–75, 83
  Cousin of Zeng Baosun, 74, 139
  Death of, 143
  Flees communist invasion of Changsha, 95
  In war with Japan, 110, 120, 122

Xishou Congtan (Collected discussions of the imperial travels to the west), 16

YMCA:
  All China General YMCA invites Zeng Baosun to lecture, 105
  Olivia Vaughan home for men compared to, 43
  In war with Japan, 121
  And World Christian Council meeting, 113
Yan Mo's Christian School for Girls, 22–24
Yeyu qiudenglu (The record of night rain and autumn lanterns), 19
Yifang School:
  Alumnae, 106
  Bombed by Japanese, 110
  Closed by Peasants' Association, 90–92
  Compared to other schools, 137–138
  Comparison to church-run schools, 76
  First reopening of, 94
  Foreign faculty, 88
  Influence of Westfield College principal Ms. Richardson, 58
  May Fourth Movement, 84–85
  Ministry of Education authorization, 81
  Miscellaneous Offerings from Yifang, 86
  New Culture Movement, 85–87
  Occupation of campus by troops, 105
  Physical description of, 77–79
  Second closing of, 105
  Second reopening of, 106
  Selection of teachers for, 58
  Student-Faculty Association, 80–81, 84, 87
  Students, 81–83
  Students return from study in Britain, 105
  Taiwan Yifang Alumnae, 146
  Third reopening of, 131–133
  Thirtieth anniversary, 136–137
  Tokyo earthquake of 1923, 85
  War preparations of, 109
  Zeng Baosun resumes duties as principal of, 100
  Zeng Baosun's adoption of Westfield College practices, 55
Yifangguan Shichao (Collected poems from the hall of culture and virtue), 5
Yinbing Shi (Ice water studio), 25
Young Men's Christian Association. See YMCA
Yu, Dalun, 21, 22
Yu, Dawang, 115
Yu, Dawei:
  Cousin of Zeng Baosun, 21, 22
  During war with Japan, 116
  Election of Zeng Baosun to National Assembly, 135
  Study in United States, 71
Yu, Mrs., 136, 140
Yu, Shouchen, 16, 21, 71
Yupi Tongjian (Imperial comments on the outlines of the *General Mirror of History*), 17
Yuewei caotang biji (Notes on minutia from my thatched cottage), 20

Zeng, Baohan, 7, 24, 36, 136
Zeng, Baohe, 22, 30
Zeng, Baoling, 5, 19, 20, 22–24
Zeng, Baomiao, 110, 122
Zeng, Baoshi, 122
Zeng, Baosu, 122
Zeng, Baosun:
  As advocate for women, xiv
  Attends Quaker meeting, 61
  Battle against cancer, 143
  Becomes principal of Provincial First Women's Normal School, 88
  Birth of, xi, 3
  On Board of Directors of Donghai University, 145
  Childhood, xi–xiii
  In Chinese Women's Prayer Association, 142
  Closing of Yifang School by Peasants' Association, 91–92
  Compares British to Chinese educational system, 65
  Confucianism of, xi–xiii
  Continuation of studies at London Day Training College, St. Mary's Training College, and Cambridge University, 64
  Conversion to Christianity, xiii–xiv
  Criticism of communist peace propaganda, 60
  Criticism of Nixon's reversal of U.S. China policy, xiv
  Departure from England, 65–66
  Develops heart irregularity, 115
  Election to National Assembly, 134–136, 144
  Encounter with Japanese soldiers, 118
  Escape from Changsha, 92–95
  Escape from Hong Kong, 119–120
  Feminism of, xiv–xvi, 135
  Festivals during childhood of, 9–13
  Illness and recovery in Shandong Province, 105
  Influenced by Reverend Timothy Richard, 61–62
  Inheritance from Louise Barnes, 115
  Institute of Pacific Relations invites Zeng Baosun to Kyoto meeting, 101
  Lectures for YMCA, 106
  Named delegate to Asian Anti-Communist League, 145
  Named vice chair of Planning Commission for the Recovery of the Mainland, 144–145
  At Newham College, 64
  Opposes returning to Mary Vaughan High School for Girls as teacher, 57
  Participation in Christian student activities in England, 60–61
  Participation in World Christian Conference, 99–100
  Passes entrance examinations for Westfield College, 46
  Poetic reflections on Nixon's visit to China, 151–156
  Preparation for entrance examinations for Westfield College, 45

Represents China on United Nations' Commission on the Status of Women, 143, 147–149
Resignation from Institute of Pacific Relations, 104
Resigns as principal from Yifang School, 90
Return to London after postgraduate studies, 65
Return trip to China, 69–72
At St. Hughes College, 64
Seventieth birthday, 146
Shares Louise Barnes' home in Hampstead, 53
As spokesperson for Christianity, xiv
Successfully takes examinations for bachelor of science degree, 57, 63
Sympathies towards Quakers, 60
In Taiwan, xiv
Third reopening of Yifang School, 131–133
Tours Manchuria, 101–102
Trip to England under tutelage of Louise Barnes, 35–38
Views about effective proselytizing Christianity, 57
Views toward conscientious objectors, 60
Visits to Scotland and England, 149
In war with Japan, 122
Zeng, Bohang, 15
Zeng, Fu, 120
Zeng, Guangjun:
  Appointment as prefect at Wuming in Guangxi Province, 15
  Death of, 94, 103
  Father of Zeng Baosun, 5
  Follower of Liang Qichao, 15
  Illness of, 103
  Leads Gangwu Army in Manchuria during Sino-Japanese War, 5
  Member of Hanlin Academy, 16
  Oldest grandson of Zeng Guofan, 5
  One Hundred Days Reform, 15
  Role in education of Zeng Baosun, 16–17
  Secures second concubine Madam Zhao, 6
  Studies in late life, 16
  Under influence of Empress Dowager, 16, 18–19
  Wife and concubines of, 7
  Writes poem lamenting death of imperial consort Zhen Fei, 16
  Youthful achievements of, 5
  Zeng Baosun's baptism, 17
Zeng, Guangluan, 15, 21
Zeng, Guangquan, 9, 21, 75, 116
Zeng, Guangrong:
  Appointment as sub-prefect to Zhejiang Province, 15
  Approval of Zeng Baosun's enrollment at Mary Vaughan High School for Girls, 26
  Beginnings of Yifang School, 75
  Conversion to Christianity, 30
  Encourages Zeng Baosun to go to England, 35
  Establishes Christian church in Changsha, 57
  Father of Zeng Baohe, 22
  Father of Zeng Zhaoquan, 5
  In One Hundred Days Reform, 15
  Preaching at Changsha, 73
  Residence at Opium Taxation Bureau, 24
  Return to Hangzhou, 20
  In revolution of 1911, 30
  In Sino-Japanese War, 22
  And sixtieth birthday of Guo Yun, 24
  Uncle of Zeng Baosun, 24
  And wife at Wenxingqiao (Changsha), 72
Zeng, Guofan:
  And adoption of Zeng Guangquan, 21
  Buddhist practices of, 9
  Grandfather of Zeng Guangjun, 5
  Great-grandfather of Zeng Baosun, 3
  Home in Xiangxiang, xii
  Library of at Fuhou Tang (Prosperity Hall), 8, 18
  Papers of, 112, 119, 120, 139
  Publication of Wang Fuzhi's writings, 77
  And Reverend Timothy Richard, 61–62
  Study of, 122
  Taiping Rebellion, xii, 77
  Temple of, 77–78, 89, 95, 110–111, 132
  Victory over Taipings at Nanjing, 107
  Writings of, 142
Zeng, Guohuang, 20
Zeng, Guoquan, 4, 6, 15
Zeng, Huimin.
  See Zeng, Jize
Zeng, Jidi, 3
Zeng, Jieshi, 20
Zeng, Jihong, 4, 18
Zeng, Jize (Marquis):
  Adopts Zeng Guangquan into family, 9, 21
  And Anglican Prelate of Jerusalem, 99
  Concludes Ili Treaty, 3
  Father of (Marquis) Zeng Guangluan, 15
  Library of at Prosperity Hall, 8–9, 18
  Residence at Hongjiajing, 4
  Son of Madam Ouyang and Zeng Guofan, 3
  Yifang School, 77
Zeng, Luchu, 75
Zeng, Rongrong, 122
Zeng, Xiping, 122
Zeng, Wenzheng.
  See Zeng, Guofan
Zeng, Yuenung:
  Appointment at Hunan University, 115
  Becomes professor of English at Taiwan National University, 142
  Becomes Quaker, 60–61
  Beginnings of Yifang Girl's Middle School, 74–76, 83, 86
  Begins study at Mingde Academy, 22
  Bombing of Yifang School by Japanese, 111
  In Changsha, 20
  Closing of Yifang School by Peasants' Association, 91–92
  Cousin of Zeng Baosun, xiii
  Dean at Yifang School, 105
  And election of Zeng Baosun to National Assembly, 135

Zeng, Yuenung (*Continued*)
  And end of Chiang Kaishek's presidency, 138
  Enrollment at Wenhua Academy, 27
  Escape from Kowloon, 119–120
  Escape to Hankou, 95
  And father in Guangxi Province, 110
  "Fifth brother" of Zeng Baosun, 5
  Greets Zeng Baosun in England, 37–39
  And heart attack of father, 116
  During Japanese occupation of Hong Kong, 118–119
  Mother's death, 75
  Outbreak of World War I, 56
  Participation in Christian student meetings in England, 60
  As president of Donghai University, 145
  At Prosperity Hall, 122–127
  Return to London, 65
  Return trip to China, 65–73
  Reunited with Zeng Baosun and family members in Hong Kong, 115
  Seventieth birthday, 146
  Son of Zeng Guangquan, 9, 21
  Student at Royal Institute of Geology, 63
  Studies with Zeng Baosun in Nanjing after Boxer Uprising, 19
  Takes examinations at University of London, 63–64
  Third reopening of Yifang School, 131–133
Zeng, Yuyang, 120
Zeng, Zhaocheng, 147
Zeng, Zhaohua, 6, 72, 107, 112, 120, 135, 139, 141–142
Zeng, Zhaohang, 121–122, 127
Zeng, Zhaoke, 7, 109–110, 125, 139, 141–142, 148

Zeng, Zhaoquan:
  Attends university in United States, 5
  Begins study at Mingde Academy, 22
  Cousin of Zeng Baosun, 9, 19, 20
  Death of mother, 124
  Death of son, 95
  Enrollment at Wenhua Academy, 27
  Independent Christian church, 95, 109
  Provides refuge for Zeng Baosun, 95
  Return to Xiangxiang, 20
  In war with Japan, 109, 122, 124
  Son of Zeng Guangrong (Jirong), 5, 9
Zeng, Zhaoshu, 138
Zeng, Zhaoyu, 136
Zeng, Zhenlian, 124–125
Zeng, Zhenluo, 124–125, 142
Zeng, Zhongxiang, 4.
  See also Zeng, Guoquan
Zeng Clan Association, 146
Zeng family:
  Entertainments, 9–13
  New Years' celebrations, 10
  Public service, 134
  Religious beliefs and practices, 9
Zhang, Hungwei, 149
Zhang, Mojun:
  Influence upon Zeng Baosun, 25
  At Wuben School, 24.
  See also Chang, Sophie M.K.
Zhao, Madam (Concubine/wife), 6, 16, 105
Zhen, Fei, 16
Zhejiang Province, 57
Zhou, Gongren, 122
Zhu, Xi, 61
Zhu, Zhusheng, 135, 142
Zuozhuan (Commentary on historical record of Confucius' home state), 20, 22

www.ingramcontent.com/pod-product-compliance
Lightning Source LLC
Chambersburg PA
CBHW080925100426
42812CB00007B/2373